The New Inquisitions

The New Inquisitions

Heretic-Hunting and the Intellectual Origins of Modern Totalitarianism

ARTHUR VERSLUIS

2006

OXFORD
UNIVERSITY PRESS

Oxford University Press, Inc., publishes works that further
Oxford University's objective of excellence
in research, scholarship, and education.

Oxford   New York
Auckland   Cape Town   Dar es Salaam   Hong Kong   Karachi
Kuala Lumpur   Madrid   Melbourne   Mexico City   Nairobi
New Delhi   Shanghai   Taipei   Toronto

With offices in
Argentina   Austria   Brazil   Chile   Czech Republic   France   Greece
Guatemala   Hungary   Italy   Japan   Poland   Portugal   Singapore
South Korea   Switzerland   Thailand   Turkey   Ukraine   Vietnam

Copyright © 2006 by Arthur Versluis

Published by Oxford University Press, Inc.
198 Madison Avenue, New York, New York 10016

www.oup.com

Oxford is a registered trademark of Oxford University Press

All rights reserved. No part of this publication may be reproduced,
stored in a retrieval system, or transmitted, in any form or by any means,
electronic, mechanical, photocopying, recording, or otherwise,
without the prior permission of Oxford University Press.

Library of Congress Cataloging-in-Publication Data
Versluis, Arthur, 1959–
The new inquisitions : heretic-hunting and the intellectual origins
of modern totalitarianism / Arthur Versluis.
   p. cm.
Includes bibliographical references and index.
ISBN-13 978-0-19-530637-8
ISBN 0-19-530637-6
1. Totalitarianism.   I. Title.
JC480.V45 2006
321.9—dc22   2005031801

Acknowledgments

My thanks to the journals *Telos* and *Esoterica* for publishing earlier versions of two chapters from this book, and to various readers for their editorial comments and suggestions. The chapter on Voegelin appeared in *Telos* in Summer 2002, and the chapter on Schmitt appeared in *Esoterica* in 2004.

This book is dedicated to those many colleagues and friends with whom I have shared enjoyable and illuminating conversations over the past few years.

Preface

This book represents an inductive intellectual journey, a form of intellectual history with relatively few precedents or analogues. Its closest analogues are—perhaps ironically—those works and authors to which it is most indebted, but of which it is sometimes most critical. I had read before nearly all the broad interpretations of political and intellectual history offered by figures such as Oswald Spengler, Isaiah Berlin, John Lukacs, and others, and had taken from each the particular insights that they offered. Intellectual history requires an interpretation, an argument, if it is to reveal insights into history and a better understanding of our present time. It is not enough to creep over the minutiae of the past and never come to any conclusions—much more valuable is to make broad sense of what one sees, to make a case. To writers like these, I am indebted.

In making my case, I have undertaken an inductive inquiry: I begin with a conundrum, and slowly, by accumulating evidence, seek to solve it. Our conundrum is nothing less than the great scourge of the twentieth century: the emergence of totalitarianism in a variety of forms. Previous ages saw nothing like the barbarism of the twentieth century as manifested in totalitarianism. For the first time, a massive technical apparatus was marshaled against individual freedom, and was responsible for the slaughter not of thousands, but of millions upon millions of people. Understandably, totalitarianism is often treated as having come nearly *ex nihilo* into the world in the twentieth century, and is depicted as having few real antecedents. One has to admit the fundamental *newness* of the gulags and the great heaps of bodies, the institutionalized murder of millions, the security state and the totalization of war in the twentieth century. Further confusing much scholarship in this area, the right tends to depict communism as the worst form of totalitarianism, whereas the left sees fascism as the worst. Even today, it is often regarded as somewhat egregious to treat communism and fascism as aspects of a single phenomenon that we can term simply *totalitarianism*.

But the more I have studied those states that can reasonably be seen as totalitarian, the more I have been convinced that what are often depicted as incommensurable and opposed systems are in fact very nearly identical in how they actually operate. Secret police, secret imprisonments, torture, show trials, insistence on public confessions, public executions, gulags, or concentration camps in which people are held incommunicado and interminably in what is sometimes figuratively called a "state of exception," but what is in fact the attempted suspension and removal of basic human rights to, at minimum, a fair trial. All of these characteristics of totalitarianism recur in National Socialist and in Communist states alike. These are among the operative "markers" of a totalitarian state, whatever putative form of government it might appear to have. Such a state might seem putatively a "liberal democracy," but the presence of these markers would indicate that the real state tends toward totalitarianism. Totalitarianism is the modern phenomenon of total centralized state power coupled with the obliteration of individual human rights: in the totalized state, there are those in power, and there are the objectified masses, the victims.

And the overarching question left by the twentieth century is simply this: where did the phenomenon of totalitarianism really come from? It is not enough to look back merely a century or two for the origins of Nazi Germany or Stalinist Russia, as most historians tend to do. One has to look more broadly at precedents in the West in order to understand the real nature of totalitarianism. What is the intellectual genealogy that leads inexorably toward the totalizing state, the single most important (and sinister) legacy of the twentieth century? As you will see, our inquiry will lead toward some unexpected conclusions that have important ramifications not only for how we understand the course of history, but also for the dangers that we still face today.

When I began the journey that this book represents, I did not expect that it would lead me where it has. It has genuinely been a journey of discoveries. The journey began with a foray into the anti-gnostic work of Eric Voegelin, which in turn led me to Carl Schmitt, then to Theodor Adorno, and on to Joseph de Maistre in a kind of spiral, each arc of which turned on the axial question of the Inquisition and of the central role that it played not only as an institution but even more as a guiding metaphor in Western history. Each time that I thought the project had reached an impasse, a new chapter revealed another dimension of the intellectual genealogy that stretches from the emergence of historical Christianity in late antiquity, through the medieval and early modern periods, straight into the twentieth and twenty-first centuries.

In my view, the fundamental politicosocial question facing us is how to avoid totalitarianism. The technical and sociobureaucratic apparatus that makes a totalitarian state possible are already in place in much of the world, and what is more, great swathes of the world's population were already subject to a totalitarian state in the twentieth century: in the Soviet Union and the lands under its domination, like Eastern Europe; in China and the lands under its domination, like Tibet or Hong Kong; in Germany, Italy, and Spain under the various forms of fascism; in various dictatorships; and even to some extent in states sometimes deemed "liberal" can we see the tell-tale markers of totalitarianism. The twentieth century, seen as a whole, suggests that periods of relative prosperity and freedom are more anomalous than they are the norm. How do we prevent the ascendance of the totalitarian state?

In order to understand the nature of totalitarianism, we need to know where it came from, and what its fundamental characteristics are. The truth is, what we're considering is nothing less than the face of evil itself, and to the extent that this is so, we cannot lay blame for the advent of totalitarianism at the feet of any single individual or institution. Yet it is not enough to say that totalitarianism is simply evil and let it go at that. The phenomenon of totalitarianism emerged in the twentieth century as an archetypal form out of the West, and it took hold in societies with a great cultural-religious inheritance: Germany, Italy, Russia, China. How could this have happened? How could the nightmares of Hitler, Stalin, and Mao have come forth out of the former greatness of Germany, Russia, and China? Clearly there is a preexisting archetype on which totalitarianism could draw, an archetype that answered some visceral need within some of humanity. What follows is an inquiry into what that archetype is, and how it functions.

We begin where this archetype has its roots: in late antiquity and in the emergence of historicist Christianity.

Contents

1. Introduction: Heresy, 3
   Heresy and the Inquisition, 6
   Czeslaw Milosz and the Captive Mind, 8

2. The Archetypal Inquisition, 13

3. Joseph de Maistre and the Inquisition, 19

4. Juan Donoso Cortés and the "Sickness" of the Liberal State, 27

5. Georges Sorel and Charles Maurras:
   The Emergence of Secular State Corporatism, 35
   Maurice Barrès and Charles Maurras: The Nationalist Substitute for Catholicism, 41
   The Secularization of Heresiophobia, 46

6. Carl Schmitt, the Inquisition, and Totalitarianism, 49
   Carl Schmitt and Early Modern Western Esotericism, 50
   Carl Schmitt and Gnosticism, 52
   Conclusions, 57

7. Communism and the Heresy of Religion, 61

8. Eric Voegelin, Anti-Gnosticism, and the Totalitarian Emphasis on Order, 69
   The Rhetoric of Anti-Gnosticism, 70
   Voegelinian Inquisitors, 77

9. Norman Cohn and the Pursuit of Heretics, 85
   The Inner Demons of Europe Once Again, 91

10. Theodor Adorno and the "Occult," 95

11. Another Long, Strange Trip, 105
    That Old Bugaboo, "Gnosticism," Yet Again, 105
    An Epidemic of Evil! 107
    Digital Revolution, 109

12. High Weirdness in the American Hinterlands, 111
    The Satanic Panic of Late-Twentieth-Century America, 112
    Illuminatiphobia, 116
    The Christian Illuminati, 122

13. The American State of Exception, 127
    Rendering to the Secular Arm, 129

14. Berdyaev's Insight, 135
    Dostoevsky Revisited, 136
    Berdyaev on Inquisitional Psychopathology, 137
    Totalitarianism of the Left and of the Right, 140
    The Betrayal of Humanity, 142
    It Can Happen Here, 143

15. Conclusion: Disorder as Order, 147
    Böhme's Metaphysics of Evil, 149
    Ideocracy's Consequences, 150
    Heresy and History, 151
    The Ubiquity of Ideopathology, 153
    Mysticism and Plato's Cave, 155

Notes, 157

Selected Bibliography, 179

Index, 187

The New Inquisitions

In its organic structure, its bureaucratic type, it is perhaps the first of its kind in the history of administration. The agents of the Inquisition are veritable functionaries, neither worse nor better than many others, who investigate and instruct and who constitute a permanent menace to the population. One could say that the Inquisition is the first form of totalitarianism of modern times.
—Guy Mathelié-Guinlet, *L'Inquisition, Tribunal de la foi*

Is the Inquisition a medieval relic, an anachronism or, on the contrary, one of the first manifestations of modernity in Europe? For me, the response is without doubt: the Inquisition prefigures the modern state in this most terrible of ways—the tendency toward totalitarianism.
—Joseph Pérez, *Isabelle et Ferdinand, Rois catholiques d'Espagne*

I

Introduction

Heresy

Among the most pivotal concepts in the history of ideas in the West is that of heresy—arguably the single most definitive concept in the early Christian period. Etymologically, heresy derives from *hairein*, a Greek word meaning "to choose." A "heretic," then, is one who chooses, one who therefore exemplifies freedom of individual thought, and by implication, who does not accept at least some of the doctrines of the corporate Church. If, on the one hand, the heretic is one who chooses, then the heretic exists by affirmation—but, on the other hand, in the context of an organized Church, the heretic is also one who may refuse. It is in this sense, more than any other, that the heretic can be termed a dualist—for as soon as the representatives of an institutionalized Church insist on a particular set of doctrines and no others, those who choose are placed between two worlds or spheres. The institutionalization of the historicist Church in turn creates the possibility of the heretical.

After all, another model is quite possible. When one looks East, to Eastern Christianity, or even farther East, to the religions of India, China, and Tibet, for example, one sees some more pluralistic models. Hinduism—if we can use that term—embodies a great variety of traditions, and is famously absorptive of new traditions. Rather than establishing a Vedantic, a Vedic, or for that matter, a Shaivite, a Tantric or some other doctrine at the expense of all the others, one finds instead what we might call an uneasy pluralism. Certainly there are forms of Indian religion that stand more or less in opposition to one another, but the tendency is nonetheless to live and let live. The same is true in, for instance, Tibetan Buddhism. A great variety of practices and traditions exist under a large umbrella, and although some are more dominant than others, still there is broad willingness to coexist. Traditional China, too, was famous for its uneasy pluralism, where Taoist, Buddhism, Confucianism, and sometimes even Manichaeism and Nestorian Christianity all could live side by side. There was no single tradition that insisted on the heretical nature of the others to the extent of establishing permanent dominance.

However, relatively early in the Christian era, we see a very different dynamic emerging. On the one side, there is a pluralistic model akin to those found in Asian religious traditions. This pluralistic model is loosely termed "Gnosticism," because what unites it is not outward—corporate, historical, and bureaucratic organization—but inward knowledge, or *gnosis*. The pluralistic nature of Gnosticism is visible in its most famous collection of treatises, known as the Nag Hammadi Library. In this collection, we see Platonic, Hermetic, Jewish moralistic, and Christian visionary treatises together, side by side. An insistence on inward spiritual knowledge or gnosis informs many of these treatises, but by no means all of them. Gnosticism has occasionally been likened to Buddhism, and there are more resemblances and even possible historical affiliations than we can consider here. Most important, for our purposes, is this: had Gnosticism become the dominant model in early Christianity, Christianity would have been a much more pluralistic tradition.

But, as is visible in the collection of writings under the rubric of "the Ante-Nicene Fathers"—so named because they preceded the Nicene Conference that decided doctrinal matters decisively in favor of historicist Christianity—we see the other end of the politicosocial spectrum. If the Gnostics tended toward an uneasy pluralism, most of the Ante-Nicene Fathers tended toward a united bureaucratic, corporate, and historicist organization. It's true that the greatest of the Ante-Nicene Fathers—St. Clement of Alexandria, and Origen—encouraged a pluralistic model that explicitly included an orthodox gnosis. And, again, had Clement's views prevailed, so, too, would some measure of Christian pluralism that would have avoided much and perhaps all of the anti-heresiological frenzies of subsequent centuries. Alas, this was not to be. Instead, with the writings of figures such as Tertullian, Epiphanius, and Irenaeus, we see a series of bitter denunciations of all those who might be deemed heretics.

Even within what came to be deemed orthodoxy, there was a spectrum of views that included not only Clement of Alexandria and Origen but also Dionysius the Areopagite—all three of whom became the basis for the mystical currents within Christianity. These mystical or orthodox gnostic currents were not concerned with hunting down and destroying other people who held dissenting views—or to put it another way, with objectifying, vilifying, and seeking to destroy others—but, rather, turned their attention inward and sought the inner transcendence of the subject-object dichotomy on which heresy-hunting is inevitably based. Thus, Clement of Alexandria, for example, embraced and encouraged an orthodox gnostic spirituality that, by widening the possibilities within orthodoxy itself, at least the possibility of a limited pluralistic clemency.

But this was not the dominant tradition within early Christianity, the tradition that ultimately became known as orthodoxy. Indeed, still today one finds Roman Catholic authors who vilify even Clement of Alexandria, and so inadvertently confirm their own indebtedness to the bitter anti-heresiological rhetoric of Tertullian, Irenaus, and Epiphanius.[1] Tertullian, in his *de Praescriptione Haereticorum*, or "On the Church's Prescriptive Rule Against Heresies of All Kinds," exemplifies in its very title the broad swathe of condemnation that he levels. A *praescriptio* is a legal term, meaning an objection or demurral, and Tertullian in many respects inaugurates the basis for a legal or juridical persecution of those who, drawing from "pagan philosophy," develop their own spiritual interpretations or understandings (ch. VII).

Perhaps most fascinating about Tertullian's anti-heresiological writing is its clear derivation from Roman legal tradition. Tertullian is essentially taking into Christianity the prosecutorial or persecutorial Roman attitude toward Christianity—which he decries at length. In *ad Nationes*, probably dated to around 217 A.D., Tertullian seeks to vindicate Christianity from the accusations of the Romans, just as he did in his *Apologia*, which has been dated to around 200 A.D. In both treatises, he writes of how Romans hated Christians until they became converted, and then they "begin now to hate what they had formerly been" (ch. I). He discusses how the Romans would torture Christians in order to extract confessions, and decries the Roman insistence on forced confession followed by punishment (ch. II). And yet we can see what Tertullian denounces as Roman practice in fact is being absorbed—in such works as *de Praescriptione Haereticorum*—into orthodox Christianity and in turn applied to "heretics." Tertullian's work in itself represents that peculiar point at which Rome is being transformed from the center of opposition to the center of Western Christianity. During precisely this shift, Christianity goes from being persecuted to being persecutor.

And in this shift, Christianity takes on a particular kind of anti-gnostic cast; it takes on rationalism and historicism as primary characteristics. Tertullian, for instance, insists that only one interpretation of the scriptures and only one set of doctrines are authentically Christian, and he heaps ridicule on the claims of the Valentinian gnostics, for instance, that there are more profound dimensions of spiritual knowledge than those accessible through reason and belief.[2] It is in such works that we begin to see the insistence on the historical nature of Christianity. Historicity and legalistic reasoning become far more primary in this tradition, which we see too in the work of Augustine of Hippo (also trained as a Roman lawyer) several hundred years later. In the period between Tertullian and Augustine, we see orthodox Christianity solidifying into the basis for a centralized bureaucratic power insistent on the primacy of a single set of doctrines and on historicism combined with what we can only call an adversarial or prosecutorial rationalism. In this, we see the foundation for the later development of the Inquisition, and for the consistent hostility toward gnosticism that has haunted Western Christianity throughout its subsequent history.

Heresy and the Inquisition

Although the word "heresy" derives from an innocuous Greek word for individual choice, it became associated with demonic influence or with the devil. The demonization of heresy began relatively early—we can see it in the works of Tertullian and Irenaeus—but by the medieval period, the attribution of heresy to the devil or to demons took on a special power. The heretic was typically depicted in orthodox writings as proud, deceptively pious, secretive, and obstinate in defending his heresy, all characteristics said to have been inspired by demonic forces. The demonization of heresies that became commonplace in the medieval period in turn made possible the hideous treatment of heretics: because they represented the devil, they could be tortured or killed.

The hardening of the Church's attitude toward heretics corresponds, in many respects, to the Church's bureaucratization and centralization during the same period. If the mainstream Church took on its bureaucratic, historicist form by way of contrast with heresies in late antiquity, in the medieval period the authority of the Church was underscored and intensified by exactly the same means, but made more effective through the bureaucratic-juridical machinery of the Inquisition.

There are two aspects of the Inquisition that are particularly significant for our later argument connecting it to the modern era. First, the Inquisition represented the peculiar legal construct of the prosecutor and the judge being the same. This accounted for a great deal of the fear that the Inquisition generated in the general populace, especially (for instance) in Spain during the period of the Spanish Inquisition. If the prosecutor and the judge are identical, and if on top of that one is unable to face one's accusers, who operate in secret, then one can see that the inquisitorial method itself has a nightmarish, even hellish quality. Second, the Inquisition represented a peculiar union of religious and secular state power. It is true that the inquisitors did not themselves kill their victims but, rather, turned the condemned over to the secular arm of the state. Yet this very arrangement—which reminds one of Pilate washing his hands of Christ's fate—itself represented a union of the religious and the secular.

And there is a final aspect of the Inquisition that connects it to modernity and that is perhaps the most important of all: the "crime" in question is fundamentally a "crime" of *thought*. That is: by definition, "heresy" is independent thought that diverges from standard Church doctrine. Anti-heresiologists seek to enforce uniformity of thought: that's the very nature of the beast. And in this enforced corporatism, more than in any other place, we see the predecessor of the totalitarian state, where again, dissent is considered a criminal act. It is true that the Soviet Union and Communist China represent violently secular states in which religion itself is controlled and often regarded as criminal— yet it is also true that expressing dissenting thought in such totalitarian states is punished by secular inquisitors with very severe penalties that include torture, imprisonment, and death. Enforced corporatism is seen as vital to the centralized, totalizing state, just as it was to the medieval Church.

Of course, one has to wonder why. Why is dissent so feared by the totalizing state? It is here that the term "ideocracy" might be introduced.[3] An ideocracy is a form of government characterized by an inflexible adherence to a set of doctrines, or ideas, typically enforced by criminal penalties. Such an ideocracy is Communist China, where state ideology enforced criminal penalties for even possessing a photograph of H.H. the Dalai Lama, let alone for professing a belief in an independent Tibet or in religious freedom. An ideocracy is monistic and totalistic; it insists on the total application of ideology to every aspect of life, and in it, pluralism is anathema. In this sense it conforms to the theory of Benito Mussolini, who said that:

> The Fascist conception of the state is all-embracing; outside of it no human or spiritual value may exist, much less have any value. Thus understood, Fascism is totalitarian and the Fascist State, as a synthesis and a unit which includes all values, interprets, develops, and lends additional power to the whole life of a people.[4]

The totalitarian state—a phenomenon of modernity—consists in the attempted extension of the secular state into all dimensions of life, and the only way this would be possible is through the imposition of a totalitarian ideology that can brook not a single dissenter or heretic. In an ideocracy, the greatest criminal is imagined by ideocrats to be the dissenter, the one who by his very existence reveals the totalistic construct imposed on society to be a lie.

Czeslaw Milosz and the Captive Mind

In his book *Captive Mind,* Czeslaw Milosz wrote about what it was like to live in the ideocracy of Eastern Europe under Soviet domination, and heresy and orthodoxy were his main themes. Milosz likened the mentality cultivated under a Communist ideocracy to a kind of acting, analogous to the Persian concept of *ketman. Ketman* is a word for the dissimulations of heretics in Persian Islam, who take great pleasure in pretending to be what they are not in order to avoid censure or punishment, and about whom Arthur Gobineau wrote:

> Ketman fills the man who practices it with pride. Thanks to it, a believer raises himself to a permanent state of superiority over the man he deceives, be he a minister of state or a powerful king; to him who uses Ketman, the other is a miserable blind man whom one shuts of from the true path whose existence he does not suspect [while] . . . your eyes are filled with light, you walk in brightness before your enemies. It is an unintelligent being that you make sport of; it is a dangerous beast that you disarm. What a wealth of pleasures![5]

Hence, for example, those under Russian occupation carry Russian books and proclaim the merits of the Russian people, even as they privately detest the Soviet Union as barbarous, and Soviets as entirely contemptible. Milosz goes on to observe that under the "New Faith" of Communism, "the varieties of Ketman are practically unlimited," and "the naming of deviations cannot keep pace with the weeding of a garden so full of unexpected specimens of heresy."[6]

Milosz's erudite and beautifully written meditation on the nature of the captive mind under the totalitarian state does draw on the concept of *ketman* from Persia, but his primary metaphor in the rest of his book is heresy and indoctrination under Catholicism. Thus, he writes, "the Catholic Church wisely recognized that faith is more a matter of collective suggestion than of individual conviction." Communist meetings function the same way, Milosz observes: their function is "under the heading of collective magic. The rationalism of [Communist] doctrine is fused with sorcery, and the two strengthen each other. Free discussion is, of course, eliminated."[7] Confusion between Church doctrines and Communist doctrines was encouraged by clerics who became Party tools, like Justinian Marina, the Romanian patriarch, who said, "Christ is a new man. The new man is the Soviet man. Therefore Christ is a Soviet man!"[8] This confusion, Milosz points out, is arguably the greatest lie in centuries, but, all the same, it illustrates how Communism drew on and perverted Christianity for its own ends. What is more, Milosz himself shows how in Communism, the "reactionary" is anyone who thinks wrongly (that is, in conflict with the Politburo police and official state dogma). False views lead to bad action, and thus those who doubt state doctrines are "criminals." Hence "Catholics who accept the Party line gradually lose everything except the phraseology of their Christian metaphysics."[9] For the Communist Party in power, nothing is "as great a menace as is *heresy.*"[10]

And so, Milosz concludes, "when one considers the matter logically, it becomes obvious that intellectual terror is a principle that Leninism-Stalinism can never forsake, even if it should achieve victory on a world scale. The enemy, in a potential form, will *always* be there; the only friend will be the man who accepts the doctrine 100 per cent. If he accepts only 99 per cent, he will necessarily have to be considered a foe, for from that remaining 1 per cent a new church can arise."[11] Communism enforces on people a numbing intellectual deadness generated by fear of the state Inquisition. In place of Christian faith, it substitutes doctrines of "historical inevitability" and "progress" on earth, but it functions similarly to the Spanish Inquisition. In the Communist system, the state that Lenin claimed would wither away is become "all-powerful. It holds a sword over the head of every citizen; it punishes him for every careless word." For, Milosz continues, "orthodoxy cannot release its pressure on men's minds; it would no longer be an orthodoxy." Communist orthodoxy *requires* an "enemy," a "heretic" for self-definition.[12] And only the widespread realization of how false and hollow are its claims will bring about the sudden and total collapse of the Soviet empire, Milosz prophesied.

What Milosz wrote about life under Communist domination—and in particular about the almost universal use of *ketman* (hypocritical subterfuge) in order to survive—is strikingly borne out in the history of Catholicism as well. The Inquisitors were constantly on guard against the tendency of Cathars and other "heretics" to provide equivocal answers to questions or to "falsely" profess their belief in orthodox Church doctrine. Of course, this created an almost impossible situation for those accused of heresy, because even if they espoused Church doctrines, this could be used against the "heretics" under the accusation that they didn't *truly* believe what they were saying. Here we see the dynamic that Milosz saw at work in the Soviet state so many centuries later: under state-enforced coercion of belief and in an environment of inquisitorial terror, even a profession of orthodoxy may not be enough to save one. The condemnation of others becomes the primary way of saving oneself. Here is the self-perpetuating mechanism of institutional terror: informants in a system of "purging" those deemed "heretical."

Milosz recognized that the new inquisitorial apparatus of the Communist state has much in common with the apparatus of earlier Catholicism, even if Communism is officially a mortal enemy of religious faith itself. But there is another dimension of this commonality that Milosz only tangentially recognizes, and it is this: both the doctrines that produced the Communist inquisition, and the doctrines that produced the persecution of "heretics" in the medieval and early modern periods were thoroughly *historicist*. In both cases, one had to profess belief in the historical Church or in the triumph of history in the New State—or be deemed heretical and subject to the most horrendous penalties. Mysticism, transcendence, even art and literature—all that encouraged people to look inward into the heights of what humanity can achieve—in such a system represents a great threat. Even the greatest mystic in Western Christian history—Meister Eckhart—was declared heretical by some Church officials. Milosz outlines how the "captive mind" under the Communist ideocracy is forced to twist itself into requisite ugly forms or also be condemned: neither authentic religion nor authentic art—both of which inherently transcend the confines of history—can be tolerated under an ideocracy.

Why? What is it about the "heretical" advocate for timelessness that so frightens the ideocrat as to produce an Inquisition? Although many reasons might be adduced, the most important of them is, I think, the need to enforce a strictly *historicist* perspective on a populace. Whether it is the Inquisition and the doctrines that produced that institution, or the Communist state and its doctrines that insist on its own Progress through history (even if it is Progress over tens of millions of corpses), or for that matter the futuristic mechanism of the Fascist state, all represent a concerted effort to eliminate individual freedom and to insist upon a corporate unity enforced by terror. To such a mentality, the greatest enemy is not external, but internal: it is the one who insists on the primacy of timelessness over time, of eternity over history. The "heretic" or rebel who has glimpsed eternity represents the greatest challenge of all for these corporate institutions, which by contrast must restrict themselves to the historical-temporal world. Thus, the totalitarian inquisitorial power pursues relentlessly those who insist on the transcendence of history through religion, art, and literature, sometimes even more than it pursues the political rebel.

Dostoevsky understood this dynamic—indeed, he foresaw its terrible consequences in the coming century. In his great novel *The Brothers Karamazov*, Dostoevsky included a chapter entitled "The Grand Inquisitor," in which he outlined precisely the connection between the Catholic Inquisition and the coming totalitarianism that was to infect not only his beloved Russia but also China, Korea, and many other countries. Dostoevsky intuited already in the nineteenth century the heart of the matter: that if Christ's kingdom is not of this world, still there are those who would attempt to enforce a new kingdom that is precisely *of* this world. Thus, the Grand Inquisitor himself says "we are not working with Thee, but with *him* [the devil]—that is our mystery." We, he continues, "shall be Caesars, and then we shall plan the universal happiness of man," through "some means of uniting all in one unanimous and harmonious ant-heap."[13] The Grand Inquisitor is one who rejects transcendence and embraces immanence—that is, historical, worldly power—in order to "help" humanity realize earthly "utopia" through the obliteration of human freedom. Dostoevsky could see totalitarianism coming, and he understood its predecessor, the Inquisition, all too well.

But what is the historical nature of this link? Where do we find the ties that bind the emergence of totalitarianism in the twentieth century with its historical precedent in the Inquisition? In what follows, we will explore such links, and see exactly how "heresy" could shift from a religious to a secular context—indeed, how a secular Inquisition could emerge in the twin forms of totalitarianism: fascism and communism. In the figures we'll investigate—pivotal authors such as Joseph de Maistre and Carl Schmitt, and pivotal historic figures such as Lenin and Stalin—we will see how the archetypal institution of the Inquisition emerges in the totalitarianism that marks the twentieth century, and that arguably is the most characteristic manifestation of modernity itself.

2

The Archetypal Inquisition

No institution of the Catholic Church is more notorious than that of the Inquisitions. The image of the inquisitors ordering or conducting tortures, and the fates of those who were burned to death in public exhibitions—including truly great figures such as the mystic Marguerite Porete (ca. 1280–1310), and the brilliant philosopher Giordano Bruno (ca. 1548–1600)—condemn the institution irrevocably and utterly, no matter whether the Vatican sponsors symposia or books that downplay or whitewash inquisitional horrors.[1] But our purpose here is not to enter into controversies between Church apologists, on the one hand, and critics, on the other. Our purpose, rather, is to consider the Inquisition's archetypal social dimensions.

As an institutional process, the Inquisition has its origin in the early thirteenth century, when the ascetic movements known as Catharism and as the Waldensians began to be seen as a real threat to the power of the Catholic Church in France. Although previous popes had shown clemency toward heretics, already Pope Lucius III in his *Ad abolendam* of 1184 had indicated that bishops should begin to investigate heretics. But when Pope Innocent III convened the Fourth Lateran Council, the third Canon it issued was devoted to the punishment of heretics, whom it said should be turned over to the secular arm if found guilty. It also said that bishops should demand that the faithful denounce heretics, and that heretics should go before a special tribunal. Finally, it said that bishops who did not prosecute heresy should be removed.[2] This was the juridical foundation for the Inquisition, but it also was very clearly part of a larger agenda to centralize Church power (a large part of which was to use secular power to enforce Church doctrine).

Here we find the first archetypal dimension of the Inquisition: from its subsequent inception as a juridical process under Pope Gregory IX around 1230 and throughout its history, the Inquisition depended on the juncture of religious and secular power. The conjunction of church doctrine and judgment with secular enforcement allowed for a convenient and lasting excuse on the part of church officials, who could say that it was not they who executed heretics but rather the "secular arm." Thus, responsibility could be cast off—and when church inquisitors began to torture suspected heretics themselves, the Church allowed them to absolve one another. Despite these casuistries, the fact remains that the Inquisition roughly united both Church ideology and secular power, thus creating a model for a society totalized into unity via force and terror.

The second archetypal dimension of the Inquisition is that it, in effect, criminalized thought. Dissent could be punished. "Heresy," after all, is not identical with schism—it is before any organizational step toward separatism. "Heresy," rather, represents a freely chosen alternative to convention or orthodoxy; it represents alternative *ideas*. Thus, at its center, the inquisitional process consisted in enforcement of an ideological unity through implied or actual violence: this is its basic nature. It is true that many targets of the Inquisition—accused witches or sorcerers, for instance, or Cathars who had created an alternative church structure—were alleged to have gone beyond dissenting ideas, and had undertaken illicit practices. Yet even here, it is often exceedingly difficult to determine where orthodoxy ends and heresy or magic begins. Discerning such distinctions was the basis for the Inquisition.

The third archetypal dimension of the Inquisitions was the imposition of torture and of the death penalty. Pope Innocent IV, in his *Ad Extirpanda,* approved the use of torture by the secular arm in certain cases, but Pope Alexander IV in 1256 gave inquisitors the capacity to mutually absolve one another. Thus, one inquisitor could torture and another inquisitor could absolve him. And although torture was approved for only a single session, inquisitors could suspend torture and then resume it days later under a "continuance." It's true that in 1306, Pope Clement V ordered an inquiry into the necessity and propriety of torture, and that John XXII in 1317 ordered that a bishop had to agree before torture could be applied. In other words, there were some efforts at constraining torture. But there is also at least some truth to H. C. Lea's no doubt exaggerated assertion that "the whole system of the Inquisition was such as to render the resort to torture inevitable."[3]

My purpose here is not to enter into the thicket of polemics or apologetics concerning Inquisitions, but rather to point out that regardless of how frequently torture was applied by inquisitors, and regardless of exactly how many people actually received the death penalty and were burned to death or otherwise horribly murdered, the fact is that indisputably, the Church did authorize both torture and murder in order to extirpate 'heresy.' Indeed, Pope John Paul II issued an official apology on behalf of the Church for exactly such inquisitorial practices at the beginning of the twenty-first century. After all, there is a consistent pattern of inquisitorial torture and approved murder that stretches over centuries.

But why did officials of the Church deem torture necessary? There are two fundamental reasons. The first is that it allowed inquisitors to hunt down others who also might be part of a heretical group, and thus to extirpate competing institutions. What made Cathars, in particular, so threatening is that they developed an organizational structure in competition with that of the Catholic Church. But the prosecution of heresy was not exclusively to hunt down particular groups—it also proceeded against individuals. And in this case, the Church insisted on confessions. If individuals were recalcitrant (or, for that matter, innocent), obviously it was difficult to extract admissions of guilt, and so there emerged extraordinary means of forcing admission.

Confession was critically important, not only to Church inquisitors, but also later to Communist inquisitors, because under consideration in both cases are *ideological* crimes. If one violates a prevailing ideology, then the only way to return to the group is by confessing one's error and recanting. The mechanism is fundamentally the same in both cases: one is compelled by fear to acquiesce to the demands of those "deputized" to enforce the ideology of the totalized society.[4] And the basic premise was recognized by Dostoevsky during the nineteenth century: the inquisitors see themselves as the "protectors" of society, as taking away from individuals the "burden" of free will and enforcing on them what is supposedly right for them. Even torture and murder are somehow justified in the name of a totalizing ideological order.

Thus we arrive at our fourth archetypal dimension of the Inquisitions: terror. In an article entitled "Patterns of the Inquisitorial Mind as the Basis for a Pedagogy of Fear," Bartolomé Bennassar details the methods and purposes of the Spanish Inquisition during the sixteenth century. The original purpose of the Spanish Inquisition was to eliminate the "crypto-Judaism" allegedly practiced by "conversos," or crypto-converts to Judaism, and more than nine out of ten victims of the early Spanish Inquisition (founded 1478–1481) were Jews or Jewish converts.[5] But by the sixteenth century, the "Holy Office . . . became an instrument for producing unanimity of words, actions, and thoughts, and for 'guaranteeing social immobility under the constraint of ideological hermeticism.'"[6] In addition to Jews or crypto-Jews, its victims included crypto-Muslims, mystics [Alumbrados], and various sects of Protestantism. The Spanish Inquisition "in order to enforce conformity with the official religious, political, and social model," chose to "foster fear at all levels of the social body."[7] A primary aim of the Spanish Inquisition in the sixteenth century was to inspire terror in the populace.

The terror that the Inquisition inspired in the population was deliberately fostered, as the Inquisitors themselves wrote. Bennassar quotes Francisco Peña, who republished Nicholas Eymerich's *Directorium Inquisitorium,* and wrote that "we must remember that the essential aim of the trial and death sentence is not saving the soul of the defendant, but furthering the public good and terrorizing the people."[8] He also observed that "there is no doubt that instructing and threatening the people by publicizing the sentences and imposing sanbenitos [humiliation] is a good method." And another official wrote in 1564 that as the Inquisition "is too much feared to be well accepted," and as "we already know that [people] do not love it, it is fitting that people nurture fear."[9] Hence arose the widespread advice of the time: *que mirase lo que dice,* or "watch what you say." Given historians now recognize that, in the mid-sixteenth century, the Inquisition did not impose torture or the death penalty at rates that exceeded those of the civil courts, one has to ask why "the whole population was so afraid of the Holy Office."

Hence we arrive at our fifth characteristic of the Inquisitions: secrecy of proceedings. The *Reportorium Inquisitorum* (Valencia: 1491) insists "witnesses must lodge their deposition in secret, not publicly, so that they may speak without restraint and tell the whole truth."[10] All charges were to be secret, and "the more secret the matters dealt with are, the more they are held as sacred and revered by all those who have no access to them," wrote an official to the Santiago tribunal in 1607.[11] And Jaime Contreras wrote that "Secrecy fostered the myth and thereby general fear and popular intimidation before the dreadful institution. This socio-psychological process.... constituted perhaps the best weapon of the Inquisition: wrapping itself up in a mist of mystery created fear or at least caution."[12] Inquisitors would not charge a summoned suspect but would force him to guess about why he had been arrested.[13] Not allowing the accused to face their accusers or to hear the evidence or charges against them generated fear, and thus the likelihood that a victim would "inform" against someone else, be it a family member, a friend, or a neighbor. Such secret proceedings intensified terror in the populace.

And the final archetypal dimension of the Inquisitions was infamy. If the proceedings and witnesses were secret at least partly in order to inspire terror, the judgments depended in large part for their effectiveness upon publicity.

The autos-da-fé—public lashings and burnings—became great notorious spectacles in Spain, but even lesser penalties depended on public shame. The "sanbenito" mentioned by the inquisitor Peña was the garb of public humiliation, adorned with the family name of the accused, and even after the individual no longer had to wear it in public, it was hung in the local church to encourage generational shame.[14] Fear of secret condemnation or betrayal, and fear of public shame: these are very much the same dynamics that we see at work in Leninist-Stalinist Russia during the first decades of Communist dictatorship.

Of course, I am not alone in making this connection between the Catholic Inquisitions and modern secular state inquisitions. Bennassar writes that "the inquisitorial mind" still exists today:

> Secrecy, mystery is the main characteristic of the political police forces of totalitarian states and even, to some extent, of some democratic ones. We readily recall the mysterious fear aroused by the Gestapo and the GPU after the Cheka, and before the NKVD, [later] the KGB. Fear is also fostered by secret police forces in countries like Argentina . . . Chile, Paraguay, and all the Gulag countries of the Eastern bloc. The inquisitorial network of familiars and commissioners has truly been "improved upon." . . . The work of persuading the defendant to confess for the salvation of his or her soul was the forerunner of the contemporary brainwashing that leads one to self-denunciation for the honor and safety of the new god, the state.[15]

Once fear is generated throughout society, people "become silent and try to adapt to the dominant social pattern, religious, ideological, or political—[they] keep quiet and follow the rules till they stop even thinking, leaving some select individuals to think rightly for them and build their happiness in this world or the next, whether they like it or not."[16] This expresses precisely the inquisitorial mentality (and its consequences) as captured by Dostoevsky in the character of the "Grand Inquisitor," a mentality that by no means disappeared over the course of the twentieth century.

Numerous recent studies have outlined how the Catholic Inquisitions really do fit into the general category of jurisprudence, and how many inquisitors were concerned about the legal niceties of their work. John Tedeschi, in *The Prosecution of Heresy*, notes for instance that the secrecy of the inquisitors was in part for witness protection, so that the accused could not retaliate. Tedeschi quotes Eliseo Masini, inquisitor of Genoa, who calls for "great prudence" in the "jailing of suspects" "because the mere fact of incarceration for the crime of heresy brings notable infamy to the person. Thus it will be necessary to study carefully the nature of the evidence, the quality of the witnesses, and the condition of the accused."[17] Inquisitors meticulously documented their findings, and were under the supervision of the Church bureaucracy. In short, there were indeed constraints on the power of the inquisitors.

But all this said, the fact remains that the Inquisitions represent a set of archetypal characteristics that recurred in the twentieth century under various secular dictatorships with much fewer limitations and with far greater virulence. Every one of these archetypal characteristics is found again in various Fascist and Communist regimes, and indeed, even recur in societies that do not quite so easily fit into either "fascist" or "communist" categories. The unity or totalizing of secular and religious bureaucracies into a single totalitarian power, the criminalization of thought, the use of torture and murder, the inculcation of terror in the populace, the use of secret evidence and witnesses, and the use of public infamy, humiliation, or "show trials" or "show executions" [autos-da-fé]—all of these can be found again in the totalitarianisms of the twentieth century.

My point here is not that the Catholic Inquisition is to blame for modern totalitarianism. It is, rather, that what we see emerging in the various Inquisitions is a *phenomenon* with particular characteristics that recurs again in the twentieth century. I believe that it is vitally important for us to understand as fully as possible the nature of this phenomenon, to throw light on *how* it recurs in the twentieth century, even in the works of authors who would seem disconnected from one another and even to be opponents of one another. For it is clearly the case that the phenomenon represented by the Inquisitions can be traced through the works of various eighteenth-, nineteenth-, and twentieth-century political philosophers—out of whose works emerged the totalitarianisms of the twentieth century. If we are not to see these same kinds of events and phenomena recur again, we must begin to analyze and understand more fully the kinds of political philosophies that give rise to them. New inquisitions do not arise *ex nihilo,* but derive from particular kinds of political philosophies.

And so, let us delve now into the labyrinthine channels through which the archetype of the old Inquisitions emerged into new, secular inquisitions.

3

Joseph de Maistre and the Inquisition

We must begin our journey in the eighteenth century with the Catholic political philosopher Joseph de Maistre, in whose dark thought at the beginning of the modern era we glimpse the origins of modern totalitarianism. Joseph de Maistre's life is easily recounted. He was born on 1 April 1753, in Savoy, to François-Xavier de Maistre, a judge who had been brought into nobility by the King of Sardinia. Maistre himself took a Law degree in Turin, and was appointed as a public prosecutor in Savoy in 1774. He was born to a deeply Catholic family, but he also joined a Masonic lodge that, in turn, offered him many personal and political connections. Maistre knew that Freemasonry was condemned by the Church, yet he joined a lodge; he wrote that heretics were among the worst of criminals, and yet he was very much influenced by Protestant mystics. We see this duality reflected throughout Maistre's work and thought. This division within Maistre had its origins (in part) in the turmoil and terror of the French Revolution. For before the French Revolution in 1789, Maistre was sympathetic to freedom of thought and to revolutionary impulses—but, by 1792, he was forced to flee his native land by the invasion of Savoy by France, after which he was separated from his wife and children for more than twenty years. Maistre lived in exile in Lausanne, where he represented the Sardinian king, until 1798, when he moved to Italy. Then, in 1802, he was sent to represent the King of Sardinia in Saint Petersburg, Russia, where he remained until 1817. In exile, he refined his antirevolutionary, ultraconservative Catholic views. He only returned to his home and family in 1817, and he died in 1821. His most important works were written during the last third of his life, many—for example, *Soirées de Saint-Pétersbourg* (a series of literary-philosophical dialogues)—during his stay in Russia.

From our perspective, the most important dynamic in Maistre's life is one of the least examined. He certainly was influenced by the Christian theosophy of Louis-Claude de Saint-Martin, whom he mentioned a number of times in his *Soirées*; and he was a Freemason who furthermore drew on pansophic ideas in his writings. Maistre accepted, for example, the concept of a golden age of humanity and the corollary to it—that our own time represents a precipitous decline. Jean-Louis Darcel and some other scholars even compare Maistre to the German theosophers Karl von Eckhartshausen and Franz von Baader.[1] But there is a striking difference between Maistre and any of these clearly esoteric theosophers, which could be summed up by the following fact: unlike any of them, Maistre was capable of writing a treatise defending the institution of the Inquisition.

What are we to make of such a figure? It is altogether too facile to liken Maistre to esoteric authors such as Baader, Eckhartshausen, or Saint-Martin, when, unlike any of them, his work has at its center not an embrace of the *inner*—mysticism or gnosis—but, rather, an uncompromising affirmation of the *outer*, of the necessity for total church and state authority.[2] Maistre's work, impelled by his horror of the French Revolution, insists on a reactionary assertion of Church infallibility and of the power of the state. Paradoxically, for Saint-Martin, who saw its horrors firsthand, the French Revolution became the occasion (as what was externally reliable was being swept away) for him to take even more the "inward road" toward spiritual life, whereas for Maistre, the social chaos of the Revolution (seen from afar) became the occasion for his call for the imposition of *external* religious and state authority. In truth, these are antithetical responses.

Yet it is important to recognize, too, that the great theosophers—Saint-Martin, Eckhartshausen, and Baader in particular—did not consider themselves heretical, nor, by and large, were they perceived by others as heretical. Admittedly, Baader did propose the dissolution of the papacy and its replacement with a synodical union of Orthodoxy and Catholicism—but this remained a reform proposal within Roman Catholicism that, of course, went nowhere at the time. Baader never left the Church, and remained a devout Catholic, like Maistre himself. Saint-Martin—referred to directly and present indirectly elsewhere in Maistre's *Soirées*—although deeply mystical, is not by any means therefore explicitly or consciously heretical. Thus, for Maistre to cite Saint-Martin is not—from this perspective—for him to engage in a dalliance with heresy. Saint-Martin, or indeed Baader, arguably exist within the ambit of orthodox Christianity. Hence, when relatively late in life Maistre wrote his *Defense of the Spanish Inquisition*, it cannot be said that he had a figure such as Saint-Martin in mind.

Still, there is a peculiar tension here, because Maistre clearly (in *Defense of the Spanish Inquisition*) endorses a demonstrably antimystical institution. It is worth examining Maistre's *Defense* carefully, because it does shed light on Maistre's viewpoint. Early on, Maistre raises what is by now the old saw that the Inquisition itself did not torture or murder people—that only the secular government did this.[3] But of course, this claim ignores the simple fact that the secular governments only instituted such procedures at the explicit behest of the Roman Catholic Church as instituted by the Fourth Lateran Council's insistence, and the insistence of Pope Innocent III, that secular governments under Catholicism institute procedures to rid themselves of heretics (or, perhaps rather, "heretics"). One cannot reasonably absolve the Church of blame for the results of the Inquisition merely because the secular arm committed the atrocities, when, after all, they did so under Church authorization and direction.

Maistre misleadingly claims that the "every man who remains quiet is left undisturbed" by the Inquisition, and that those who were prosecuted, tortured, and murdered, had only themselves to blame.[4] But alas, accounts and assessments of the Spanish Inquisition attest otherwise. Bartolomé Bennassar writes at length about the terror generated in the population by the very words "official of the Holy Office." He notes that the sentences of the Inquisition were more or less similar to those of the civil courts but observes that the terror in the population was far greater than the sentences themselves would account for. Why? Bennassar points out two primary reasons: secrecy, and infamy.[5] Witnesses were kept hidden from defendants and thus one could not confront or cross-examine one's accusers. And the penalties of the Inquisition relied on not only torture and murder but also public humiliation for one's family. These two together—fear that anyone could be an accuser against whom one could not respond, and fear of public humiliation—served to make the Inquisition a terrifying institution whose reach extended deep into the general population.

But the most important dimension of Maistre's work, for our purposes, is his insistence that heresy is arguably the greatest of crimes. He writes that "the heresiarch, the obstinate heretic, and the propagator of heresy, ought to be classed among the greatest criminals."[6] And Maistre asserts that by suppressing heretics, the Inquisition created a much more stable, ordered society. Had the Inquisition been in sufficient power against Lutheranism, the Thirty Years' War would have been prevented, and so, too, the French Revolution would never have taken place, he thinks.[7] Spain was the "happiest," "most ordered country in Europe," under the Inquisition, Maistre argues—the Inquisition "saved" and even "immortalized" Spain.[8] Yet at what cost?

There is a fundamental question here. It is true that the suppression of heresy and the enforcement of a "pedagogy of fear" on a population does ensure order, at least in some respects. Yet it can only ensure order exactly as Dostoevsky's Grand Inquisitor said, by eliminating freedom of thought and, in effect, by shifting responsibility from the individual to the Inquisitors. Freedom of thought, in this view, is too great for the individual to bear, and so the Church must assume corporate responsibility for determining what is acceptable and what is unacceptable thought. Exactly the same argument can be applied to the imposition of any centralized secular state power on society: at the heart of Maistre's endorsement of the Inquisition is the Hobbesian belief that man is fundamentally evil by nature and must be restrained by an outside force, be it the Church in the form of the Inquisition, or, by extension, the fascist government, or the Communist Party.

At the crux of Maistre's endorsement of the Inquisition is his belief that once Catholicism has become predominant in a society, "things change. Since religion and sovereignty have embraced one another in the state, their interests must necessarily be confounded."[9] Thus the ideal state, in Maistre's view, is one in which there is a tribunal to maintain orthodoxy in what has become a national religion, indeed, something akin to a unified theocratic state. Although in the stage of proselytizing, Catholicism is to be meek and mild, when in the stage of state control, Catholicism must incorporate state violence via a tribunal to enforce religious orthodoxy.[10] In his view, the interests of state and religion become one. And if one accepts this unity, then, indeed, heresy becomes not merely a matter of freedom of thought, but in effect a crime against the state.

Maistre detests individualism. In his view, democracy is the "harshest, most despotic, and most intolerable" form of government because it is anarchic, and "whoever says that man is born for liberty is speaking nonsense."[11] A state exists, he argues, only by virtue of sovereignty, and individuals cannot have sovereignty over themselves: they must be restrained by an outside, a sovereign force.[12] One cannot have a "multiheaded" leadership—the idea itself is ridiculous, Maistre contends. He goes so far as to claim that "There is no sovereign without a nation, just as there is no nation without a sovereign."[13] Maistre's broader logic is this: God is sovereign over man; and among men, there must therefore also be a sovereign. Thus, he believes, monarchy is the most natural of state institutions, just as the papacy is the most natural form of religious leadership. At heart, Maistre rejects individualism and notions of liberty as Protestant and as fundamentally heretical: what he insists on is an organically unified religious state. In this larger context, then, Maistre's vigorous defense of the Inquisition is not, as some have claimed, an anomalous work disconnected from his thought as a whole, but in fact belongs very much to the center of Maistre's worldview.

Yet can we go further and, with Isaiah Berlin, see Maistre as an originating source for twentieth-century totalitarianism? At the very least, there is some cause for such a belief. Émile Faguet wrote in 1899 of Maistre that "his Christianity is terror, passive obedience, and the religion of the state," and Samuel Rocheblave wrote of Maistre's "christianisme de la Terreur."[14] Certainly there is something authentically new emerging in Maistre's work: a nonclerical defense of the Inquisition and of centralized and unified state power. The terror of the French Revolution generated in Maistre its antithesis. Given that the masses rose up in the French Revolution, then the counter must be the imposition of divine authority and authoritarian suppression of individualism and of dissent. The tyranny of the masses must be opposed by an authoritarian force. In Maistre's view, constitutions, republicanism, democracy, individualism, and all the institutions of liberalism are to be scorned and opposed because man is intrinsically suited to monarchic or authoritarian centralized power conjoined with religious authority.

And there is more. Maistre feverishly opposes those whom he terms "la secte." By this, he means dissenters, those who subvert established order—secular heretics. Among them, he lists Protestants, Jews, Jacobins, intellectuals, scientists—anyone whose faith is in individualism or rationalism rather than in the Church. "This," writes Berlin, "is 'la secte,' and it never sleeps, it is forever boring from within."[15] "La secte" therefore, Maistre thinks, must be suppressed and, if possible, extirpated. As Berlin later puts it, from this perspective "men must submit freely to authority; but they must submit. For they are too corrupt, too feeble to govern themselves; and without government, they collapse into anarchy and are lost."[16] Here we see a confusion of the secular state and religion; here we see the emergence of the persecutorial state that hunts down dissenters.

And there is still more. For in Maistre we see the conceptual emergence of the inquisitorial secular state. Maistre writes that "Government is a true religion. It has its dogmas, its mysteries, its priests. To submit it to the discussion of each individual is to destroy it. It is given life only by the reason of the nation, that is, by a political faith of which it is a symbol."[17] What is more, "Man's first need is that his growing reason be put under the double yoke [of church and state]. It should be annihilated, it should lose itself in the reason of the nation, so that it is transformed from its individual existence into another—communal—being, as a river that falls into the ocean does indeed persist in the midst of the waters, but without name or personal identity."[18] Berlin observes that Maistre's opposition to individualism, "far beyond traditional authoritarianism," is "terrifyingly modern." He goes so far as to conclude that "Maistre's deeply pessimistic vision is the heart of the totalitarianisms, of both left and right, of our terrible [twentieth] century."[19]

Of course, Berlin's influential essay is subtler than its title might suggest. Berlin recognizes that Maistre predicted the brutality of the Russian Revolution and its consequences, and he offers some illuminating remarks on Maistre and Voltaire as, paradoxically, two sides of the same coin. Maistre foresaw that if religious and civil authority were overthrown in czarist Russia, the results would be terrible—and so he proposed that the authorities only gradually introduce Western liberal thought so as not to overthrow the social order and create an atheistic tyranny of the masses. Berlin also observes that Voltaire and Maistre proposed fundamentally cynical and even heartless perspectives that were *together* the intellectual origins of modern totalitarianism. Berlin does not lay the blame for totalitarianism entirely at the feet of Maistre by any means. His argument, rather, is that we see totalitarianism foreshadowed in Maistre's works.

I believe that Berlin is quite right in this.

Some forty years after Berlin's essay was published, an expert on Maistre, Richard Lebrun, responded. Lebrun wrote that Berlin's assessment of Maistre is "seriously misleading" for a variety of reasons, but primarily because Berlin asserts that "Maistre believed in authority because it was an irrational force."[20] According to Lebrun, Berlin "distorts Maistre's overall position by overemphasizing what he characterizes as the 'irrational' aspects of Maistre's theorizing."[21] Lebrun sees Berlin's depiction of Maistre as more "lurid" than "lifelike." In these assessments, Lebrun is right: Berlin does overemphasize the irrationalism of Maistre in order, I think, to better conform Maistre's thought to the prevalent depiction of fascism during the mid-twentieth century as a predominantly backward-looking, irrationalist movement rather than as a futurist movement deeply imbued with the spirit of industrialism.

But, paradoxically, Lebrun's point actually confirms the deeper insight that Berlin had into the connections between Maistrean thought and twentieth-century totalitarianism. If Maistre's thought is not so easily characterized as simply "irrationalist," then it is similar to fascism in yet another way. For Italian Fascism and German National Socialism were very much intent upon the imposition of order upon society and upon a quasi-religious rejection of political dissent as a kind of heresy. In its totalization of society, Fascism represented not an atavistic primitivism, but an industrialist futurism, even a secular millennialism that cannot be accurately dismissed as mere "irrationalism." The reality is more complicated than that, both in the case of Maistre and in the cases of twentieth-century fascism.

In any case, already a solid body of research has emerged that shows how Maistre formed a major source for the work of one of the most prominent legal theorists during Hitler's Third Reich: Carl Schmitt (1888–1985). As Stephen Holmes has put it in *The Anatomy of Antiliberalism,* Maistre represents a "truly brilliant" originator of the antiliberal tradition, and Schmitt in turn represents Maistre's "most influential twentieth-century admirer."[22] And Graeme Garrard summarizes neatly the connections between these two figures. He writes that:

> there is no doubt that Maistre and Schmitt were kindred spirits in many ways. . . . It is beyond question that they had a great deal in common, both personally and ideologically. . . . Both believed in Catholicism as the one true faith, admired the Church as a model political institution, and denounced Protestantism for contributing to the fatal destabilization of the social, political, and religious order of modern Europe. Maistre and Schmitt were also both jurists.[23]

It is true, as Garrard argues, that Schmitt selectively chose parts of Maistre's work to cite, and even that Schmitt and Maistre diverge in views because they belong to very different eras and societies, but such observations do not change (and in some respects, underscore) the fundamental connections between these two authors.

It is with good reason that Schmitt drew extensively on the works and thought of Maistre. Maistre was not as anti-Semitic as Schmitt, he was no decisionist, and he was more ambivalent toward Freemasonry and related European esoteric currents—this is true.[24] But these are adventitious differences that derive from their respective eras. More important are the facts that Maistre and Schmitt both saw the Inquisition as a fine juridical model, that both despised liberalism and individualism, and that both insisted on a state corporatism whose origins are unquestionably in Roman Catholicism. We will analyze Schmitt and his work in more detail shortly, but for now it is sufficient to say that his work represents an extension and a development of themes that first appear in modernity in the work of Maistre, and that reappear in even more fiery and extreme form in the work of the other primary predecessor whom Schmitt cites: Juan Donoso Cortés.

4

Juan Donoso Cortés and the "Sickness" of the Liberal State

Juan Donoso Cortés is the next major figure in the lineage of authoritarianism that began with Maistre. Donoso Cortés was born in 1809 in the arid province of Extremadura; his father was a successful lawyer and mayor of the town of Don Benito.[1] He grew up in relative prosperity—his father held land that brought in an income—and Donoso Cortés went on to study law at the University of Seville, from which he was graduated in 1828. He lived the good life thereafter in Madrid and then back in Don Benito, running up debts, writing poetry, and continuing intense reading of both romantic and conservative writers. In 1829, he accepted a professorship in the humanities, and married a wealthy young woman who gave birth to a child, María, that died at two, and who herself died in 1835. After these deaths, the most important women in Donoso's life were royalty: the Queen (or Queen Mother), in particular María Christina, in whose favor he rose to high political prominence. In 1837, he was elected to parliament, and in the 1840s, he played a major role in Spanish politics. His work took a decisively authoritarian turn after the revolutionary year of 1848—for the following year, 1849, saw his famous speech and letters defending dictatorship and Catholic authoritarianism against disorder and against what he derided as "philosophical civilization." Deeply religious, Donoso Cortés was known for his piety, charity, and personal asceticism; he was internationally famous for his defenses of order and authority in the tradition of Maistre; and it came as a shock when he died in 1853 at the young age of forty-four.

The most important work of Donoso Cortés, at least for our line of inquiry, was his "Speech on Dictatorship," given 4 January 1849. In this oration, he asserted that, faced with the risk of revolutionary excess, law alone is not enough to preserve order. Thus, "when [the letter of the law] is not enough [to save society], then dictatorship is best." Donoso explicitly set aside any assertion of his own ascent to power, but insisted that "in [revolutionary] circumstances, I say that dictatorship is as legitimate, good, and beneficial a form of government as any other. It is a rational form of government that can be defended in theory as in practice."[2] He holds—in a tradition that was to be followed by Carl Schmitt in the twentieth century—that laws may be set aside in exceptional circumstances, because what matters is "society. Everything through society, everything for society, always society, society in all circumstances and on all occasions." Of course, Donoso is here insisting on social totalism.

He then makes absolutely explicit why he insists on a "clear, luminous, and indestructible theory of dictatorship" by employing a metaphor of illness and health in society. Donoso declaims that "invading forces, called illnesses in the human body and something else in the social body (but essentially being one and the same thing), have two forms." One is when "illnesses are complete spread throughout a society by individuals," while in the other, "acutely diseased form," "these illnesses are concentrated in and represented by political associations."[3] In the first case, resistance to widespread illness in the social body is also widespread: it is "dispersed throughout the government, the authorities, the law courts," that is, "throughout the entire social body." But when, in the second case, the illness is concentrated in political associations, then, necessarily "the resisting forces concentrate themselves into the hands of one man." Dictatorship, he continues, is found in every society on earth, and is even, if he may say so, "a divine fact" in the person of God Himself. Social illness or disorder has to be combated by the unified society in the person of the dictator who can impose his (society's) unified will on the disorder and eradicate it.

Donoso's thought is typically dualistic. Hence, he posits that there are only two forms of repression in the world: religious and political. These he likens to two linked "thermometers." When "the religious thermometer rises, the thermometer of political repression falls."[4] Thus, Jesus and his disciples had no government whatever, because they had internal (religious) discipline. But when there is no religious discipline, then tyranny and slavery rule. The more corrupt the society becomes, the more government and with it political repression must grow. Hence, he continues, "if government was not necessary when religious repression was at its height, now that religious repression does not exist, there will be no form of government powerful enough to maintain order, for all despotisms will be weak." This, he continues, is "placing the finger in the wound:" that is, he is simply diagnosing the illness in society as it actually is.[5] Only a "healthy religious reaction" will save society. And such a miraculous healthy religious reaction, such a return of "religious repression," he sadly says, he cannot expect.

Donoso concludes that his audience must choose between "a dictatorship of insurrection and a dictatorship of the government."[6] Had he the choice, he would of course choose freedom over dictatorship, but since "freedom does not exist in Europe," then "I choose the dictatorship of the government as the least wearisome as well as the least outrageous." Donoso chooses to reject the "dictatorship from below," and to accept instead "one that comes from above," one that is "noble," that represents a "dictatorship of the saber." It is not for nothing that Donoso has been accused of being a kind of Manichee in his extreme dualism (he was so accused in his own lifetime): and we see his dualism here again, as in so many other places. True to form, in his final line, he urges his audience to vote, always, "for what is more healthy."

Let us pursue a bit more carefully, now, this theme of social health and disease in Donoso's work, since it is the *leitmotif* of his most famous speech. For here, in this theme of health, we have a key to unlock a door whose opening will reveal some hidden dimensions of Donoso's thought and life. We may begin by noting that, near the end of his "Speech on Dictatorship," Donoso remarks that he will conclude because both Congress and he himself are tired. "Frankly, gentlemen," he continues, "I must declare here that I cannot continue because I am ill. It is a miracle that I could speak at all."[7] And he adds, a bit later, that his illness would not permit him to add too much more. Indeed, he concludes his speech only a handful of paragraphs later, with the observation that he and his fellow legislators "will vote for what is more healthy."

These references to Donoso's own illness are jarring, given all that he has said about the repression of illness in society. With what was he ill? And could his own illness be reflected into his most famous speech? Our answers to such questions come by consulting biographical investigations into Donoso's last years of life. It is true that during his last years of life, he was very devout, charitable, and ascetic. But, as John Graham detailed in his biography of Donoso Cortés, in fact in the latter years of his life, Donoso was suffering from the acute stages of a venereal disease—which he kept a secret, and which he sought to treat on his own.[8] The symptoms of this disease, probably syphilis, were appalling. Among his family papers are the names of a series of drugs recorded in his own hand, and as recently as 1971, his preserved library included worn copies of medical treatises on the urinary tract and genitals.[9] He meticulously recorded his symptoms, which included "blood in the urine, swelling of the testicles, utter loss of control over sexual appetites and functions at all times of the day, and much pain." His symptoms also included "diarrhea, bloating of the stomach, general weakness, sleeplessness, sharp pains in the [legs], and some paralysis."[10] The loss of control must have been terrifying, especially because some of the symptoms must have been occurring at the very time that he had garnered the most international fame and notoriety, near the end of his life. Indeed, "his illness in 1849 is the most severe one he recorded."[11] How difficult it must have been to seek to master the disorder in his own body, even as he declaimed against the disorder and illnesses of society as a whole. What his opponents and enemies would have done with such knowledge! No wonder he kept the nature of his illness a secret.

But there is more to consider here. Is it not possible, indeed, likely, that Donoso's own struggle to master and to extirpate the raging illness in his own body might well have been projected outward into society as a whole? He struggled to impose his will-to-health upon the various horrific symptoms of his own disease, but if he could not be the dictator of his own body, he could at least insist on the stability and health of society around him. Donoso's dualism now appears in a different light. When he argues against socialism and communism and revolutionary disorder, he is in some sense arguing also against the illness that has infected him, and insisting on a cure by sheer imposition of will, by penance and mortification, by hair shirt—by dictatorial *fiat*.

Although psychological explanations may not always be entirely useful as explanatory tools, in this particular case it would seem that psychology can play an even greater than usual role in revealing what is actually at work in Donoso's writing.

It is not as though this theme is found only in the "Speech on Dictatorship." The same metaphor of illness runs through, for instance, Donoso's "Letter to the Editors of *El Pais* and *El Heraldo*." There, he refers to all the various forms of rationalism and in particular of philosophy as "doctrines of perdition" that are "poisoning" society. Thus, "European society is dying. Its extremities are cold. Its heart will soon stop beating. Do you know why Europe is dying? It is dying because it is poisoned."[12] The poison? "Every anti-Catholic word uttered from the mouths of philosophers. [Society] is dying because error kills. And this society is grounded in errors. Everything that it holds to be incontestable is false." And so "the disaster that must come will be the disaster *par excellence* of History. Individuals can still save themselves because they can always save themselves. But society is lost."[13] These words read somewhat more poignantly if we consider that Donoso himself was dying, that he was dying because of a venereal error years before, one that had irrevocably poisoned him, and that his own heart soon after ceased to beat.

By 1852, he is writing even more harshly against "rationalism," against "freedom," against "liberalism," and against "parliamentarianism," all of which he terms variant forms of "insanity."[14] He writes of the "health of the organism" [society] as being more important than the health of any particular organ [institution]; and he affirms even more totally the immoveable and complete unchanging truth of Catholicism in the face of all modern rationalist heresies.[15] And he protests that he has never defended tyranny, only that he writes of things as they actually are, not through a gauzy romantic haze. What he is fundamentally attacking, he writes to Cardinal Fornari, is "heretics" and "heresies," "ancient errors that appear before our eyes today."[16] Society is "poisoned with the venom" of "irksome heresy."

The theme of revolution as fever or as illness in society is by no means limited to Donoso's work. We find it, for example, in the earlier writings of the great German theosopher Franz von Baader. But in Baader, we do not find the kind of extremism that we see in Donoso Cortés—quite the opposite. In Baader's view, revolutions may represent an "inflammation" in society, but what is called for is not therefore "dictatorship" or "repression," so much as an organic return to natural balance and health. And Baader was Catholic, like Donoso—yet he did not insist on papal infallibility but rather called for a conciliar union of Eastern Orthodoxy and Roman Catholicism, and for an end to the institution of the papacy itself. Baader is useful here, in other words, as an instance of how a devout Catholic might reach very different conclusions and responses from those of Donoso, even if beginning with the same metaphor of health and illness.

But Donoso took a different course: driven at least in part by his own decaying body, he strove to impose infallible Catholic dogmatic order on the world around him by way of his writing. He insisted, as Maistre did before him, on the importance of extirpating modernist "heresy" and "poison" from the social body. There is, in the compressed fury of his writing, often a sense that he would extirpate if he could people as well as ideas. In his masterwork, *Essays on Catholicism, Liberalism, and Socialism,* he writes that "it is absurd to endeavor to extirpate the evil from the society in which it exists by incidence only, without touching the individuals in whom it was originally and essentially."[17] He cites among the Church Fathers, Tertullian, and he extols the infallibility of the Church and its power at triumphing over heretics.[18] The "doctrinal intolerance" of the Church has alone "saved the world from chaos."[19] Not surprisingly, Donoso also approves of Augustine and his dualistic notion of the "City of God" from which the Donosian and Maistrean line of thought takes its origins.

What we see in Donoso is a total reaction against the perceived chaos of modernity and individualism. Everywhere he looks is heresy; everywhere he finds heretics. Modernity itself is, in his mind, nothing but a concatenation of errors, and so it is little surprise that rather than insisting upon the Inquisition to stamp out particular errors, Donoso sees the wrath of God coming down on all of humanity and in particular upon European civilization. An inquisition requires the possibility of imposing doctrinal order on society, but when things have gone too far, then nothing can ensue but the pallor of death itself, apocalyptic visions of vast wars and calamities and lunatic despotism. It is perhaps indicative that there is some truth in his vision that his prophecies of European disaster, of the baleful effects of communism and of tyranny, of world war and of totalitarianism, were borne out by history less than a century later.

But Donoso was not a man who went for complexities or subtleties: for him, the world was utterly divided into the saved and the damned, into Catholic or philosophical civilizations, into doctrinal orthodoxy or total heresy. A man of extremes, his vision was nothing if not totalizing and absolute. Donoso's antimodernism was visceral, and he could see nothing worth redeeming in modernity. Protestantism, individualism, science, rationalism, philosophy—these were all to him delusional, errors to be rejected by those who placed their entire faith in the Church. Like Maistre before him, Donoso saw the world not as progressing, but as caught in a precipitous decline. Humanity, ever more separated from its religious salvation, has to have a powerful dictatorial force to hold it back from the total abyss. A secular dictatorship is better than what he sees as the only alternative: the unleashing of total chaos.

In Donoso's writing, as in Maistre's, we see the origin of the line of thought whose next incarnation is the German political philosopher Carl Schmitt. Thus it is no surprise that Schmitt wrote in detail, and multiple times, on Donoso's work and its significance. Of his articles on Donoso, among the most important is "The Unknown Donoso Cortés," in which Schmitt offers an overview of Donoso's importance in relation to his own political philosophy. In a no doubt deliberately misleading aside, Schmitt claims that the origin of George Sorel's work—and by extension, of fascism, state corporatism, and communism—lies not in figures such as Maistre and Donoso but, rather, in the antiquated and genteel socialism of Proudhon (whom Donoso vilified as Satanic, while ignoring Marx)! The truth is, of course, that there is a direct line from Maistre and Donoso through Sorel to both fascism and communism, and Schmitt knew this all too well. But he wanted to defend Donoso, and throw the reader off track, for Schmitt saw in Donoso's fierce dualism his own distinction between "friend" and "enemy."[20] Thus Schmitt concludes his essay by insisting that we should acknowledge the "purity and greatness" of Donoso, who represents "the exceptional phenomenon of a singular political intuition rooted in secular horizons."[21]

But even this final sentence of Schmitt's essay on Donoso is deceptive, for we know all too well (as Schmitt himself certainly also did) that Donoso was far from being "rooted in secular horizons." The very assertion is comical, given the fanaticism with which Donoso asserted the absolute primacy of the Catholic Church. Indeed, Donoso's insistence on the infallibility of the Church and of the Pope, attested to in his letter to Cardinal Fornari, is widely credited with influencing the Catholic Church's declaration of the doctrine of papal infallibility in 1870. Thus Donoso would seem to be the furthest imaginable from someone who is "rooted in secular horizons." Donoso was embroiled in the hugger-mugger of daily political intrigue in Spain, and he was insistent on defending the concept of a more or less secular dictatorship. But for all that, any reader of *Ensayo sobre el catolicismo, el liberalismo, y el socialismo* could not fail to see that Donoso was *rooted* only in Catholicism.

How do we then explain the apparent contradiction between Donoso's defense of secular dictatorship, on the one hand, and his totalistic embrace of Catholicism, on the other? Here the work of Schmitt becomes especially valuable because we see in it the actual conduit from the Maistrean/Donosian line right into the work of a primary theorist of state totalism in the twentieth century. What Schmitt, as a fascist thinker, embraced above all in Donoso is none other than Schmitt's own projected thought. Schmitt praises Donoso for being rooted in secular horizons and for coldly endorsing dictatorship—but it is Schmitt who moved from Catholicism to secular state corporatism and who accepted Nazism and Hitler's dictatorship. Schmitt praises Donoso for his "decisionism," as opposed to the mere "discussions" of parliamentary democracy that they both detest—but it is Schmitt who is the decisionist, a term and an idea very much bound up with the twentieth, not the nineteenth, century.[22]

Donoso Cortés is an important figure because he represents the awakening of the idea that was to grow and darken the secular horizon of the twentieth century in the state corporatism of both communism and fascism. In him, we see emerging even more clearly than in Maistre the assertion of Dostoevsky's Grand Inquisitor that man ought not be free but must live under the imposed order of state corporatist dictatorship. Because man is by nature utterly fallen, an authoritarian state must be imposed that will decide the proper course for errant individuals and thus impose on humanity the "happiness" of the antheap. Such an imposition is, exactly as Donoso makes it out to be, coldly "rational" just like the slaughter of millions in the twentieth century—

ruthless industrial efficiency. How can reasoning people conceive of and carry out the slaughter of millions? Only by *rationalizing* it. This kind of thinking, like it or not, has its origins at least in part in the work of figures such as Maistre and Donoso, and more broadly in the bloody tradition of the persecution of heretics.

But in order to see another conduit in this path from the Inquisition to totalitarianism, let us turn to yet another figure instrumental in the emergence of state corporatism in the twentieth century, whom we have already met in passing, but now must meet formally: Georges Sorel.

5

Georges Sorel and Charles Maurras

The Emergence of Secular State Corporatism

It was Wyndham Lewis who, in 1926, published his assertion in *The Art of Being Ruled* that in the work of Georges Sorel (1847–1922) is nothing less than the "key" to the political thought of the era.[1] Yet others, in his own lifetime and after, have dismissed Sorel as merely a "chatterbox," little more than a garrulous fool. What are we to make of such a figure, who was at various times a supporter of radical syndicalism, Bolshevism, communism, and fascism, who influenced both Lenin and Mussolini, and whose work is said to be instrumental for the emergence of totalitarianism even during his own lifetime? It would be a mistake to attribute too much of an intellectual system to Sorel, for his work is often disorderly and rambling. Any greater coherence lies in Sorel's elastic ability to project his fundamental enthusiasms for a "workers' revolution" into whatever movement might seem at the moment a suitable vehicle, whether on the "left" or the "right." But in fact Sorel also represents something quite important for our argument here: he represents an important link in the lineage that runs from Maistre and Donoso to both communism and fascism.

At first glance—and even after repeated closer looks—Sorel appears to be a figure of multiple intellectual personae. Indeed, Jack Roth arranged his book *The Cult of Violence: Sorel and the Sorelians* (1980), with sequential biographically organized sections for each chapter: "the man," "the idea," and "the impact." Thus, chapters on integral nationalism, Bolshevism, communism, fascism, and so forth, each begin with a section entitled "the man," giving the distinct impression that Sorel's association with a new movement, somehow gave birth to a new man—over and over. Such an impression would not be entirely mistaken. Sorel's intellectual life was a series of infatuations with one radical movement after another, culminating in the adoption of at least some of his ideas by both Lenin and Mussolini, as well as by various influential figures just before and during the period of National Socialism in Germany.[2]

Sorel himself was neither a revolutionary nor a man of action. Trained as an engineer, he retired early from that occupation in order to devote himself to his publishing career as a controversialist and radical. It is, of course, paradoxical that Sorel was consistent in his anti-intellectualism even as he himself was fundamentally an intellectual. He extolled the working class even as he despised the intellectuals; and yet at the same time his thought turned frequently to the notion of a revolutionary sect, an elite and ascetic group that could ultimately transform the world through a kind of apocalypse or secular millennium. Despite his own abstemious moralism, especially in regard to sexual mores, Sorel was interested in the Mafia or the Camorra as potential models for clandestine revolutionary sects that, like the furtive organization of early Christians, might bring about his imagined new world order.[3]

Sorel's conjoining of the Mafia and early Christianity at first glance may seem rather counterintuitive, but this is in fact a very revealing linkage. Freund remarks that Sorel's lifelong interest in semisecret criminal organizations derived from their "halbmilitärische" character, and he even went so far as to suggest that the early Christian church resembled the Mafia, using in particular the word "apaches." Politicocriminal organizations are "extralegal" and thus can break through social convention as a more or less unified body not subject to the constraints of parliamentary democracy, or checks and balances. One can understand Sorel's interest in criminal or secret religious organizations because they represent models for the ways revolutionary political organizations (themselves often illegal) necessarily have to work—and what is more, reveals very much how both fascism and communism actually did come to power. Sorel saw the early Christians, furtively allied against Rome, as inherently similar to contemporary revolutionaries.

Thus, not surprisingly, in a pattern that by now already is becoming familiar, he identified with Tertullian and Irenaeus, and attacked that mossy enemy, the Gnostics. One begins to see traces of this identification in *La ruine du monde antique* (1894), but it becomes more visible in *Le système historique de Renan* (1905–1906) and especially in "Le caractère religieux du socialisme," an essay first published in 1906, but published in 1919 in a much more extensive version.[4] Sorel explores, in *La ruine du monde antique,* and in *Le système historique de Renan,* exactly how it was the messianic religious organization of Christians was able to emerge in late antiquity, and what it was that held them together. He looked specifically to the Church Fathers, and there found the idea of the eucharist as the means of union, the creation of a corporate body of Christians. Sorel already in his work on Renan was aware that "the Gnostics created highly complex mythologies with Reason, Truth, the Abyss, Wisdom, etc.," but he dismissed them as "only fantasy" and endorsed instead a strict historicism and a narrow understanding of how Christianity was to be understood.[5] Thus, he asserts that "The Gnostic theories are of little interest," and, further, "the Gnostics were not Christians."[6]

One can readily understand why Sorel would dislike the Gnostics. The Gnostic writings we possess now, notably in the *Nag Hammadi* collection discovered in 1945, reveal that indeed many of the Gnostics were fundamentally otherworldly in inclination, visionaries who regarded this world as a vale of tears and a place of deception and ignorance. Sorel, by contrast, is interested in this-worldly revolutions: he searches restlessly from one contemporary revolutionary movement to the next in order to find the one that might overturn liberal society and establish his imagined earthly millennium. He valorizes violence, and imagines that in Fascism or in Communism, it might be possible to bring about a this-worldly secular millennium. Thus, he searches among the Church Fathers for evidence of how Christianity emerged from the ruins of antiquity, and finds that he shares with the early church a rejection and denunciation of sexual freedom, and an assertion of the primacy of historicism as opposed to the visionary, otherworldly Gnostics.

And so when Sorel turns to comparisons of contemporary radical groups that he dislikes, he finds them to be akin to the Gnostics. He attacks, for example, the Saint-Simonians and other utopian groups "whose adventures can serve to throw some light on the obscure history of Gnosticism."[7] Sorel thinks that the Saint-Simonians were "proud masters of an alleged superior science of the moral world," syncretists akin to "the Egyptian and Syrian Gnostics" before them who sought "the secret of the absolute" by mixing "all theogonies and all cosmogonies."[8] Sorel believes that both the Saint-Simonians and the Gnostics were "devoid of all critical spirit" and that the Saint-Simonian doctrines thus "could only be a mish-mash as 'confused and pernicious' as Gnosticism had been."[9] Renan had been somewhat sympathetic to the otherwordliness of Valentinus, but Sorel has not the slightest use for speculative Gnosticism.

It is revealing that Sorel lumps together Saint-Simonians and the Gnostics of antiquity with early modern "prophetic enthusiasm" and "initiations," all of which belong (in his view) not to religion but to the "realm of magic."[10] Sorel, in other words, is quite hostile to the slightest hint of otherworldliness or mysticism, which he thinks of as, variously, "neuropathic excitation," "hypnotic suggestion," "delirium," and "magic." Thus, he absorbs from Catholicism into his restless revolutionary worldview exactly what we might have expected: an anti-heresiological inclination bound up with a thoroughly modern secular millennialism. Entirely in the tradition of anti-Gnostics Tertullian, Irenaeus, and Epiphanius, Sorel writes that "in my opinion Gnosticism gives us an example of those machinations of bold, unscrupulous and articulate men who procure for themselves women and money by speculation on the forces which impel so many on the path of magical superstition. The metaphysical apparatus was there only to conceal the true intentions of the adventurers."[11] Not surprisingly, Sorel reveals not the slightest sympathy for nor understanding of Gnostic or mystical inclinations: for him, such spiritual movements can be reduced to materialism, to outright fraud, deception, and prurient motives disguised as piety. He evinces not the slightest self-awareness that thus he transferred early Christian anti-heresiology into various nineteenth- and twentieth-century revolutionary movements.

We can see in Sorel's work a kind of puritanical spirit—an incipient form of the totalistic spirit that infuses modern revolutionary movements such as communism and fascism. And, indeed, this makes sense when we consider that the totalizing revolutionary is by nature all too willing to adopt a kind of secular asceticism in the service of the millennial revolution imagined to be just around the corner. Sorel recognized that "socialism is often compared with Catholicism; both claim to be unable to realize their true nature until they reign without opposition over the whole world." Thus, "the existence of capitalist and military states [sic] alongside Communist societies is scarcely conceivable."[12] Communism, Sorel recognized, had appropriated at least some of the universalism of Catholicism: neither religious nor secular ideology could brook heretical alternatives. Thus, he intended to develop the idea that the future of communism is to be found in "its resolute transformation into a metaphysics of behavior," in other words, in its extension throughout the whole of life as a kind of secular religion.

It is perhaps only a little surprising to find, then, references to the works of Donoso Cortés and Maistre in Sorel's most well-known and influential work, *Reflections on Violence*. Donoso, in particular, appears during Sorel's strange discussion of the Inquisition in relation to state violence. Sorel outlines a history of state-sponsored violence that claims—in the line of Donoso and of Maistre before him—that the Inquisition was "relatively indulgent, having regard to the customs of the time."[13] In Sorel's narrative, "from the Inquisition to the political justice of the monarchy, and from this to the revolutionary courts of justices, there was a constant progress toward greater severity in laws, the extension of the use of force, and the amplification of authority."[14] The Church had harbored doubts about "exceptional methods;" monarchies had few scruples; and revolutionaries such as Robespierre required only the slightest of dubious "proof" in order to assure "the triumph of the republic and the ruin of its enemies."[15] Sorel evidently prefers, instead of these juridical processes of the state, "proletarian acts of violence" that are "simply acts of war." "Everything in war," he continues in a bizarre passage, "is carried on without hatred and without the spirit of revenge."[16] Sorel thinks that class warfare is thus somehow an improvement on state violence.

Although Sorel reproaches Maistre with being too clever, in truth, the concluding chapter of *Reflections on Violence*—"Unity and Multiplicity"—continues Sorel's lifelong quest to find a secular substitute for Catholicism that for all that, resembles the unitary state imagined by Maistre.[17] Sorel likes to see the history of Catholicism in a military light: it triumphed with "elite troops, perfectly trained by monastic life, ready to brave all obstacles, and filled with an absolute confidence in victory."[18] Communism also, he thinks, should develop such a military-style "division of functions," and a similar overarching social unity that dominates "the economic-juridical life of the whole of society," so that the "leaders" of the "class struggle" "create the ideological unity that the proletariat requires in order to accomplish its revolutionary work."[19] Maistre would have been appalled by Sorel's imagined totalizing secular state, and yet he certainly would have recognized its reference points in Catholicism all too well.

Sorel represents a bridge between the antirevolutionary state totalism imagined by Maistre and Donoso Cortés and the "revolutionary" state totalism of communism and fascism. Both Lenin and Mussolini were indebted to Sorel and his notion of revolutionary violence led by a pure and dedicated (nonintellectual) elite. Indeed, Mussolini remarked that "I owe most to Georges Sorel. This master of syndicalism by his rough theories of revolutionary tactics has contributed most to form the discipline, energy, and power of the fascist cohorts."[20] Even when "Sorelism" fell into disfavor among some Fascist apologists, Mussolini himself "continued to speak of Sorel as his foremost mentor."[21] As to Sorel himself, he extolled both Lenin and Mussolini. Sorel thought that Lenin was "saintly," almost ascetic in what Sorel believed was Lenin's "disinterested" and charismatic advocacy for the masses.[22] Thus Sorel published, in 1918, his "Defense of Lenin," occasioned by an article that claimed Lenin and Trotsky had certainly read Sorel's work during their stay in Switzerland. In Sorel's "Defense of Lenin," he compares Lenin to the great leaders of Russia like Peter the Great, he claims that the number of those the Bolsheviks shot was inconsequential compared to the greatness of Lenin's aspirations, and he acknowledges by way of self-defense that Lenin's terrorism might not have been inspired only by Sorel's own *Réflexions sur la violence*.[23]

Why did Sorel shift his allegiance from Lenin and the Bolsheviks to Mussolini and the Fascists? Deceived by each new revolutionary movement that came along, Sorel was incapable of learning from the experience. As Richard Vernon put it, Sorel's career was one long chronicle of self-deception:

> he was deceived about the significance of revolutionary syndicalism ... he was deceived about the nature of the Action Française.... he was deceived, as many were, about the place of the Soviets in Lenin's Russia, which he took to be a decentralized and pluralistic order; he was deceived, too, about the nature of Italian Fascism, which very soon proved to be a prime example of the pastiche and superficial politically directed "revolution" which he had consistently despised.[24]

Sorel invested quasi-religious faith in the transformation of bourgeois society through revolutionary violence: he imagined a political sect that would, through what he conceived as therapeutic violence, bring about a new society with new mores. Democratic or republican political organization tended to generate social decadence, and Sorel, like the National Socialists in Germany and the Fascists in Italy, saw hope only in the violent struggle that, he imagined, alone could make people heroic warriors and unify society so as to bring about a new form of corporatist or "integral" social integration such as that possessed by Catholic societies during the medieval period. Thus Sorel was ready, indeed, eager to be deceived by every nascent totalitarianism that came along.

It should be noted that Sorel does not endorse violence for its own sake, even though he devoted numerous pages to defending violence as an expression of class war. He hoped for a "Cromwellian army" of rabble that would restore to society some higher values that had mostly disappeared with the waning of Christianity and in particular of thoroughly Catholic societies. If Christianity was not capable of imposing moral order on society, then what could? Sorel imagined a *ricorso*, or social renewal through violent upheaval that in turn brought into being a revolutionary, totalized society infused with new revolutionary values. And he imagined a disciplined elite, along the lines of Lenin's Bolsheviks, who would govern society on behalf of the masses whom, he thought, they would represent in a kind of new social unity. War was the means through which this new social order would come about. Thus Sorel was predisposed to embrace whatever new movement came along that might represent such sweeping social changes—and thus he was destined to be perpetually disappointed by reality. A hater of self-deceiving intellectuals, he was himself the most self-deceived intellectual of all.

We see in his disdain for parliamentary democracy and political parties, in his longing for a unified state informed by a juridical "sentiment" that enforced morality, in his encouragement for and defense of violence, in his belief that only war was sufficient to bring about profound social revolution, in his belief in a society that encouraged "heroism," and, most of all, in his desire for a new, totalized or "integral" unified and moralistic society, not only the traces of Maistre and Donoso before him but also a conduit directly through him to German Nazism (in particular to the Nazi political theorist Carl Schmitt) and to the Soviet state. All of these individuals—Maistre, Donoso, Sorel, Maurras, and Schmitt—longed for a unified Catholic society that could no longer exist, if it ever did—and all of them encouraged the creation of a new, pseudo-religious social order that, if it possesses none of the loving bonds or the otherworldliness of Christianity, certainly continues and intensifies the imposition of social order through force that was inaugurated by the Inquisition. What we see slowly being born here is the political religion of secular millennialism that is the driving force of totalitarianism.

Maurice Barrès and Charles Maurras: The Nationalist Substitute for Catholicism

These three—Sorel, Barrès, and Maurras—are among the most prolific writers of that era. Sorel's work and influence we have already seen, and now our attention must turn to two more figures instrumental in the founding of the French nationalist movement Action Française: Maurice Barrès (1862–1923) and Charles Maurras (1868–1952). I will only briefly sketch their works, and then delve immediately into their importance for our purposes: to trace yet another transformation of Catholicism into a parodic form of political religion.

Barrès is similar, in many respects, to Sorel—above all, both are notoriously difficult to pin down. For all the volumes of fiction and nonfiction produced by Barrès and Sorel, one is generally hard-pressed to determine exactly what they thought or meant. This is especially true of Barrès, who first came to public attention with the publication of his trilogy, *Culte du moi* (1888–1891). In it, as the title would suggest, he celebrated the subjective—it is a paean to egotism. This was followed by another trilogy, *Le Roman de l'énergie nationale* (1897–1902), and *Sacred Hill* (1913; trans. 1929). In these later works, Barrès had become an advocate of "integral nationalism" along the lines of Charles Maurras, and by this period of his life, had come to see Catholicism as a hindrance to the necessary emergence of French nationalism. Unlike Sorel and Maurras, Barrès also took on a real political role: elected to the French parliament, he served there until the end of his life as an egregiously outspoken character who, in the end, got a state funeral. Barrès was notoriously amorphous and indeterminate as a writer, despite his fifty-six books. Jules Renard said Barrès was "a great writer, but what does he mean? One understands each phrase, but the total meaning is obscure."[25] Barrès himself wrote that "Life has no sense," and he reflected what he saw as life's absurdity in his writing.

Yet, in the latter half of his life, Barrès came to speak and to stand for French national unity and a strong leader. Disillusioned with an electoral system and with the parliamentary democracy in which he served, he stressed again and again the importance of national unity. Like Maurras, Barrès detested what he saw as the decadence, partisanship, and demagoguery of the Republic. As with Donoso Cortés before him, Barrès, along with Maurras and the other nationalists saw the Republic as sick, indeed, as decomposing under the cancerous plutocracy and deceitfulness of the ruling elite, as well as foreign influence. Anti-Semitism played no small role here, but it was accompanied by its complements, anti-Masonry and anti-Protestantism. Barrès, like Maurras, wanted to eliminate from France the four *Etats Confédérés*, the Freemasons, the Protestants (mainly Swiss, English, and German), the Jews, and the "métèques," a word coined by Maurras and first published in Barrès's journal, referring to recently naturalized visitors to France. Thus, the nationalists refined their xenophobia as the essential complement to their "integral nationalism." In order to affirm France, they had to create enemies to denounce—that old and familiar dynamic.

Although Barrès is significant in the emergence of "integral nationalism," it is Maurras who really was responsible for it more than anyone else. Whereas Barrès (like Sorel, only worse) is often obscure in his writing, Maurras is not. Maurras, whose prolific work is little short of astonishing (he is said to have published some twenty thousand articles in his lifetime), is remarkably consistent in his temperament and ideology. He wrote consistently in favor of French nationalism and national identity, in favor of monarchy, in favor of the imposition of social order, against what he perceived as alien or foreign influences, and against the forces of anarchism or disorder. These political themes emerged out of and are reflected in his prodigious literary writing as well, notable within which is his rejection of what he saw as Romantic individualism and self-indulgence. Maurras saw Catholicism in ways quite akin to those of Maistre and Donoso Cortés, as well as Sorel and, later, Carl Schmitt: Roman Catholicism exemplified the principle of order in society. Maurras loved about Catholicism its Latinity, its continuity of tradition, the unity of society that it represented, its hierarchic, undemocratic character, its formal beauty—everything, one may say, except its religious heart. For what Maurras sought, what he advocated throughout his life, was nothing less than a political religion.

Maurras was born in Martigues, in Provençe, in a small fishing village. He enjoyed a most pleasant and bucolic childhood, although his father died when Maurras was six; and from his mother he drew a lifelong love of poetry and literature. When he was seventeen, his mother moved the family to Paris, chiefly so that he might receive the best education. Hard of hearing, Maurras immersed himself in study and entered into what he later called an almost Buddhist contemplative way of life.[26] During this period of intense reading, he came into contact with works that formed the inner basis of his perspective, among them the works of Maistre, Bonald, Bossuet, Renan, and Comte. He concluded that most important in the continuity of culture is what he termed "Tradition," meaning that which in the human inheritance is beautiful and true. Thus, he writes that "Le nom de Tradition ne veut pas dire la transmission de n'importe quoi. C'est la transmission du beau et du vrai."[27] He opposed what he saw as sickly in literature, and insisted instead on a renewal of the "ancient Roman synthesis" of "Gallic strength" and "the tradition of 'Rome the Great,' " under the twin signs of beauty and truth.[28]

It appears at first paradoxical that Maurras could extol Catholicism with such vigor, and yet not himself be Catholic. What is one to make of this? He claimed, on the one hand, that the Catholic Church is the "incarnation and terrestrial apotheosis of Thought," and that its wise maxim was "experience and tradition, order and progress."[29] Yet, on the other hand, he detested the emotional and irrational dimensions of Christianity, what he termed "Biblism," and which he associated with what he called the "Jewish spirit," or, more characteristically, the "Semitic leprosy."[30] Maurras insisted on the integral unity and worth of Latin civilization as a Greco-Roman inheritance, and thus detested also the Reformation and Protestantism, which he associated with the spirit of fragmentation that he attributes also to Jews. Maurras affirmed Catholicism as a purely political concept, for his was a secular Catholicism defined by contrast with its enemies, Jews, Masons, Protestants, and at heart, a Catholicism without Christ. Thus, it is not so surprising that, for all his extolling of Catholicism, Maurras's works were placed on the Papal Index as proscribed.

Already by the late 1890s, a violent, inquisitional spirit had shown itself in Maurras, awakened along with the anti-Semitic wave that had passed through France in the wake of the Dreyfus affair. Thus, he wrote in newspaper columns published in 1899 that Jews should be subject to a "bloody repression" that Maurras claimed to be "inevitable." "Although certain inexpiable crimes entail the penalty of penalties, it must be as short and as moderate as possible," he added.³¹ A chronicle of the Dreyfus affair, Joseph Reinach, Maurras found particularly objectionable, and so wrote that he should go immediately to the guillotine, that "the daily outrage of this German Jew against the soul of the fatherland designates him for capital punishment. Let the penalty be inflicted as soon as possible. I desire and demand it."³² Maurras drew from Catholicism the inquisitional idea that "political criminals" or "political heretics" (scapegoats of Action Française: Protestants, Masons, Jews) were to be eliminated from French society, by bloodshed if necessary.

Not surprisingly, Maurras decried the advent of Protestantism as a watershed moment. In *Romantisme et Révolution,* he inveighed against the decline that he saw from *les traditions helléno-latines* and medieval Catholicism to the Protestantism of Huss, Wycliff, and Luther, who belong to what he claimed to be the more barbarous Germanic and Anglo-Saxon worlds.³³ Maurras, like Sorel, looked for a kind of renaissance or resurgence of a more traditional world, but he also evinced a pessimistic antimodernism that perceived Romantic and Protestant individualism as inherently leading toward anarchy and revolution.³⁴ It is not that Maurras himself was deeply Catholic, but, rather, that he saw in Catholicism (as did Schmitt) the basis for an organic unity in society that, in modernity, had been dissolving since at least the seventeenth and eighteenth centuries.

This period is, of course, precisely when Europe saw an explosion of esoteric movements, among them Freemasonry. But Maurras's anti-Masonry is not simply a matter of anti-esotericism, although he had denounced astrology, too. Indeed, Maurras had attracted a body of followers who reportedly were inclined toward "ardently prophesying the Fall of Democracy and the Return of Monarchy, by Astrology, prophecy, crystal-gazing, palmistry, card-shuffling, phrenology, psychometry, and every kind of medium-ship."³⁵ Rather, Maurras's anti-Masonry derives from his belief that a unified monarchic society requires that society's members not be hindered by outside allegiances or secret counteralliances, especially with organizations such as Freemasonry. Ironically, this perspective, which was widespread in Action Française, itself generated a variety of secret groups within Catholicism itself, like the Sodalitium Pianum, or Fellowship of the Pine, "a secret international federation of integral Catholic groups. Dispersed throughout the Church, its members and agents kept careful watch on all Catholics suspected of "demo-Christianity."³⁶ It is perhaps paradoxical that the Maurrasian/Action Française fear of Masonry as a secret organization itself *generated* secret counterorganizations.

But anti-Masonry in French nationalism during this period is entirely bound up with anti-Semitism. On this subject, Michel Winock offers an excellent overview. He observes in *Nationalism, Anti-Semitism, and Fascism in*

France that Action Française in general was known for "its exaltation of the 'show of force' and authoritarian powers, and perhaps even more, its teaching of a certain style consisting of invectives, outrageous acts, slander, and ad hominem attacks."[37] Or, to put it another way: many in Action Française were what Mark Twain would have called "good haters." Robert Brasillach, one member of that circle, said that "Fascism is for many a vital reaction, a sort of anti-antifascism."[38] One was defined not only by what one was for—authoritarianism—but also by what one was against: an enemy. Thus Maurras called the leader of the Front Populaire, Léon Blum, "human detritus," and another member of Action Française said that Blum "incarnates everything that turns our blood cold and gives us goose flesh. He is evil, he is death."[39] And these chilling words were announced at a meeting of the Solidarité Française: "if ever we take power, this is what will happen: at six, suppression of the Socialist press; at seven, suppression of Freemasons; at eight, M. Blum will be shot."[40] These speakers are nothing if not Twain's "good haters."

Such hyperbole is an extreme form of the secular anti-heretical rhetoric that we are tracing here. At least the Inquisition generally offered "heretics" the possibility of recantation and some kind of rehabilitation. But in national socialist and authoritarian movements of the early to mid-twentieth century, the enemy was imagined as irredeemably evil, as inherently less than human. The consequences of such an attitude are obvious, not only in the Nazi slaughter of Jews, but also in the gulags and countless murders of Stalin's Soviet Union. To be a dissident or in the opposition to the totalitarian worldview is to become the subject of virulent and total hatred: somehow, through ideology, one is objectified and so regarded as less than human. Modern anti-Masonry and anti-Semitism have clear antecedents in Catholic anti-heresiology and in the Inquisition, but the intensity of invective at certain points in the twentieth century is shocking: at its worst, it constitutes nothing less than a total disavowal of common humanity.

It is true that one does not find a great deal of anti-occultism as such in Maurras's work, but that is almost certainly a reflection of his own secularism. Because Maurras endorsed a secular Catholicism—if one could put it that way—one ought not be surprised that his projected enemies were envisioned as fundamentally secular, too. Thus, Jews were despised in the French nationalist right because they represented big banking interests and were said to be a group of people "without a homeland," just as the Masons were detested not for the esoteric dimensions of Masonry, but because they represented a secret society seen as separate from a projected national unity. Somehow—one is never quite certain how—the two even became fused, so that various writers of the time fulminate against nothing less than "Judeo-Masonic" interests, whatever those might be. And whatever they are, they exist in a secular, not a religious world.

The Secularization of Heresiophobia

What we see in Sorel, and even more so in Maurras as well as more broadly in the nationalist movement Action Française, is the secularizing of what in earlier periods was the persistent Catholic (and subsequently also the Protestant) fear of heresy and schism. In earlier eras, the pervasive fear was that a competitor to the Church or to orthodoxy (however that category was conceived) would rise up to threaten the prevailing institutional hierarchy. But in the late nineteenth and early twentieth centuries, we see heresiophobia being transferred from a religious to a state category. In Sorel's work we see again the influence of Tertullian's and Irenaeus's fear of heresy, but this fear of divergence from accepted orthodoxy is not any longer religious: it is depicted as (and it is already) fundamentally political. Maurras commented directly on Sorel's *Réflexions sur la violence* in his *La Contre-révolution Spontanée*, and observed that unlike that which Sorel encouraged, "our violence stands in the service of reason."[41] And this politicization of religion becomes even more explicit in the voluminous writings of Maurras and of his fellow writers in Action Française.

Thus, whereas Sorel is only nascently anti-Semitic, Maurras and Action Française are virulently so, and indeed widen anti-Semitism to incorporate Freemasonry and even Protestantism as categories threatening to the unified, totalized state. "Heresy," in this secular, politicized sense is simply that which diverges from the projected Maurassian national construct united under a single party and a dictator-monarch. Whatever "unites" the nation-state into a single entity is good, and whatever "divides" it by preserving a separate identity or allegiance, like Judaism, Masonry, or Protestantism, is conceived of as bad. Of course, all three of these traditions do maintain traditions of independent thought and conscience that, in forms like Anabaptism, often totally refuse military service as well as, sometimes, even industrial society itself (as in the case of the Amish). But in the new political religion, the imagined, totalized national state becomes "orthodoxy," and independence becomes "heresy." "Heretics," once again, have to be expunged.

Hence Maurras cites the history of French "civil war," by which he means the extirpation of "heretics" like the Albigensians, the Camisards, and the Templars, who are "enemies" of the unified French identity. "Hérétiques" and "insurgés" are fundamentally alike: they divide. By contrast, what he supports is the "unité Catholique," the projected indivisibility of French society under a monarch or dictator who is the secular equivalent of the Pope.[42] It is not that Maurras cares about the concept of heresy itself as a religious idea: what concerns him is the *political* notion of heresy as schism or sectarian division that splits one group away from society as a whole. Thus, he represents very clearly an example of the secularization of heretic-hunting.

Of course, as we have already seen in the case of Sorel, this anti-"heresiological" dynamic is found on both the left and the right. As Michel Winock points out, Maurras and Action Française exemplify the anti-Semitism characteristic of those who long for a closed society, the anti-Semitism of the "counter-revolutionary, traditionalist, and Catholic society." But, Winock rightly points out, "anti-Semitism also raged on the left" in France: socialist universalism was as hostile to the independence of Jewish identity as was the Maurrasian right, and indeed, those in Europe who extolled Stalin failed to recognize that at that very time Stalin was busily engaged in the extermination of Russian Jews.[43] The larger point of my argument here holds: the inquisitional model reemerges in a secular context in authoritarian or totalitarian movements on both the right and the left. What matters is the dynamic in question, far more than the labels of Fascist or Communist.

Thankfully, Action Française never took over France in the way that Mussolini's Fascist party overtook Italy, or that Hitler's National Socialism overcame Germany. If they had, however, we can easily predict that there would have been similar consequences, probably somewhere between those of Italian Fascism and Nazism. The extreme virulence of French nationalist rhetoric would have translated into real victims, of that one can be reasonably sure. It is ironic, I suppose, but nonetheless true that Jacobins (and some anti-Jacobins) engage in the same kind of rhetoric and that their ascent to power inexorably results in victims. Those who wish to impose monarchic-dictatorial authority upon society and thus enforce systemic order, automatically engage the rhetoric and, if they gain power, the mechanism of the Inquisition. For a variety of reasons, totalitarianism requires enemies, and a primary theoretician of state "enemies" is not French but German: the well-known juridical scholar, Carl Schmitt.

6

Carl Schmitt, the Inquisition, and Totalitarianism

The work of Carl Schmitt, on its face, presents us with enigmas; it is esoteric, arcane, words that recur both in scholarship about Schmitt and in his own writings. Jan-Wenner Müller observes that Schmitt "employed what has been called a kind of philosophical 'double talk,' shifting the meaning of concepts central to his theory and scattering allusions and false leads throughout his work."[1] And Müller goes on to remark about Heinrich Meier's work on Schmitt that ultimately Meier, too, "lapsed into the kind of double talk, allusiveness, and high-minded esoteric tone so typical of Strauss and, to a lesser extent, Schmitt."[2] Indeed, Schmitt himself writes, in *The Leviathan in the State Theory of Thomas Hobbes* that "like all great thinkers of his times, Hobbes had a taste for esoteric cover-ups. He said about himself that now and then he made 'overtures,' but that he revealed his thoughts only in part and that he acted as people do who open a window only for a moment and close it quickly for fear of a storm."[3] This passage could certainly be applied to Schmitt himself, whose work both makes direct reference to Western esoteric traditions, and itself has esoteric dimensions. These esoteric allusions and dimensions of Schmitt's thought are, in fact, vitally important to understanding his work, but the question remains: what place do they have in it?

Carl Schmitt and Early Modern Western Esotericism

Much has been made of the exoteric-esoteric distinction in the thought of Leo Strauss. Some authors suggested that a Straussian esotericism guided the neonconservative cabal within the George W. Bush administration, after all a secretive group that disdained public opinion and that was convinced of its own invincible rectitude even in the face of facts.[4] It is true that Strauss himself distinguished between an esoteric and an exoteric political philosophy. In perhaps his most open statement, Strauss writes, coyly, of how "Farabi's Plato eventually replaces the philosopher-king who rules openly in the virtuous city, by the secret kingship of the philosopher who, being a 'perfect man,' precisely because he is an 'investigator,' lives privately as a member of an imperfect society which he tries to humanize within the limits of the possible."[5] Strauss's "secret kingship of the philosopher" is, by its nature, esoteric; as in Schmitt's, there is in Strauss's work a sense of the implicit superiority of the esoteric political philosopher.

But in fact those who are searching for esotericism have much more to find in the work of Schmitt, not least because Schmitt's references to classical Western esotericism are quite explicit. Schmitt refers directly to Kabbalism and to Rosicrucianism, to Freemasonry, and, most important for our purposes, to Gnosticism. It is quite important, if one is to better understand Schmitt, to investigate the meanings of these explicitly esoteric references in his work. Although there are allusions to classical Western esoteric currents such as Jewish Kabbalah, Rosicrucianism, and Freemasonry scattered throughout Schmitt's writings, those references are concentrated in Schmitt's 1938 *The Leviathan in the State Theory of Thomas Hobbes*. There are a number of reasons why Western esoteric currents should form a locus in this particular work, among them the fact that many of these traditions (notably, Rosicrucianism, Freemasonry, and Christian theosophy) emerged precisely in the early modern period of Hobbes himself and so correctly, as Schmitt recognized, represent historical context as well as contribute to Schmitt's larger argument.

But what *is* Schmitt's larger argument regarding these esoteric currents? There is little to indicate, at first glance, that Schmitt is derogating these esoteric currents—even the references to the Kabbalistic interpretation of *leviathan*, which come on the wake of Schmitt's notorious 1936 conference on Judaism and jurisprudence, are not immediately recognizable as anti-Semitic. Schmitt's own overview of his argument is instructive. He summarizes the first chapter as covering the "Christian-theological and Jewish-cabbalistic interpretations" of the symbol of leviathan, and "the possibilities of a restoration of the symbol by Hobbes."[6] A *restoration* indicates a prior fall: this is our first clue. Schmitt's treatise on Hobbesian state theory is also an occasion for Schmitt's diagnosis of modernity as sociopolitical decline, and in this decline (in Schmitt's view), esoteric currents played a part. Hence, he references the seminal twentieth-century French esoterist René Guénon's *La Crise du monde moderne* (1927), and specifically Guénon's observation that the collapse of medieval civilization into early modernity by the seventeenth century could not have happened without hidden forces operating in the background.[7]

Both Schmitt and Guénon came from a Catholic background and perspective—and Guénon's broader thesis was that the advent of early modernity represented one stage in a much larger tableau of decline in which modernity (representing the *kali yuga* or final age) would conclude in the appearance of the Antichrist and the end of the world. In this Guénonian tableau of decline, the emergence of individualistic Protestantism represented an important step downward from the earlier corporate unity of Catholicism, and a similar perspective inheres in Schmitt's work, no doubt why he alludes to Guénon in the first place. Hence, in the important Chapter V of *Leviathan*, Schmitt refers to the "separation of inner from outer and public from private" that emerged during the early modern period, and in particular to "secret societies and secret orders, Rosicrucians, freemasons, illuminates, mystics and pietists, all kinds of sectarians, the many 'silent ones in the land,' and above all, the restless spirit of the Jew who knew how to exploit the situation best until the relation of public and private, deportment and disposition was turned upside down."[8]

At this point, we can see Schmitt's perspective is implicitly critical of the subjectification and inward or contemplative turn characteristic of those who travel "the secret road" "that leads inward." He opposes the split between private spiritual life and public life, which Schmitt associates with Judaism as well as with Protestantism, and the profusion of esoteric groups during this period—and by implication, affirms a unified, corporate inner and outer life that is characteristic of Catholicism. Schmitt remarks that "as differently constituted as were the Masonic lodges, conventicles, synagogues, and literary circles, as far as their political attitudes were concerned, they all displayed by the eighteenth century their enmity toward the leviathan elevated to a symbol of state."[9] He sees Protestantism and the variety of esoteric groups or currents during the early modern period as symptomatic—like Guénon, he sees the emergence of modernity as a narrative of cultural disintegration.

Like Hobbes himself, Schmitt is pessimistic about the human condition. Still, in Schmitt's view, Hobbes was not proposing that human beings flee from the state of nature into a monstrous state leviathan, but, rather, was arguing for total state power only insofar as it guaranteed protection and security. Hence, Schmitt writes, one's obedience to the state is payment for protection, and when protection ceases, so too does the obligation to obey.[10] The leviathan serves to diagnose the artificial, gigantic mechanism of the modern state, and to symbolize that state as an intermediate stage that can restrain or postpone the larger decline that modernity represents. In *Leviathan,* Schmitt isn't extolling the leviathan state or totalism, but, rather, coyly stops short— even though it is clear that he seeks a political alternative to the split between inner and outer life represented by the inward turn of esoteric groups and individuals, and by the subjectification represented by Romanticism during the early modern period. Schmitt belongs to the world of jurisprudence, to the realm of weighing and deciding, and one can see this in his treatment of esoteric groups, in which he acknowledges their differences—but he clearly has "placed" them in his larger narrative as indicative of the fragmentation represented by modernity.

It becomes clearer, then, how Schmitt could have seen in National Socialism a secular alternative to modernity. Nazism represented for him, at least potentially, the reunification of inner and outer life, a kind of modern reunification of the mythic and spiritual with the outer public life. It at first seemed to conform to the Hobbesian notion that in exchange for obedience, one receives protection from the state; it represented a new form of corporatism as an alternative to the sociopolitical disintegration represented by parliamentary democracy in the Weimar era; and it even offered an apparent unity of esoteric and exoteric through its use of symbolism and mythology in the service of the state. But to the extent that he allied with the Nazis, Schmitt was consciously siding with the Inquisitors, and with totalistic state power. In retrospect and by comparison, perhaps the "secret road" inward as represented by eighteenth-century esotericism was not quite so bad as all that. Yet, to understand more completely Schmitt in relation to the esoteric, we must turn to a subject he treats somewhat more explicitly: Gnosticism.

Carl Schmitt and Gnosticism

Schmitt writes that oppositions between friend and enemy are "of a spiritual sort, as is all man's existence."[11] In *Politische Theologie II,* he writes that Tertullian is the prototype of the theological possibilities of specific judicial thinking, and refers to him as the "jurist Tertullian."[12] Heinrich Meier discusses Schmitt's indebtedness to Tertullian and in fact remarks that "Tertullian's guiding principle *We are obliged to something not because it is good but because God commands it* accompanies Schmitt through all the turns and vicissitudes of his long life."[13] What is it about Tertullian that Schmitt found so fascinating that he returned to his work again and again? Divine authority as presented by Tertullian divides men: obedience to divine authority divides the orthodox from the heretics, the "friends of God" from the "enemies of God," and the political theologian from the secular philosopher. Here we are reminded of perhaps Tertullian's most famous outcry: "What then does Athens have to do with Jerusalem? What does the Academy have to do with the Church? What do the heretics have to do with Christians?"[14] Tertullian was, of course, a fierce enemy of Gnosticism, and his works, especially *De praescriptione haereticorum*, belong to the genre of heresiophobic literature.

With Tertullian's anti-gnosticism in mind, we should turn to the afterword of Schmitt's *Politische Theologie II*, in which "gnostische Dualismus" figures prominently. There, Schmitt remarks that Gnostic dualism places a God of Love, strange to this world, in opposition to the lord and creator of this evil world, the two conflicting in a kind of "cold war."[15] This he compares to the Latin motto noted by Goethe in *Dichtung und Wahrheit*, "nemo contra deum nisi deus ipse"—only a god can oppose a god.[16] With these references, Schmitt is alluding to the Gnostic dualism attributed to the Gnostic Marcion, who reputedly posited two Gods, one a true hidden God, the other an ignorant creator God.

What is important here, for our purposes, is the underlying theme of heresy and orthodoxy. As is well known, for Schmitt, especially from *Der Begriff des Politischen* onward, the political world is defined in terms of the well-known Schmittean distinction between friend and foe. But not so often remarked is that this friend-foe distinction can be traced directly back to the anti-heresiology of Tertullian. Tertullian devoted a considerable number of pages to the refutation of Marcion in five books, and in particular attacked what he perceived as Marcionitic docetism. In "Against the Valentinians," Tertullian attacked "certain heretics who denied the reality of Christ's flesh," first among these heretics being, again, Marcion.[17] For Tertullian, historicity is paramount: the docetic view that Christ did not come in the flesh but belongs to another world—this is unbearable to him. Tertullian devotes hundreds of pages to detailing and attacking the works of those he designates heretical, and (perhaps ironically, given Tertullian's venomous diatribes) compares them to scorpions full of venom.

So virulent is Tertullian in his hatred of those he perceives as heretics that he goes so far as to imagine that "There will need to be carried on in heaven persecution [of Christians] even, which is the occasion of confession or denial."[18] Here we begin to see the dynamic that impels Tertullian's hatred of those he designates as heretical. On the one hand, Tertullian belongs in the context of Roman persecution of Christians as a whole—but, on the other hand, he in turn carries on an intellectual persecution of heretics whom he sees as scorpions, that is, as vermin.[19] Thus we see Tertullian's perception of himself as defender of the historicist orthodox, the strength of whose identity comes, on the one hand, from affirmation of faith in the historical Christ against the Romans, on the other hand, from rejection of the Gnostics who seek to transcend history and who affirm, for example, a docetic Christ. Tertullian's very identity exists by definition through negation—he *requires* the persecution of "heretics." Tertullian is the veritable incarnation of a friend/enemy dynamic, and he exists and defines himself entirely through such a dynamic. We can even go further, and suggest that the background of persecution by the Romans in turn inevitably impels the persecuted historicist Christians to themselves become persecutors of those whom they deem heretics—a dynamic that continues throughout the subsequent history of Christianity (from the medieval condemnation of Eckhart right through the various forms of early modern and modern antimysticism within Protestant and Catholic Christianity alike).[20] Tertullian, for all his fulminations against what he imagines as Gnostic dualism, is in fact himself the ultimate dualist [or duelist]. He cannot exist without historical enemies, without persecutors and without those whom he can persecute in his turn.

Thus, we begin to see the reasons for Schmitt's endorsement of Tertullian as the paradigmatic jurist theologian and political theologian. For Tertullian, Christ's historicity is paramount—exactly as is the case with Schmitt himself. In *Nomos of the Earth,* Schmitt proposes the *historical* importance within Christianity of the concept of the *katechon,* or "restrainer" that makes possible Christian empires whose center was Rome, and that "meant the historical power to *restrain* the appearance of the Antichrist and the end of the present eon."[21] The concept of the *katechon* is derived from an obscure Pauline verse: II Thessalonians 2.6–7, "And you know what is restraining him now so that he may be revealed in his time. For the mystery of lawlessness is already at work; only he who now restrains it will do so until he is out of the way." This passage is in the larger context of a Pauline warning against the "activity of Satan" among those who are "sent" a "strong delusion" *by God himself* [!] "so that all may be condemned who did not believe the truth" (II.2.11). The *katechon* represents, for Schmitt, an "historical concept" of "potent historical power" that preserves the "tremendous historical monolith" of a Christian empire because it "holds back" nothing less than the eschatological end of history.[22] The Pauline context in Thessalonians can be read to support institutional Christianity as a prosecutorial power. In any case, the *katechon* makes intellectually possible (in Schmitt's view) the emergence of the Christian empire oriented toward Rome and itself now a juridical, prosecutorial, or persecutorial imperial power within history.

Now, I am not arguing that Schmitt's work—and, in particular, his emphasis on the role of antagonism and hostility as defining politics, nor his emphasis on historicity—derives only from Tertullian. Rather, I hold that Schmitt refers to Tertullian because he finds in him a kindred spirit, and what is more, that there really is a continuity between Schmitt's thought and the anti-heretical writings of Tertullian. Both figures *require enemies*. Schmitt goes so far as to write, in *The Concept of the Political*, that without the friend-enemy distinction "political life would vanish altogether."[23] And in the afterword to *Political Theology II*, Schmitt—in the very passages in which he refers to Gnosticism and in particular to dualism—ridicules modern "detheologization" [*Die Enttheologisierung*] and "depoliticization" [*Die Entpolitisierung*] characteristic of a liberal modernity based upon production, consumption, and technology. What Schmitt despises about depoliticizing or detheologizing is the elimination of conflict and the loss thereby of the *agonistic* dimension of life without which, just as Tertullian wrote, the juridical *trial* and *judging* of humanity cannot take place. Tertullian so insists on the primacy of persecution/prosecution that he projects it even into heaven itself. Schmitt restrains himself to the worldly stage, but he, too, insists on conflict as the basis of the political and of history; and both are at heart dualists.

Why, after all, was Schmitt so insistent on what he called "political theology"? In the very term, there is a uneasy conjunction of the worldly sphere of politics with what usually would be construed as the otherworldly sphere of theology. But Tertullian represents the forced convergence of these two spheres—in some central respects, Tertullian symbolizes the point at which Christianity shifted from the persecuted *by* Rome to the persecutor *from* Rome, the shift from Christ's saying that His Kingdom is not of this world, to the assertion of Christendom as a political-theological entity and of the possibility of Christian empire—that is, of the compression together and perhaps even the merger of politics and theology. This forced convergence of politics and theology could not take place without the absolute insistence upon an historical Christ and on the paramount importance of the horizontal, that is, of history itself (as opposed to and indeed, founded on the explicit rejection of the transcendence of history or of the vertical dimensions represented by gnosis).

The work of Schmitt belongs to the horizontal realm of dualistic antagonism that requires the antinomies of friends and enemies; his work imagines the world as perpetual combat. Schmitt is a political and later geopolitical theorist whose political theology represents, not an opening into the transcendence of antagonism, but, rather, an insistence on antagonism and combat as the foundation of politics, reflecting Tertullian's emphasis on antagonism toward heretics as the foundation of theology. When Schmitt writes, in *The Concept of the Political*, that "a theologian ceases to be a theologian when he ... no longer distinguishes between the chosen and the nonchosen," we begin to see how deeply engrained is his fundamental dualism.[24] This dualism is bound up with Schmitt's insistence upon "the fundamental theological dogma of the evilness of the world and man" and his adamant rejection of those who deny original sin, that is, "numerous sects, heretics, romantics, and anarchists."[25] Thus, "the high points of politics are simultaneously the moments in which the enemy is, in concrete clarity, recognized as the enemy."[26] The enemy, here, just as in Tertullian's work, is those deemed to be heretical.

Here we should recognize a certain irony. Tertullian, we will recall, railed against the Gnostics because they supposedly were dualists and because some of them reputedly held that humanity was deluded and that the world was evil.[27] Yet much of mainstream Christianity, like Tertullian himself, itself came to espouse a fierce dualism and an insistence on the evil nature of humanity and of the world. Even when it is clear, as in the case of Valentinus, that his thought includes the transcendence of dualism, Tertullian cannot bring himself to recognize this transcendence because his mind works on the level of the juridical only—he is compelled to attack; indeed, his entire worldview is constructed around those whom he rejects, ridicules, refuses to recognize as in any way legitimate—around those whom he sees as his enemies. And this fierce dualism, this need for that which is construed as heretical, as the enemy, is exactly what Schmitt's work also reflects.

As perhaps Tertullian once did, Schmitt, too, came up against the command of Christ to "love your enemies" (Matt. 5.44; Luke 6.27). His interpretation of it is befitting a wily attorney—he takes it only on a personal level. "No mention is made of the *political* enemy," Schmitt writes. "Never in the thousand-year struggle between Christians and Moslems did it occur to a Christian to surrender rather than to defend Europe," he continues, and the commandment of Christ in his view "certainly does not mean that one should love and support the enemies of one's own people."[28] Thus, Christ can be interpreted as accepting political antagonism and even war—while forgiving one's personal enemies along the way. Schmitt conveniently overlooks the fact that nowhere in the New Testament can Christ be construed as endorsing, say, *political* war against Rome—His Kingdom is not of this world. Is it really so easy to dismiss the power of the injunction to love one's enemies?

There is more. For Schmitt's distinction between the personal and the political here makes possible what his concept of the *katechon* also does: Christian empire. Here we see the exact point at which the Christian message can be seen to shift from the world-transmuting one of forgiving one's enemies to the worldly one that leads inexorably toward the very imperial authority and power against which Christ himself stood as an alternative exemplar. "My Kingdom is not of this world," Christ said. But somehow a shift took place, and suddenly Christ was being made to say that his kingdom *is* of this world, that rather than forgiving one's enemies, one should implacably war against them. Thus, we have the emergence of Christian empire. But the collapse of feudalism and of the medieval *polis,* and the emergence of modernity ultimately meant the depoliticization of the world—the absence of enemies, of heretics, of those against whom others can define themselves—none other than the cultural vacuum represented by technological-consumerist modern society.

Conclusions

Rather than attempting to blame the victims—the Gnostics and "heretics"—for the advent of modernity and for totalitarianism, it might be more reasonable to take a closer look at the phenomenon of the Inquisition and of historicist Christianity (particularly millennialist Christianity) for the origins of modern secular chiliasm. After all, it wasn't the heretics or the Gnostics who burned people at the stake, or created institutional torture chambers, or who slaughtered the Albigensians. Rather, it was the institutional church that did this. Our analysis of Schmitt's work has brought us, unexpectedly, back to this same general terrain.

It is worth remarking, however unpleasant it might be to admit it, that as Mao or Pol Pot did when their policies meant the deaths of millions, so, too, the Church itself did when it rendered victims to be burned at the stake for heresy—all of these institutional murderers believed at least in part that they killed people for their own good, or at least, for the better good, and in order to realize some better state upon earth in the near future. How is it that the medieval Church was so unwilling to allow the Albigensians their freedom and their own traditions? Why was it so impossible to regard them as Christian brethren and not as enemies to be slaughtered? By slaughtering those deemed heretics, one hastens the historical millennium of Christ's kingdom upon earth, or so the logic goes. Secular chiliasm in the technological modern world like that analyzed by Pellicani is only a more extensive and brutal form of the same phenomenon, whose origins are to be found in historicist Christianity, not among those victims of it that were deemed heretical.[29]

Schmitt's work belongs to the juridical tradition of Tertullian and he inherits Tertullian's need for enemies, for heretics by which one can define oneself. Thus, it was not too difficult for Schmitt to organize the 1936 conference to weigh the "problem" of "the Jews"—he was predisposed toward the division of "us" and "them" by the triumphant Western historicist Christian tradition that peremptorily and with the persistence of two thousand years, rejected "heretics" who espoused gnosis and, all too frequently, rejected even the possibility of transcending dualism. Indeed, Schmitt's work allows us to see more clearly the historical current that was operative in National Socialism as well as in Mussolini's Fascist party—and that brought Schmitt to open his 1936 conference remarks with the words of Hitler: "In that I defend myself against the Jews, I struggle to do the work of the Lord."[30] The murder of heretics has a theological origin; the murder of secular opponents has a political origin—but often the two are not so far apart, and so one could even speak of political theology in which to be the enemy is to be *de facto* heretical.

Thus, after the "Night of the Long Knives" and after Goebbels and Himmler carried out the murder of various dissidents, Schmitt published an article defending the right of the Third Reich and its leader to administer peremptory justice—and, in an interview published in the party newspaper *Der Angriff*, defending none other than the Inquisition as a model of jurisprudence.[31] Schmitt argued there that when Pope Innocent III created the juridical basis for the Inquisition, and when thereafter the Inquisitional apparatus came into being, it was perhaps the "most humane institution conceivable" because it required a confession. Of course, he goes on, the subsequent advent of confessions extracted by torture was unfortunate, but in terms of legal history, he thought the Inquisition a fine model of humane justice. He managed to overlook the fact that the prosecuted "crimes," both in the case of the Inquisition and in the case of National Socialism in mid-1930s Germany, were primarily "crimes" of dissidence—that is, of *projected* nonconformity.

Here we begin to consider the larger question of ideocracy as characteristic of modernity. Ideocracy has nothing to do with Gnosticism or gnosis—but it might well have something to do with those who require enemies in order to define themselves, and with those who are willing to torture and slaughter in the name of some forthcoming imagined religious or secular millennium. It is rigid ideocracy that we see at work in the unreadable pronouncements of Communist China defending their occupation of Tibet and the insanity of the Cultural Revolution; it is rigid ideocracy at work in the pronouncements of Stalinist Russia, behind which millions on millions lie dead. Secular millennialism requires a rigid historicism—faith in history is necessary, a belief that one can remake this world and human society into a new historical model, even if the price is murder and torture. Schmitt was a subtle thinker and very learned, no question of that. His work offers us insights into the nature of modernity, into geopolitics, and into politics as combat. But his work also, unexpectedly, throws considerable light on the intellectual origins of modern ideocracies in early and medieval historicist, anti-heresiological Christianity.

7

Communism and the Heresy of Religion

Karl Marx's famous assertion that "religion is the opiate of the masses" had consequences that one suspects he could not have imagined. Marx envisioned a revolution that would sweep away the social structures of the past and that would inaugurate a new form of communal society. But he could not have guessed—when he wrote at the beginning of the *Communist Manifesto* that communists are "hunted" throughout Europe as dangerous revolutionaries—that Communists themselves in only a handful of decades would become the hunters or inquisitors, and that their own fearful victims would be those who embraced religious belief and practice. Whereas figures on the right from Donoso Cortés to Schmitt and Voegelin identified with the Catholic inquisition and encouraged hunting down "heretics" or "Gnostics" in order to preserve social order, for figures on the left, Catholicism and, indeed, religion itself became the "heresy" from the dialectical materialist doctrines of Communism. Thus Communist inquisitions were not far away, once the Communists took power.

Despite the deep foundation of Russian Orthodoxy within Russian culture, during the mid- to late nineteenth century, there emerged a nascent hostility to organized religion. In part, this antireligious sentiment was bound up with the emergence of Russian nihilism in the 1860s, and with the fiery anarchic sentiments of figures such as Mikhail Bakhunin (1814–1876), who urged the destruction of both state and religious hierarchy. Behind these various antireligious currents in Russia lay the rejection of otherworldly aims and an insistence on the primacy of economic and material concerns. The stage for Communist antireligion also was set by Marxists such as Georgy Valentinovich Plekhanov (1856–1918), who saw the Russian Orthodox Church as an obstacle to social transformation and who would accept no compromise with religious traditions.[1]

But it was only with the ascent to power of Vladimir Ilyich Ulyanov [Lenin] (1870–1924) that the Communist movement could manifest the antireligious sentiments that already influenced a good part of the revolutionary thought in Russia. As Nicholas Berdyaev points out, Lenin (like Stalin) was raised in a religiously devout Russian Orthodox household, but he converted his religious devotion into party devotion, becoming a kind of secular ascetic.[2] Trotsky speculated that Lenin's "conversion" to a rigid revolutionary materialism was a reaction to the early death of Lenin's father and the imprisonment and execution of Lenin's older brother, who was barely twenty-one.[3] His religious faith shaken to the core, Lenin shifted his faith to an earthly revolution. Lenin thus became a proselyte for the perspective advanced by Marx: that religion merely served to keep people subjected to capitalist exploitation and to deaden the masses' sense of outrage at basic socioeconomic inequality. And this sense was heightened after the defeat of the 1905 revolutionary effort in Russia. Luukkanen puts it this way: "From Lenin's point of view, the post-revolutionary situation after 1905 had given rise to *a multitude of doctrinal heresies including one of the most serious ideological sins, compromise with religion*" [italics added].[4] This summarizes what was happening in the Bolshevik movement: religion was itself already perceived as "heresy."

Lenin's rejection of religion was pathological. He called it "necrophilia," and fought bitterly against any Bolshevik compromise with religious traditions, perceiving the great efflorescence of Russian religious thought during this period (exemplified by such extraordinary creative figures as Nicholas Berdyaev [1874–1948] and Sergei Bulgakov [1871–1944], but more generally by the mystical syntheses of Orthodoxy and mysticism, especially in the tradition of Jacob Böhme) as genuine opposition or betrayal. This, the Russian "silver age," was arguably the most creative period of religious and philosophical thought of modern times, and Lenin was right to perceive it as a real threat to his ideologically rigid conception of a Bolshevik revolution. Lenin's writings and speeches are laced with venomous attacks on religion, so it is little wonder that when the Bolsheviks took power they began to institute an antireligious inquisition.

But first it was necessary to consolidate centralized power, and one sees this from the beginning in Lenin's movement and his writings. He insisted on the importance of an elite, "a small, compact core of the most reliable, experienced, and hardened workers . . . connected by all the rules of secrecy with the organization of revolutionaries." The leadership elite must be "professionals," that is, devoted entirely to the revolutionary cause, and they alone must direct the revolution. The masses were seen as "children who had to be protected from their own misguided inclinations."[5] And once the Bolsheviks had seized power and established a single-party system under the dictatorship of Lenin, they began to implement exactly what Lenin had defined dictatorship as: "nothing more nor less than authority untrammeled by any laws, absolutely unrestricted by any rules whatever, and based directly on force."[6]

On seizing power, the Bolsheviks instituted a policy of terror. It is true that early in the revolution, the Bolsheviks abolished the death penalty, but Lenin was outraged by the news and according to Trotsky, kept repeating, "How can one make a revolution without firing squads?"[7] Trotsky said Lenin insisted on "the inevitability of terror at every opportunity," and brightened up at a subordinate's suggestion to change the name of the Commissariat of Justice to the "Commissariat for Social Extermination." Of course, such a commissariat already existed: it was the secret police, or Cheka, which by this time had taken the initiative in shooting opponents and in spreading terror throughout the country. At this time, the terror was intended to consolidate centralized dictatorial power, and was directed at political dissidents: the suppression of religion came later.

Lenin argued that violence was essential for revolution, and wrote of the Communist dissenter Kautsky that he "betrayed his cloven hoof" in opposing the use of violence. Lenin writes, in "The Proletarian Revolution and the Renegade Kautsky," that "The proletarian revolution is impossible without the forcible destruction of the bourgeois state machine and the substitute for it of a *new one* which, in the words of Engels, is 'no longer a state in the proper sense of the word.' "[8] He goes on: "the revolutionary dictatorship of the proletariat is *violence* against the bourgeoisie; and the necessity of such violence is *particularly* called for, as Marx and Engels have repeatedly explained in detail."[9] It is interesting that Lenin employs the rhetoric of Christian heresy ("cloven hoof") in condemning Kautsky and insisting upon the need for inflicting violent horrors on the population.

Lenin insisted on absolute and total obeisance to party ideology. He said that "to belittle the socialist ideology *in any way,* or *to turn away from it in the slightest degree,* means to strengthen bourgeois ideology."[10] Thus, Robert Wesson observed concerning Lenin's vision for a new world that ideological compromise "was viewed as a concession to economism and consequently heresy."[11] Indeed, much of the force of Lenin's elite cadre of "Bolsheviks" derived from their strict adherence to a single totalizing ideology that formed the basis for the subsequent notion of "purging." The violence that Lenin called for was the expression of an ideological fanaticism with a millennialist fervor: the Bolsheviks were bringing into being a "new era" and a "new humanity." To do this entailed murdering "heretics" and unrepentant members of the "bourgeoisie."

The "grand inquisitor" of the Communists was Felix Edmundovich Dzerzhinsky (1877–1926), head under Lenin of the Vecheka or Cheka, the "All-Russian Extraordinary Commission" established on 20 December 1917, and empowered on 22 February 1918 to "arrest and shoot immediately" all members of "counter-revolutionary organizations." A "secular ascetic," Dzerzhinsky reportedly said when Lenin appointed him head of the Cheka, "We don't want justice, we want to settle accounts." Dzerzhinsky explicitly said in the summer of 1918 that the Cheka was not a court or a juridical body, and so "cannot reckon with whether or not it will inflict injury upon private individuals, but must concern itself only with *one thing*—the victory of the Revolution over the bourgeoisie . . . even if in so doing its sword accidentally falls on the heads of the innocent."[12] Thus Dzerzhinsky confirms in his own words exactly what Nicholas Berdyaev had observed: that the fanatical Inquisitor always seeks to reduce the complexity of life to just *one thing*.

And it was at this time (1918) that Lenin's authoritarianism became explicit. Lenin declared to Gorky, after an assassination attempt on Lenin's life, "Whoever is not with us is against us." In this spirit, Lenin charged the Cheka with being the regime's Inquisition, rounding up and eliminating potential rivals or critics. And when European socialists like Kautsky indicated their distress at the brutality of the Bolshevik regime (see Kautsky's *The Dictatorship of the Proletariat*) Lenin responded with typical ridicule and fury. Tellingly, in "The Proletarian Revolution and the Renegade Kautsky," Lenin cited Engels in this way:

> A revolution is undoubtedly the most authoritarian thing there is, an act whereby one part of the population imposes its will upon the other part by means of *rifles, bayonets*, and *cannons—all very authoritarian means*; and the victorious party must perforce *maintain its rule by means of the terror* that its arms inspire in the reactionaries.[13]

This is the brutal authoritarian spirit that brought into being the Cheka and the inquisitional dimensions of the Soviet Union.

At the same time, one has to keep in mind that even though Communist atheism did have predecessors in, for instance, the Russian nihilism of the nineteenth century, Russian Orthodoxy is deeply rooted, and so Lenin could not simply obliterate religious faith with the peremptory wave of a hand. Rather, the Soviets primarily established various means of undermining religious authority, such as the "Liquidation Commission," a subsection of the Commissariat of Justice that was headed by P. A. Krasikov (1870–1939), a bitterly antireligious figure. The "Liquidation Commission," despite its sinister name, was initially responsible for instituting the separation of church and state.[14] And the Soviets soon undertook a policy of confiscating Russian Orthodox Church valuables and property. More effective forces allied against religion were in the Soviet security apparatus, which infiltrated religious groups or sects across Russia. Still, it was not simply a case of constant attack on religion: there were figures in the Soviet government during this period that were conciliatory.

But Solzhenitsyn was not entirely wrong to regard the totality of the Russian Communist system as a kind of antireligious gangsterism.[15] Although it is true that there was conciliatory rhetoric toward religion on the part of Lenin and even Stalin, this was in order not to foment a rebellion among the peasants or for other strategic reasons. Even during periods when there were relatively little in the way of public attacks on religion, Trotsky in particular plotted to divide the clergy and to undermine the Russian Orthodox Church. The basic Soviet policies toward religion were by and large hostile, entailed the widespread confiscation of church land and wealth, and sometimes reached the level of witch-hunts and purges, primarily out of fear that the Church or some sect would constitute a threat to centralized Soviet power.

Among the worst of these early periods were the Russian Civil War of 1917–1921 and the "Red Terror," a bloody campaign against the "bourgeoisie," or "class enemies," notable among which were clergy. Thousands of "bishops, priests, monks, and nuns perished as a result of anarchy and the Red Terror," Luukkanen records. Furthermore, "potential leaders of ecclesiastical protests in particular were vigorously persecuted" by the Cheka. Bolshevik terror "tended to be 'pre-emptive' in nature. All potential class enemies were in danger of being liquidated even before they became engaged in actual counter-revolutionary actions."[16]

Another such period came early in the reign of Stalin, when once again various officials were accused of being soft on religion. As various scholars have put it, a "search for 'heretic' scapegoats epitomized the Cultural Revolution," during which the "heretics" were not only Soviet officials who were insufficiently antireligious, but also priests and their congregations.[17] Those active in religious traditions were accused of being disloyal to the party, and of various trumped-up "political crimes" that effectively turned on its head the notion of "heresy": in the past, "heresy" was deviation from traditional religious doctrines, but now, religion itself had become a "deviation" from Communist Party dogma. This period, in the late 1920s, was only a prelude to the horrors of the 1930s under Stalin.

What characterizes the Stalinist period above all is the pervasive paranoia that is the result of the appalling violence directed not only at "bourgeois" members of society, at the intelligentsia, and at the clergy (a pattern from the days of Lenin), but also and with great ferocity and irrationality, at Party members themselves. The numbers speak for themselves: a recent estimate holds that from the 1920s to the 1950s, 20 percent of all adult males passed through or died in Gulags; fifteen million were condemned to forced labor; a million and a half died in prison; over three and a half million people were condemned by the secret police courts, and roughly two-thirds of a million were murdered, many during the nightmarish years of the "Great Terror" of 1937–1938.[18] The late 1930s also were characterized by bizarre show trials, public "confessions" by former officials, and a terrifying atmosphere of denunciations, "trials" without evidence, assumption of guilt unless one could prove one's innocence before hostile functionaries, and what Nicolas Werth calls "trials for political sorcery," as well as "execution quotas approved region by region by the Political Bureau."[19]

One of the most bizarre dimensions of the "Great Terror" under Stalin was the purging of Party members. By February 1937, nearly one and a half million members had been excommunicated from the Party, nearly as many as remained in the Party! But not all of the 680,000 who were executed by Stalin's terror squads were ex-Party members; the "enemies" included members of non-Russian ethnic groups, former clergy, "ex-landowners," and others who could be construed as belonging to the past rather than as Party loyalists.[20] Werth notes "most of the victims of the Great Terror were individuals placed on file by the political-police services. When the quotas were higher than the number of suspects, the NKVD either used depositions extorted during interrogations, or resorted to police raids in public places, a common practice throughout the 1930s."[21] Torture was by no means ruled out, any more than it was ruled out by the Catholic inquisitions.

But there is a fundamental difference between the Stalinist purges and the Catholic inquisitions. At its worst, the Inquisition did instill fear in a society such as Spain, for instance, at least at certain periods. Even so, the fear was constrained by at least some form of internal logic: it was widely understood, at least in a rough way, what "heresy," "witchcraft," "conversion to Judaism," or "sorcery" were held to consist in, and the Inquisition restricted itself more or less to such general areas. Under Stalinism, however, there was no such internal logic—indeed, the very point of the Stalinist purges, mass murders, show trials, and all the rest was to throw all of society into a state of terror. Nothing was stable, except perhaps the presence of the whims and scheming of Stalin himself at the center of the whirlwind.

By now, it is obvious that words such as "heresy" and "persecution" are widely used by scholars in discussing the nightmarish dimensions of life under Leninism and Stalinism. Scholar after scholar uses words derived from aspects of the Inquisition in order to describe the seizure, imprisonment, torture, quasi-juridical process including secret charges and witnesses, and executions of "political criminals" or heretics. Are these comparisons to the Inquisition accurate? If anything, they underscore how much more horrific were the Communist inquisitions than their Catholic predecessors. If the Catholic Inquisitions relied upon means like secret informants and confessions extracted under torture, the Stalinist inquisitions often did not even bother with these: it was often enough merely to be accused. At their worst, the Stalinist inquisitions reveal a society gone pathological.

Seen as a whole, inquisitorial Communism is worse because it seems almost limitless in its madness: anyone could be a victim, and the numbers of dead and imprisoned are consequently many, many times higher than those of any Catholic Inquisition in centuries past. For all the perversity of condemning people to torture and death in the name of religion, still there were limits to what a misguided Catholicism or, later, Protestantism could give rise to. By contrast, secular millennialism has no such limits—indeed, once people are taken up by a secular millennialist ideology, greater evils soon follow on the heels of lesser ones, and there are no constraints imposed by the reproofs implicit in religion. It is obvious that an Inquisition flies in the face of the Sermon on the Mount, but there is no comparable reproof within Communism's history, only precedents.

But with all that said, the underlying logic of inquisitions remains the same, whether they are in the service of a religious or a secular millennialist bureaucracy. Although there are clear differences between them, the religious inquisitions do foreshadow the untrammeled brutality and destructiveness of the twentieth-century secular inquisitions to come. Their implicit logic privileges an imagined millennialist future over the lives of its victims in the present or past; it fiercely denies and attacks affirmations of transcendence, while asserting instead the primacy of the strictly historical. When the Vatican condemned (for a brief time) Meister Eckhart, certainly among the greatest of Christian mystics, it was asserting the primacy of the historical over the explicit gnostic transcendence that Eckhart represented, and it was thus presaging the tyranny of "dialectical materialism" that produced the Soviet or, for that matter, Chinese Communist inquisitions.

For the parallels between the various Communist inquisitions and their religious predecessors go beyond merely structural aspects. There is also an underlying continuity in the emphasis (in the ideology of both political and religious inquisitions) on the historical march toward a millennial future, and on the consequent need for an enforced unity of society in order to make this millennial future possible. In both late antiquity and in political modernity, the victims are the "Gnostics," that is, those who assert the lasting value of the transcendent in the face of powers that insist upon the total primacy of the historical or temporal. Thus the Communists instituted a merely "technical" education for an instrumentalized humanity. It was not for nothing that Berdyaev, Bulgakov, and their émigré colleagues believed Communism to be a form of "demonism." For it was not religion alone that Leninist or Stalinist (or Maoist) Communism sought to destroy, it was also the humanities and the transcendent dimensions of humanity that they sought to deny or to obliterate.

Hence we find that the dynamics of heretic-hunting and the torture, imprisonment, and execution of "heretics" are by no means limited to fascist governments. One might expect to find the inquisitional model transposed into political forms sympathetic to Catholicism, but it is surprising to find the inquisition's inverted secular mirror image in Communism, here turned against Catholicism and Christianity as the "heretics." But what we are considering here is a much more complicated set of refractions and ramifications of the inquisitional archetype. What matters most for the emergence of the inquisitional dynamic is a dictatorial form of leadership, a fanatical insistence on ideological "purity" or unity, and a belief that people ought to be controlled and even exterminated for their own or for the greater good. When these factors come together, the stage is set for another new inquisition. That is what we see in the history of Russian Communism. But as we shall see, the seeds of an inquisition are also present in works sometimes deemed to be on the "right." A case in point: the work of Eric Voegelin.

8

Eric Voegelin, Anti-Gnosticism, and the Totalitarian Emphasis on Order

In conservative circles during the mid- to late twentieth century, one finds a recurrent use of the word "Gnostic" as a peculiar derogatory epithet. This obsession with anti-gnosticism derives from Eric Voegelin, to whom modernity is the venue for a very long-lived ideological threat, a threat to social Order that reappears from age to age, and that is associated with the religious phenomenon of late antiquity (contemporaneous with early Christianity) called Gnosticism. Thus, one finds during the late twentieth century, in various conservative political works, allusions to the "Gnostic" nature of the Soviet Union, of Marxism, of Hitler, of Stalin, of various leftists, and so forth. But, as we shall see, these derogatory references to "Gnosticism" bear no relation to the actual phenomenon of Gnosticism or of gnosticism, and in fact disturbingly resemble such proto-totalitarian, anti-heresiological impositions of Order as one found in the Inquisition or in witch trials.[1]

Over the last half of the twentieth century, scholars learned a great deal about the religious phenomenon of late antiquity known as Gnosticism.[2] Before the discovery and dissemination of the extraordinary discovery of the Nag Hammadi library—a collection of actual Gnostic writings found in Egypt in clay jars in 1945—it was possible to hold to a single view, arguably a caricature of Gnosticism along the lines of that proposed by Hans Jonas. But by the late twentieth century, the simplistic characterization (derived from its opponents of late antiquity, like Irenaeus and Epiphanius) of this complex and diverse movement as dualistic, anticosmic, pessimistic, and the like was largely discarded, at least in serious academic analysis. Yet in one arena of political discourse one finds anachronistic and peculiar uses of the word "Gnosticism" that are preserved from another era intact, like a dusty 1952 Studebaker kept intact in an old garage. I refer, of course, to the derogatory use by Eric Voegelin and his followers of the words "gnosis," "Gnostic," and "Gnosticism" as describing, bizarrely enough, the forms and origins of modern totalitarianism. The contributions of Voegelin's other work are eclipsed by his total confusion over what Gnosticism (or gnosticism) is, and in fact unfortunately reveal more than traces of the very totalitarianism that he uses the term "Gnosticism" to condemn.

The Rhetoric of Anti-Gnosticism

To begin, we will need to consider Voegelin's abuse of "Gnosticism" as a rhetorical weapon. His most widely known set of direct references to "Gnosticism" occur in an essay entitled "Science, Politics and Gnosticism," published in 1958, though he had published other references to what he labeled "Gnostic" politics or political movements many years earlier. When we look carefully at this essay, and at the introduction to it that Voegelin wrote for its American publication, we find something rather surprising. From the title, one would expect to find that Voegelin was going to demonstrate some kind of concrete connection between the three subjects of the essay—in other words, that he would outline Gnosticism and then show how "it" emerges in the modern period in science and politics. In the introduction, he does briefly (drawing, significantly, as we will later see, on the anti-Gnostic Irenaeus) sketch the outlines of Gnosticism as the realization of "gnosis itself—knowledge."[3] But knowledge of what? Voegelin does not say. Instead, we find that "the [Gnostic's] aim is always destruction of the old world and passage to the new," and that gnosis is "the means of escaping the world."[4] At the end of this misleading characterization, Voegelin then warns the reader that:

> self-salvation through knowledge has its own magic, and this magic is not harmless. The structure of the order of being will not change because one finds it defective and runs away from it. The attempt at world destruction will not destroy the world, but will only increase the disorder in society.[5]

Let us unpack Voegelin's characterization of gnosis here and show why it is so thoroughly misleading.

First: what is gnosis, anyway? Voegelin writes that it is "knowledge," implying that it is just another form of ordinary knowledge, or information. But in fact the word "gnosis" in its generally accepted scholarly sense refers to knowledge of God or to put it another way, transcendence of the subject-object division. The word "knowledge" entails a subject knowing an object, but gnosis may perhaps better be termed the realization of inner union between the individual consciousness and divine revelation. The word "revelation" implies a "revealer," and in the various Gnostic writings one finds numerous instances of the divine revealer, in general, Christ. Gnosticism certainly cannot be described as "self-salvation"—throughout the Gnostic writings, one finds the theme of divine revelation and the need for both human effort toward realizing gnosis, as well as the need for corresponding divine grace or angelic help. But most interesting of all is Voegelin's claim that the "Gnostic" seeks destruction of the old world or even more startling, "world destruction," and that such "Gnostic" attempts are a futile effort to disturb the order of being and the order of society.

This is interesting perhaps most of all because there is no evidence for the idea that Gnostics (as represented in the actual writings we possess) were engaged in any such effort at world destruction at all. It is arguable that Gnosticism, as part of the larger emergence of Christianity in late antiquity, represented a shift from Platonism or Hermetism in that Gnostics in the Nag Hammadi library writings often insisted on the decisive revelatory power of Christ, separating them to some extent from the other religious traditions of the era. But in fact Platonism and Hermetism are directly represented in the Nag Hammadi collection, and when one looks closely at the actual collection, one finds nowhere in it an urge toward "world destruction" or even the deliberate disruption of social order. Rather, one finds an insistence on direct inner spiritual experience as opposed to, say, worldly or social power. One finds numerous instances of visionary revelations, and some ethical admonitions as well as what we may call "mystery sayings" like those of Christ in the Gospel of Thomas.

The obvious disconnect between Voegelin's characterizations of Gnosticism and contemporary scholarly understanding becomes, frankly, ridiculous when we turn to the actual essay "Science, Politics and Gnosticism." The essay meanders from Plato to Marx to Nietzsche with nary a mention of, let alone a definition of, gnosis or Gnosticism until we find such gems as this in a discussion of Nietzsche:

> In this "cruelty of the intellectual conscience" can be seen the movement of the spirit that in Nietzsche's gnosis corresponds function-

ally to the Platonic *periagoge,* the turning-around and opening of the soul. But in the gnostic movement man remains shut off [!] from transcendent being. The will to power strikes against the wall of being, which has become a prison. It forces the spirit into a rhythm of deception and self-laceration.[6]

Thus Voegelin asserts, without reference to anything authentically gnostic, that Nietzsche represents a "gnosis" that is "shut off" from transcendence. Furthermore, he represents a "will to power" that leads to "deception," and all of this in turn leads up to the pronouncement that "To rule means to be God; in order to be God gnostic man takes upon himself the torments of deception and self-laceration."[7] In all of this, "gnosis" and "gnostic" are tossed in and misused as if they meant things to which they certainly bear no relation whatever. Gnosis here is described as being "shut off" when earlier Voegelin himself admitted that this is a word meaning "freedom" and "salvation." The scholar of Gnosticism or of gnosis looks on with bewilderment at such *non-sequiturs:* what on earth is Voegelin up to?

The bewilderment intensifies. In discussing Hegel, Voegelin pronounces him also a "gnostic," and then offers the following: "Gnosis desires dominion over being; in order to seize control of being the gnostic constructs his system. The building of systems is a gnostic form of reasoning, not a philosophical one."[8] "*Gnosis*" desires something? A strange formulation made stranger by what follows. The subsequent tautology goes: gnostics reputedly had systems; Hegel had a system; therefore Hegel is a gnostic, and further, *all* system-builders are gnostics. Interesting as an example of fallacious reasoning, but rather frustrating for the scholar familiar with Gnosticism or gnostic religious traditions. What accounts for Voegelin proclaiming that "gnosis desires dominion over being"? Did he not earlier write that the gnostic seeks to escape the world, and shortly after that of the gnostic's will to destroy it? And is not all of this in rather total disregard of anything we have learned of gnosis as inner spiritual revelation and union with the divine? Little wonder that, as Gregor Sebba wrote, "nowhere in the thousands of scholarly papers, books, and reviews [by scholars of gnosis] does there seem to be any evidence that Voegelin's early and later work on gnosticism has even been noticed. There is good reason for that."[9] There is indeed. Voegelin's work is totally irrelevant to the actual study of Gnosticism or gnosis. It has an entirely different agenda.

In order to understand this agenda, we might consider the rather obvious clues that are scattered throughout Voegelin's work. In *The New Science of Politics,* another work that featured Voegelin's peculiar view of "gnosticism," we find an entire chapter entitled "Gnostic Revolution—The Puritan Case." In it, Voegelin asserts that *the entire Reformation movement and the whole of modernity* must be "understood as the successful invasion of Western institutions by Gnostic movements."[10] "This event," he continues portentously, this "revolutionary eruption of the Gnostic movements" "is so vast in dimensions that no survey even of its general characteristics can be attempted in the present lectures."[11] The scope of this claim is rather remarkable, in the way of most sweeping and unsubstantiated claims. Voegelin goes on to offer a brief sketch of Richard Hooker's *Ecclesiastical Polity*, an overview of sixteenth-century Puritanism, and from it determines with absolute certainty and no real evidence that Puritanism as a whole was gnostic! Given the hostility of Calvin himself and of Calvinism in general to mysticism in general, let alone gnostic thought, one can only conclude that in Voegelin's view, Calvin and Calvinism (and the entire Reformation movement to boot) were gnostic even in the midst of their hostility to gnosticism, precisely the kind of rhetorical inversion that Voegelin attributes to none other than—gnosticism.[12]

In "Ersatz Religion," Voegelin extends his condemnation as "gnostic" not only to Hegel and Protestantism but also beyond it to virtually the entirety of the modern world. Now *everything* bad is "gnostic." He begins this odd essay with the pronouncement that "By gnostic movements we mean such movements as progressivism, positivism, Marxism, psychoanalysis, communism, fascism, and national socialism."[13] Given such a list, one realizes where the scholar Ioan Culianu found reason for his frustrated outburst at those who claimed any old thing at all is gnostic.[14] But the ubiquity of gnosticism is the logical conclusion if one believes, as Voegelin does, that "all gnostic movements are involved in the project of abolishing the constitution of being, with its origin in divine transcendent being, and replacing it with a world-immanent order of being, the perfection of which lies in the realm of human action."[15] Such a definition stretches "gnostic" so far as to make it transparent and thus a label for any effort at social reform. Voegelin is indeed describing something one can see at work in modernity—that much is true. But its origin will turn out to be somewhere other than in gnosticism (or Gnosticism).

Let me offer another clue as to Voegelin's only barely veiled agenda here. Voegelin corresponded at great length over many years with Alfred Schutz, to whom on 1 January 1953 he wrote concerning his views on Christianity. In this revealing letter, Voegelin elaborates on his distinction between "essential Christianity," on the one hand, and what he construes as "the gnosis of historical eschatology," on the other.[16] He goes on to write that "The sectarian movements and certain trends within Protestantism insist that eschatological Christianity is the essential one, while what I call essential Christianity is for them the corruption of Christianity by the Catholic Church." And if this were not clear enough, Voegelin near the end of his letter says it directly: "this essential Christianity can be identified with Catholicism" with only a few reservations.[17] Curiously, he goes on to mention Eckhart and Nicholas of Cusa (certainly gnostics within the Catholic tradition itself) but because they do not correspond to his peculiar political definition of gnosticism, he does not directly attack them. In any case, the gist of all this is clear: Protestants and modernity are gnostic; Catholicism, except perhaps in certain cases, is not.

Now we begin to see the larger picture here. But what is revealed when we step back enough to see the whole may not be exactly what Voegelin had in mind. First, we should note that in this letter, and in much of his later work, Voegelin confuses gnosticism and "historical eschatology" or millennialism. This, it turns out, is a quite interesting confusion, not least because gnosticism (using the broadest meaning of the term, the perspectives of those who seek or espouse gnosis) is precisely *opposed* to an historicist view of Christianity. Is there any serious scholar who has studied the history of gnosis and has not recognized the clear division between those who espouse "horizontal" historical faith (*pistis*), on the one hand, and those who espouse gnosis ("vertical" realization), on the other? This division, after all, is at the very heart of many Gnostic writings themselves. Indeed, Christ in the Gospel of Thomas directly tells his disciples that they seek him somewhere else (historically or "horizontally") when the truth is right there before them in the "vertical" present moment. One finds this also in the Gospel of Philip and other Nag Hammadi texts.

Why would Voegelin invest Gnosticism (or gnosticism) with exactly the historicizing characteristics to which gnostics are in fact most opposed? Clearly there is some kind of rhetorical inversion at work here, a sleight of hand. But let us consider the question of "historical eschatology" for a moment. Where do we in fact find the origins of this Christian tradition of historical eschatology? The answer is certainly not in gnosticism—it is, rather, within Catholicism. Voegelin himself frequently cites Joachim of Fiore, the medieval Calabrian abbot who envisioned history as unfolding in three successive ages: that of the Father, of the Son, and of the Holy Spirit. He anticipated a "third age" immediately in the future, and this millennialism is a theme implicit in Christianity as a whole, which has after all generated many and perhaps countless millennialist perspectives. But one could just as well argue that this millennialist tendency is precisely a *result* of the loss of gnosis ("vertical" direct spiritual realization for oneself) as a possibility within Catholicism. The rejection of an orthodox gnosis (even that represented by St. Clement of Alexandria) and the emergence of a Catholic hierarchic corporate social structure with an emphasis on historical faith and the mediating power of the Church—it is *here* that we find the origins of "historical eschatology."

Let me make this even more explicit. The Gnostics of late antiquity, and gnostics of all kinds, insist on the necessity that the individual seek direct inner spiritual realization (gnosis) for him or herself. This is not to say that such traditions necessarily represent anarchy or total individualism: rather, they tend toward a simple communal organization not unlike that of Jesus and his disciples. We see this not only in the relatively small gnostic groups of antiquity but also in more recent gnostic traditions such as the Christian theosophy of Jacob Böhme.[18] Such groups exist in order to help one another toward spiritual realization; they do not have worldly or historical aims; their aims are "vertical." It is when this gnostic impulse is *absent* that we see the "horizontal" and historical-eschatological development of a corporate, hierarchic Church structure that actively opposes and even for a considerable length of time, by way of the Inquisition, persecutes and murders those who espouse one or another form of gnosis.

Now, once we realize that Voegelin is falsely accusing gnostics of the very thing (historicism) that belongs in fact to the "essential Christianity" of Catholicism that he embraces, suddenly a very different possibility emerges. What if Voegelin's attacks on gnosticism were in fact a rhetorical deception or mistake that disguises the true origins of totalitarianism? Without any question, the gnostics of late antiquity and the various heretical and gnostic groups and individuals—that I have made the principal subject of my study for years—represent the *dissident* element within Christianity. They are the ones who are willing to stand alone and even die in defense of their inner realizations; historically, they are the victims. If we were to look back in history and think about modern totalitarianism's origins in the West, where exactly might we look? Where, for instance, do we find the totalization of society in a corporate body that expels or murders its dissidents? Is it possible that the Inquisition signals the real predecessor of modern totalitarianism? Certainly it is more reasonable than attributing these origins to the *victims* of these earlier machines of enforced social order.

Such an analysis would not be unprecedented, of course. Alain de Benoist, as is well known, finds the origin of totalitarianism back in the emergence of monotheism itself, in the totalizing God who will have no other gods before him, and who commands the Jews to kill their enemies, to "put the inhabitants of that city [where people serve other gods] to the sword, destroying it utterly, all who are in it and its cattle. . . . Burn the city and all its spoil."[19] Certainly I am not willing to go quite so far as de Benoist in indicting monotheism, yet one cannot help but be compelled to acknowledge that there is a real tension at work here between one perspective that insists on dogmatic formulations based on historical eschatology resulting in murder of those who believe differently, and another that champions direct spiritual realization for oneself and for others. This opposition, it would seem, is implicit within Jewish, Christian, and Islamic monotheism from antiquity to the present: one sees it again and again. This opposition is what the whole of Voegelin's work disguises by confusing "gnosticism" with historicist millennialism.

Once one is in possession of this key, Voegelin's work takes on an entirely different set of implications. Voegelin's insights into the emergence of modern totalitarianism suddenly suggest that the ideological constructs of Fascism and Communism have their origins in prior doctrinal systems enforced on pain of torture and murder; that in historicist-eschatological Christianity are the origins of the Marxist or Fascist historical faith in a future state that justifies almost any means of achieving it in this world, including mass murder. Who more clearly reveals what Voegelin calls the "cruelty of the intellectual conscience" and the will to "domination": the Inquisitor torturing and (by way of the state) murdering a woman gnostic like Marguerite of Porete, or her, the victim? One can easily see why—since he embraced an "essential Christianity" substantially identical with Catholicism—rather than look to historicist Christianity for the origins of totalitarianism, Voegelin would seek to blame the victims, the gnostics who in fact represent the dissident *opposition* to totalism! Of course, when one thinks about it, this rhetorical move seems quite bizarre. I can think of no historical instance in which a gnostic individual or group (using the word in its proper sense) killed or sought to kill anyone; but I can think of numerous examples of the Inquisitions resulting in torture and murder.

As it turns out, though, the attribution of virtually everything bad in the modern world to "gnosticism" has an interesting genealogy. Voegelin is only one branch on a fairly large family tree. Generally, apologists for Voegelin's perspective begin with Ferdinand Christian Baur (1792–1860), whose book *Die christliche Gnosis, oder die christliche Religions-Philosophie in ihrer geschichtlichen Entwicklung* (Tübingen, 1835) explained the history of religion as an Hegelian gnostic phenomenon developing in a dialectical evolutionary movement toward unity with the Godhead.[20] Baur's Tübingen school of Protestantism eventually manifested itself as an extreme form of antisupernaturalism, particularly in his followers, but in *Die christliche Gnosis* Baur sees Gnosticism in antiquity through Hegelian goggles, thus forging a link between Gnosticism and Hegel that later Voegelinians could use even if the rest of Baur's work was more or less discarded.[21] Harking back to Baur is convenient for ideological reasons in that he was an Hegelian at the time he wrote that book, but in fact an earlier and more extensive analysis of gnosticism is to be found in Gottfried Arnold's *Unparteiische Kirchen-und-Ketzerhistorie* (1700), which is somewhat more inconvenient for Voegelinism because it is fairly sympathetic to the gnostics discussed in it.

The next major branch on this tree is Hans Jonas, who also saw Gnosticism through very particular lenses, in his case, those of early-twentieth-century existentialism. Jonas's view of Gnosticism in his primary and immensely influential book *Gnosis und spätantiker Geist* (1934), published in English as *The Gnostic Religion: The Message of the Alien God and the Beginnings of Christianity*, defined Gnosticism as a dualistic, world-rejecting phenomenon. Jonas's depiction of Gnosticism—with its emphasis on the Gnostic mythology of the ignorant demiurge, the malevolent archons, the fallen Sophia, and the effort of the gnostic seeker to reach the kingdom of light—indeed, depicted a form of Gnosticism that is visible in the Nag Hammadi library in such works as The Gospel of Philip and even more clearly, The Hypostasis of the Archons. But this form of "classical Gnosticism" is only one of many different currents, and in Jonas's rendering bore a strong resemblance to twentieth-century existentialist philosophy. Even in late-twentieth-century efforts of Voegelinians to justify Voegelin's bizarre political renderings of gnosis and gnosticism, when countless other resources are available, it is to Jonas's form of "classical Gnosticism" that they repair.[22] Sebba writes that "in our inquiry, *Hans Jonas* holds a special position." This is so—even though Jonas's depiction of Gnosticism has long been superceded by the discovery of the Nag Hammadi Library and other research—because Jonas's existentialist Gnosticism can be used to support Voegelin's idiosyncratic views, and many later scholars cannot.

Voegelinian Inquisitors

Another apologist for Voegelin's political misuse of gnosticism is Stephen McKnight, who seeks to justify this misuse by extending it to the whole of Western esotericism, beginning with the *prisca theologia* of the Renaissance. He notes that recent scholarship

> diminishes the status of ancient Gnosticism as the primary source of modern epistemological and political disorder. In pointing to a broadening and deepening of the sources of esoteric religion and pseudoscience, I am not attempting to correct or disparage Voegelin's work. On the contrary, I think I am working very much in the

Voegelinian mode.... Morever, as will become clear in the course of this essay, Voegelin was already acknowledging problems with a unilinear emphasis on Gnosticism and encouraging the exploration of other esoteric traditions like magic, alchemy, and Renaissance neoplatonism.[23]

McKnight rather understates the facts concerning recent scholarship on Gnosticism, which does not support Voegelinism at all, as actual scholarship in this field is much more complex and nuanced than Voegelinism will allow. But what we see in McKnight is an interesting direction: rather than simply attacking "Gnosticism," he seeks to extend the field of what we may call heresiology to magic, alchemy, Ficino—whatever can be roped in as a purported "source of modern epistemological and political disorder."

Interestingly, in a revealing paper given in 2001, McKnight discusses a lecture given by Voegelin in 1971 in which it becomes clear that Voegelin had himself begun to realize his ascriptions to "gnosticism" were untenable in the light of subsequent scholarship and the discovery of the Nag Hammadi Library. McKnight quotes directly Voegelin's second thoughts from an audiotape he had made of the lecture at which Voegelin reflected on his earlier works on "gnosticism." Voegelin remarked on

> the dogmaticization which sets [in] whenever a book is published," [which was] perhaps more dangerous with regard to this subject [Gnosticism].... Because immediately the problem of gnosis as characteristic of modern political ideas ... was absolutized, and everyday I get questions of this kind: is, for instance, the Russian government a Gnostic government? Of course things are not that simple—gnosis is one element in the modern compound, but there are other elements ... for instance, the apocalyptic traditions and Neoplatonic experiences and symbolizations.[24]

In other words, Voegelin by 1971 had discovered that modern scholarship was by no means according with his idiosyncratic perspective, so he sought to expand his witch-hunt for the sources of the evils of modernity among the Renaissance Neoplatonists, practitioners of magic and alchemy, and the like. But by this time the Voegelinian misuse of "gnostic" had ossified into political dogma, and even he himself could not stop it. What is more, he still held to his basic thesis that esotericism of various kinds was to blame for the ills of modernity—one merely should look beyond the word "gnostic" itself. Thus we have McKnight's project to identify the "source of modern epistemological and political disorder" with "other esoteric traditions like magic, alchemy, and Renaissance neoplatonism."

At this point, we should pause and consider these authors' emphasis on "order" and fear of "disorder." It is interesting because it is precisely the kind of totalistic thinking that one finds in the communist and, although perhaps to a slightly lesser extent, in the fascist state. In the totalitarian state, there is no room for the dissident; the dissident is the source of "disorder," and according to this logic must be imprisoned, tortured, or killed. It is interesting, therefore, that this is precisely the logic of the Inquisition, which also sought to impose social and religious order at all costs, including that of human life. This obsession with order haunts the works not only of Voegelin but of his followers as well, and leads McKnight (just as Voegelin before him) into attributing strange things to gnostics, as when in his conclusion to this article, McKnight claims that "the gnostic regards the search for innerworldly fulfillment as a sign of ignorance (*agnoia*), not *gnosis*."[25] Once again, we are in the land of Voegelinism, where gnosis is proposed to have nothing to do with the inner spiritual life so that it can be shaped into a term of political abuse for dissidents.

The Voegelinians do not hesitate to take this fetish for order and rejection of dissidence to its extreme, either. Gregor Sebba, another Voegelinian apologist whose work I noted earlier, makes even more explicit what is implicit in McKnight's remark just cited: Sebba writes that "The *gnosis* of the gnostic is *agnoia*, ignorance of the truth. But it is not innocent ignorance: he *wills* the untruth, although he *knows* the truth. But why then does he will the Evil? Why is there Evil at all? . . . The history of ancient gnosticism has become the history of the discord."[26] This is an extremely revealing remark, because it makes absolutely no sense—except if the author sees himself as a modern Irenaeus, a heresy-hunter. Here the idea of imposed order is counterposed to the gnostic who is now openly identified with "Evil." Not just evil, but capitalized evil, evil incarnate, opposed to the One Truth of the historical Church or of the totalitarian state. Discord, dissidence, these are unbearable to the totalitarian order. The Voegelinians, in their hatred for the least sign of the esoteric, here reveal themselves akin to the very totalitarianism whose origins they purport to be exposing!

A similar, typically sweeping application of Voegelinism is to be found in a book whimsically entitled *Gnostic Wars: The Cold War in the Context of a History of Western Spirituality* by Stefan Rossbach. This work of about 225 pages of main text does not even discuss the Cold War of the Soviet Union against the United States until page 186. Most of the book is devoted to a survey of "gnosticism" in the West, predictably spending a great deal of time on Hans Jonas, Hegel, and Marx, but with brief stops at the Cathars and Puritanism—in other words, the usual Voegelinian anti-gnostic train ride through history with the usual stops. But it still comes as a surprise when, with no proof, Rossbach, in the epilogue, announces that

> *Gnosis* promotes the soul, in its self-understanding, to an absolute position high above the un-reality of cosmic ignorance and suffering.... [Hence] if *gnosis* elevates the soul above the cosmos, beyond Plato's *chorismos*, the unbridgeable gap which the classical thinkers perceived between the human and the divine realms mutates into a gap between those with *gnosis* and those without. The common bond of mankind is effectively broken between these two groups as soon as both consider themselves in possession of absolute vision. They will then fight a war driven by *gnosis*, a "Gnostic war."[27]

One finds such an announcement totally ridiculous, given that the book is purportedly about the Cold War, yet demonstrates no convincing connection at all between the emergence of the totalitarian, rationalistic Soviet Union and anything gnostic or Gnostic. One is reminded of Voegelin's own frustration, expressed in 1971, with those who "every day" plagued him with "questions of this kind: is, for instance, the Russian government a Gnostic government?" "Of course," the by then slightly more enlightened Voegelin intoned, "things are not that simple."[28] But it would appear from *Gnostic Wars* that things are that simple after all!

By now we are familiar with this sort of wild leaping about in place of logical progression, because Rossbach's is fairly typical Voegelinism. First, gnosis is defined as what it is not—it is here pronounced to have nothing to do with knowledge of the divine or union with the divine. Then the "classical" "gap" between human and divine realms somehow "mutates" into "those with *gnosis* and those without." Both groups are then projected to see themselves as in possession of absolute vision, even though before the focus was solely on the bad gnostics. But this shift of focus to a battle between two groups is necessary in order to force "gnosticism" to fit the Cold War of the mid- to late twentieth century. Finally, the groups must fight a war, even if one can find not a single instance in the history Rossbach recites of an actual war between gnostics and anyone. Of course, he does not mention the Western war *on* gnostics that mars its history; the Inquisition for some reason doesn't merit notice, because it doesn't fit with Voegelinism.

But not all the anti-gnostics are quite so immediately obvious in their simplistic demonization of the gnostic currents of the West. There is another development in the general current of anti-gnosticism that also requires mention here, and that is represented in the multivolume, rather opaque works of Cyril O'Regan, a professor at Notre Dame. O'Regan's perspective is more an outgrowth of what I have come to call "hyperintellectualism," the hypertheoretical manifestations of the "linguistic turn" in literary theory and philosophy. O'Regan spends almost no time at all demonstrating with any evidence that Jacob Böhme is a Valentinian Gnostic—his central claim in *Gnostic Apocalypse: Jacob Böhme's Haunted Narrative*—and almost all his time constructing his own abstract linguistic-rhetorical edifice, using terms such as "Valentinian narrative grammar" and "deformations of Valentinian grammar." At first, even the specialist in the work of Böhme is perplexed: what is O'Regan up to here?

Then, slowly, it becomes clearer what he is up to. Historical details get almost no play here at all: on the first page (and actually throughout the book) the names of major figures are misspelled.[29] Recent scholarship in the field is ignored.[30] But such details are not so important: more important is what is inadvertently revealed in the language of O'Regan's discourse. He claims that "Böhme's visionary discourse constitutes a metalepsis of the biblical narrative, in that its six-stage narrative of divine becoming disfigures every single episode of the biblical narrative, as interpreted in and by the standard pre-Reformation and Reformation theological traditions."[31] Böhme's work shows "how apocalyptic, Neoplatonism, and the Kabbalah can live together in a master discourse that displays Valentinian transgressive properties."[32] Never mind that there is here no significant evidence that any of these specific historical traditions—any of them—actually appear in Böhme's work in any meaningful way, only the attempt at ascription. The key word here is "transgressive." Böhme is made out to be a "Valentinian" and therefore "transgressive." Trangressive of what? Of order, one gathers, represented by the projected unity of the whole of "pre-Reformation and Reformation theological tradition" (which we all know is but a single uniform perspective).

This author certainly can generate all kinds of jargon—in a single line we read of "apocalyptic inscription, apocalyptic distention, narrative deconstitution of negative theology," all part of a self-described "sophisticated conceptual apparatus of general constructs."[33] And this apparatus, O'Regan tells us on the same page, "amounts to taking a machine gun to swat a fly." This is interesting, because presumably Böhme is the fly. On the next page we read that the Böhmean "mode of thinking is irredeemably past." Böhme represents "an impossible hope for a form of knowledge—perhaps any form of knowledge—that would escape the hegemony of an all-controlling rationality."[34] In other words, O'Regan now pronounces the fly dead. There is, in his mind, no possibility that Böhme's thought could be meaningful for anyone today or in the future—

it represents merely a "deranging of biblical narrative" that is somehow "parasitic" just like he thinks Valentinianism was. Using Voegelin's term, he writes that Gnostics are "pneumapathological."[35]

And so we find ourselves, despite all the jargon and the rhetorical convolutions, back in the same general territory as Voegelinism. O'Regan seeks to demonstrate a *Gnostic Return in Modernity* in order to show what? The total tyranny of rationality, as he suggests above? The impossibility of realizing or understanding what Böhme's work represents? The ponderous prose here has an underlying agenda that is very much akin to that of Voegelin's misguided efforts. What we see in these works is a concerted effort by a number of authors to totally dismiss and beyond that, annihilate all that they construe as gnostic. They represent a kind of hegemonic near-totalitarianism that we can certainly trace back to the anti-gnostic rhetoric of the early Church Fathers such as Tertullian, Epiphanius, and Irenaeus.

Consider, for instance, yet another anti-gnostic effort at witch-hunting, this one by a student of Christopher Lasch, Catherine Tumber, and entitled *American Feminism and the Birth of New Age Spirituality* (2002). Here, too, we see trotted out once again the Voegelinian old saws about "gnosticism" (with a small "g," but often also with a big "g") having a "dominant mood" of "nihilism and despair," a product of a "bitter mood of aristocratic withdrawal and profound cosmic alienation." Tumber at least dimly recognizes that such views "appear to have little in common with the sunny optimism, the nearly ideological cheerfulness that marked late nineteenth-century American gnosticism."[36] Still, such bizarre self-contradictions don't bother her in the least, for Tumber is armed with the rhetorical weapons of fervent anti-gnosticism. By the end of her book, Tumber is making wild claims right and left, asserting unaccountably that modern mass consumerism and "bohemian subculture" derives from "gnosticism," as did the New Thought movement of the nineteenth century and the New Age movement of the twentieth. Indeed, the whole of feminism is based in "self-deluding" "gnosticism" that, clearly wrongly in Tumber's view, "seeks inner peace."[37] One wouldn't want social order inconvenienced by inner peace!

But the real tendency toward witch-hunting comes only at the end of the book, when we discover that Marcus Garvey was a "gnostic," and that, in breathless if ungrammatical prose, "not only can self-proclaimed feminist heretic Mary Daly and professed pagan Starhawk be classified as gnostic, but gnostic tendencies can be detected in the work of Nation of Islam leader, Louis Farrakhan, and the founder of Black Theology, James Cone." Oprah Winfrey [!], Gloria Steinem—[and] "middle-class women" as a whole—"revived" "the corrupt spirituality of gnosticism."[38] Never mind that there is not the slightest support for these pronouncements, only the flinging about of the word "gnostic" as if tossing the epithet, like tossing the epithet "witch," were enough to condemn whomever she wishes. But in fact Tumber has only "established" that "gnostics" are like Communists in the America of the 1950s under McCarthyite witch-hunting: everywhere and nowhere at once. "Gnostics" provide convenient enemies, which one needs if one is to establish Order by rooting them out.

All of this would be rather amusing and a little sad, if it were not for the fact that this anti-gnosticism had and still has both a following and consequences. When we look at the history of Buddhism, we find something quite different: a range of perspectives is possible, and a general consensus emerges within a tolerance of alternative but related views. This is quite akin to the more pluralistic perspectives one finds within Gnosticism, as evidenced by the range of works in the Nag Hammadi Library, and for that matter, within the pluralism of gnostic traditions in the West more generally. But Western Christianity developed an apparatus to crush dissent, to annihilate a plurality of views, to obliterate those who espoused a gnostic path toward spiritual realization. This apparatus has its roots, I believe, in early Christian efforts to establish an orthodoxy based on historical faith, an orthodoxy that framed itself by exclusion and attack, an orthodoxy framed by those who hated the gnostic traditions that emphasized inner spiritual realization.

Out of this anti-gnostic orthodoxy of antiquity, whose adherents so feared direct spiritual realization for oneself—emerged the panoply of anti-gnostic individuals and social structures of the medieval period. During this period, we see the witch-hunts and the burning of heretics under the oppressive apparatus of the Inquisition. The same dynamic of antidissidence, of enforced adherence to overarching rationalized dogma is replicated in new ways in modern totalitarianism. But whereas even in the medieval period one was comparatively free so long as one's gnostic inclinations did not come to the attention of the Inquisitors, in the modern period totalitarianism has the capacity to reach into every aspect of society, to lay its deadening hand upon not only the outward aspects of freedom like where one goes and what one does but what is more, upon what and how one thinks. That is what is implied by O'Regan's pronouncement that we *cannot* any longer realize what Böhme realized; gnostic life, he thinks, is closed to us. One begins to wonder if this is a form of totalitarian closure of possibilities differing in form but not in kind from the Chinese Communist destruction of virtually all religious traditions in the lands under their dominion, most notably Tibetan Buddhism, with its gnostic experiential religious traditions.

And so we have moved toward conclusions rather different than those of

Voegelinism, ones that offer valuable insights into the origin and nature of totalitarianism. The struggle to make real on earth the millennial or utopian reality envisioned in an historical future, the willingness to kill those who dare to be dissidents to an imposed social order—what is the historical origin of these tendencies? To be sure, no doubt these are also simply human tendencies, the worst human tendencies, one might argue, as they resulted in millions on millions of dead bodies tossed in mass graves or allowed to rot where they fell. But an historical lineage certainly also could be traced from Christian millennialism-apocalypticism to secularized Hegelian evolutionism, and from that to Marx's effort to imagine a utopian society in the historical future. From Marx it was not long to Lenin and Stalin, to Hitler and to the elimination of those who are seen as "parasitic," and finally to a totalized society in which dissent is intolerable if the society is to reach the millennial future imagined to be just around the next bend.

The genealogy of anti-gnosticism and its secular reflections is complex, to be sure, but if are seeking the origins of totalitarianism, it is here we must look. Certainly we can begin to see why Voegelinist anti-gnosticism represents what I term a "pseudoconservative" wrong turn because it is not based in conserving anything from the past except the spirit and perhaps by extension the apparatus of the Inquisition transposed to a more or less secular ideological realm. The anti-gnostic is viscerally hostile to inner spiritual life, regards the gnostic (however the word is construed) as the Enemy, and thus represents a particularly interesting modern form of intellectual totalitarianism, one opposed to even the least indications of seeking inner peace or of otherworldliness, one that reduces the whole of life to this-worldly social concerns. This is a fascinating dynamic, and one that we can see not only in Western Christianity but also in Islam. For in Islam, as in Christianity, the origins of modern totalitarianism are found with the witch-hunters and anti-gnostic ideologues. Yet time and again, contemporary authors want to blame the victims—one of the more complex instances of which is the well-known work of Norman Cohn.

9

Norman Cohn and the Pursuit of Heretics

On the face of it, Norman Cohn's *Pursuit of the Millennium*—first published near the height of the Cold War in 1957—might appear to be a compendious and more or less objective survey of various heretical, specifically chiliastic Christian movements from the medieval through the early modern periods. And, indeed, that is precisely what it is, at least on one level. I recall reading with some interest its descriptions of the extraordinary panoply of heresies that flourished up to and into the eighteenth century: in it, Cohn, having consulted numerous primary sources, outlines "heretical" groups and individuals from the medieval Brethren of the Free Spirit to the Ranters of early modern England. Still today, it remains one of the most readable overviews of heretical groups during that period of history. But by its end, and seen in a broader context, the book also reveals its larger agenda.

The historical context for *Pursuit of the Millennium*—a popular scholarly book that sold numerous copies and was reprinted many times—is quite important. Why, one might ask, would a book that consisted mostly of painstaking details about obscure heretical groups and individuals during the medieval period become the scholarly equivalent of an enduring bestseller? One is hard-pressed to think of a single comparable example, and so one turns to the question of historical context in order to understand this phenomenon. *Pursuit of the Millennium* was published shortly after the McCarthy period in the United States, during that period when "witch-

86 THE NEW INQUISITIONS

hunting" for Communists was still not far from its peak, and when fear in England, Europe, and the United States about the worldwide spread of Soviet-style Communism was not far from its zenith.¹ The popularity and influence of Cohn's book fits very well into the Cold War dynamic.

Among the interesting aspects of Cohn's most well-known book is the understated, even minimal, nature of its argument. The book begins with the following assertion:

> Between the close of the eleventh century and the first half of the sixteenth it repeatedly happened that the desire of the poor to improve the material conditions of their lives became transfused with phantasies of a new Paradise on earth, a world purged of suffering and sin, a Kingdom of the Saints.
>
> The history of those centuries was of course sprinkled with innumerable struggles between the privileged and the less privileged, rising of towns against their overlords, of artisans against merchant capitalists, of peasants against nobles.²

Thus, the book would appear to be about social revolutions not all that dissimilar to the Bolshevik revolution in Russia, for instance. By the end of the first page, however, the author asserts that the book will be about chiliasm or millennialism, and by the second page, we see its chief argument: "the more carefully one compares the outbreaks of militant social chiliasm during the later Middle Ages with modern totalitarian movements, the more remarkable the similarities appear."³ Here is Cohn's thesis, it would seem.

Yet when we examine *Pursuit of the Millennium* from beginning to end, we find virtually no evidence or even effort to support this thesis. The thesis is asserted briefly in the foreword, and again in the conclusion as if it has been demonstrated—but when we search the voluminous body of the book itself, what we find is simply a detailed overview of various "heresies" interspersed with the histories of occasional, mostly unrelated more or less revolutionary social movements. Cohn makes no serious effort to demonstrate with evidence that there are genuine parallels between medieval chiliasm and modern totalitarianism: he simply asserts those parallels as proven in the beginning and at the end of his book.

Now one could speculate that Cohn wanted the reader to draw conclusions for himself, and so did not need to directly make his own case. However, such a strategy would mean that the parallels between modern totalitarianism and heretical movements of the Middle Ages are quite clear from his evidence, and this is not the case at all. We have seen how the archetype of the Inquisitions directly appears in intellectual lineages that flow into Nazism and Communism, manifesting itself in the form of modern totalitarian inquisitions under Lenin, Stalin, Hitler, and others. But where is the evidence of any influence of Christian heresies on Communism or Nazism? Anyone looking for such direct evidence in *Pursuit of the Millennium* is going to be disappointed.

What we find—instead of evidence of any connections whatever between medieval heresies and modern totalitarianism—is a peculiar shotgun marriage between the "mystical anarchism" of the putative medieval sect "Brethren of the Free Spirit," on the one hand, and early modern Anabaptism, on the other. Here I will not delve into more recent scholarship that calls into question whether the antinomian "Brethren of the Free Spirit" actually existed as an organized group, or whether they were largely a useful fiction of antinomian disorder created so that the institutional bureaucracy of the Catholic Church would have a suitable nemesis. Rather, we must look at the historical links that Cohn proposes between the "Brethren of the Free Spirit" that purportedly existed in the thirteenth century, and the Anabaptist social rebellions of figures such as Thomas Müntzer.

Cohn does assert of one sixteenth-century band of Westphalia robbers that "the mystical anarchism of the Free Spirit provided these people, as it once provided the Bohemian Adamites, with a communal code. Claiming that all things rightly belonged to them, they formed themselves into a robber-band which attacked the residences of nobles and priests and ended by practicing sheer terrorism."[4] But where is the actual evidence that there is a link between late-sixteenth-century German thieves, on the one hand, and a much earlier purported medieval antinomian heresy, on the other? The connections here, as throughout Cohn's book, rest entirely on unsubstantiated false syllogisms: medieval heretics were antinomian; early modern robbers were antinomian because they were thieves and disrespectful of social hierarchy; therefore these two groups are fundamentally identical. But even if there were a connection between the Brethren of the Free Spirit and various Anabaptist rebellions against quasi-feudal authority, so what? There still is no demonstrated connection or even parallel between either of these and modern totalitarianism.

Thus, nearly the entirety of Cohn's argument is to be found in his seven-and-a-half-page conclusion. There, he writes,

> where revolutionary chiliasm thrives best is where history is imagined as having an inherent purpose which is preordained to be realized on this earth in a single, final consummation. It is such a view of history, at once teleological and cataclysmic, that has been presup-

posed and invoked alike by the medieval movements described in the present study and by the great totalitarian movements of our own day.[5]

Here, in my view, Cohn makes a good point. In modern totalitarianism, we do see what I term "secular millennialism," a chiliasm whose claim to represent historical "progress" is rooted primarily in a secular, social evolutionist view of history. And we also consistently see in modern totalitarianism the need for victims, scapegoats whose elimination is imagined to bring about this coming secular millennium, be it a "third reich" or a "workers' paradise" or the "end of history."

But there are profound, insurmountable differences between the variant forms of modern secular millennialism, on the one hand, and medieval religious currents that emphasized direct individual spiritual experience, on the other. However, Cohn almost totally ignores or elides those differences. Regardless of whether the "Brethren of the Free Spirit" actually existed as any kind of organized group, it is certainly true that they did not found a competing church or even create a sectarian structure. Rather, if they existed, they consisted in small, dispersed groups whose primary focus was, as Cohn himself acknowledges, direct individual spiritual revelation, sometimes also called "deification."[6] Given that the overwhelming focus of these medieval mystics— among whom one might count Marguerite of Porete, author of the beautiful treatise *Mirror of Simple Souls*—was to live a reclusive spiritual life devoted to God, how does one make the gigantic leap to blaming them for a much later revolutionary social movement like, say, militantly atheistic Communist totalitarianism in the twentieth century? In truth, one can't blame them.

Cohn seeks to tie the "Brethren of the Free Spirit" by implication to Nietzsche and thus also perhaps to fascism by claiming that the medieval heretics sought to make themselves into "an élite of amoral supermen," but in fact the evidence he cites shows nothing of the sort. What it shows, rather, is that those figures he cites were intent on realizing direct union with God. Like Meister Eckhart (who himself was condemned by the Inquisition at one point), some individual mystics were given to hyperbole, and so spoke of being "Goded with God," or of "no longer having any need of God."[7] Such declarations, however shocking they might seem, have numerous parallels not only in mystical Christianity but also in mystical Judaism and in mystical Islam. There are inherent contradictions when monotheists attempt to express union with the divine, but this hardly makes the mystic into what Cohn calls him, a "nihilistic megalomaniac!" What it makes the mystic is simply that: a mystic, one who dares to express direct spiritual experience in writing.

But Cohn mixes together different movements, periods, and figures with a thin helping of "depth-psychology," and creates a farrago of confusion. The section on "mystical anarchism" is typical: it begins by declaring with great authority that

> from the standpoint of depth-psychology it could be said that orthodox mystic [sic] and heretical adept both started their psychic adventure by a profound introversion, in the course of which they lived through as adults a reactivation of the distorting phantasies of infancy. But whereas the orthodox mystic emerged from this experience—like a patient from a successful psychoanalysis—as a more integrated personality with a widened range of sympathy, the adept of the Free Spirit introjected the gigantic parental images in their most domineering, aggressive, and wanton aspects and emerged as a nihilistic megalomaniac.[8]

Without evidence, the "Free Spirit" mystic is convicted of "introjecting" "gigantic parental images" and becoming a megalomaniac. Not having any actual examples of any of this, Cohn then adduces the example of a *nineteenth-century* libertine and con man who regarded himself as "the sword of God" sent to cleanse society of Catholicism, who "had a great taste for luxurious living," and who had many followers in Eastern Europe.[9] All very well, but it has little or nothing to do with medieval mystics. Cohn then discusses sexual libertinism in the medieval period, and concludes with Calvin's assertion that some spiritual libertines wanted to hold all things in common and thus believed in theft.

Clearly, even though at first Cohn's narrative looks to be an effort at a more or less objective discussion of medieval mystical movements, in fact it is yet another effort to go back in history and blame the victims. And victims there were. Regardless of whether the "Brethren of the Free Spirit" actually existed as an organized group in any meaningful sense, it is certain that such libertines were useful as a bogeyman in order to provide grist for an Inquisitional mill. I mentioned Marguerite of Porete, clearly a gentle soul—but I also should note that she, like many others, was burned at the stake for being akin to, if not herself directly, a libertine heretic. And indeed, when we look through Cohn's own book, we see numerous examples of heretics, on the one hand, and social reformers, on the other, being tortured, burned to death, and otherwise cruelly and despicably treated.[10]

Obviously, I am not arguing here against Cohn's discussion of Thomas Müntzer and various agrarian or peasant rebellions, nor against Cohn's assertion that revolutionary chiliasm has flourished in periods of severe social disruption, when a messianic social leader has come along in order to galvanize followers. But I do have very serious doubts about his confusion of revolutionary social movements, on the one hand, with various complex forms of mysticism, on the other. It is telling that on the very last page, Cohn notes "it is outside the scope of this study to consider what happens when a paraonoiac mass movement captures political power. Only in the story of the radical Taborites and of the New Jerusalem at Münster can one perceive hints of the process which seems to be normal in modern totalitarian states."[11] Here you have it: there *is* no connection between mystics, whether "Brethren of the Free Spirit" or not, and modern totalitarianism. The only real connection—and in my opinion, it is so vague and forced as to be of little value—is with various peasant rebellions.

Although Cohn asserts that various mystics were "paranoiac" or "megalomaniacal," he cites not a bit of convincing evidence for it. Thus we are compelled to ask the question: why was it necessary to drag various heretical groups and individuals into the book to begin with? They bear no connection to Hitler, or to Stalin, or to Pol Pot, or to Mao. No Communist or Fascist authors or authorities cite them; and their *modus operandi* bears no relationship at all to the modern totalitarian state. The heretics were isolated individuals, hunted by the Inquisitions, forced to communicate furtively; their writings were burned and so, often, were they. They had some right to be fearful, but I have seen no evidence of heretical "paranoia." The paranoia, it would seem, was very much on the part of the authorities, both the clerical and the secular authorities who were, after all, jointly responsible for the Inquisitional apparatus responsible for tortures, show trials, and horrific public executions of people who, in retrospect, like their fellow victims of totalitarian regimes, are often rehabilitated and recognized as worthy of respect after all. Of course, by then it is always long since too late.

Hence it becomes very interesting if we turn our attention from the mystics (where Cohn directs us) to the Inquisition (which he studiously ignored in this early book). Which of these two groups might better be described as "paranoiac" or "megalomaniacal?" Hmm. Nowhere in the book is there the slightest indication that, when we look back into Western Christian history, there is one institution that stands out as enforcing the coercion of thought through torture, show trials, and individual or mass executions. That institution was not run by heretics, and it was not run, for that matter, by peasant rebels, unsavory as they might have been.

Seen from a bit of judicious distance, *Pursuit of the Millennium* reveals how unconsciously and thoroughly modern intellectuals still are often imbued with the perspectives shaped by the Inquisitions. When he wrote this book, Cohn undoubtedly saw himself as a modern, secular scholar equipped with the "objective" language of Freudian psychoanalysis, and so he was. Yet for all that, his book unconsciously confirms and even recapitulates the accusations of the Inquisitors against those accused of being "spiritual libertines" or "mystical anarchists," placing the usual suspects in the dock all over again, albeit this time also accused of responsibility for modern industrial totalitarian bureaucracies. On grounds of common sense alone, it is clearly absurd to blame the mystics for totalitarianism—but, as we have seen, its patent absurdity has not prevented numerous modern authors, from Voegelin to Adorno, from repeating the same error over and over. And that is more remarkable still.

The Inner Demons of Europe Once Again

Yet when we turn to Cohn's later book, *Europe's Inner Demons* (1975), we find an entirely different story. Published nearly twenty years after *Pursuit of the Millennium*, *Europe's Inner Demons* convincingly demonstrates that underlying the inquisitional currents of Christianity ran "the urge to purify the world through the annihilation of some category of human beings imagined as agents of corruption and incarnations of evil."[12] Cohn shows that from the period of early Christianity, European civilization bore within it a specific fantasy: "that there existed, somewhere in the midst of the great society, another society, small and clandestine, which not only threatened the existence of the great society but was also addicted to practices which were felt to be wholly abominable, in the literal sense of antihuman."[13] As we will see in a later chapter, this fantasy by no means disappeared during the modern era: we see it not only in anti-Semitic propaganda, but also in the persistent anti-Masonic and anti-"Illuminati" conspiracy theories that emerged anew in late-twentieth-century American evangelicalism.

Particularly fascinating about *Europe's Inner Demons* is Cohn's demonstration that the archetype of the clandestine, antihuman secret society is portable and fluid: the phenomenon recurs again and again in European history, but the parts are played now by one group, later by another. Thus, for example, early Christians were characterized by the Romans as practicing orgies, incest, cannibalism, and worship of an ass and of their leader's genitals—in other words, as belonging to a totally inhuman group that ought to be stamped out. Hence the brutal Roman persecutions of Christians. Yet what were the consistent accusations of institutional Christians against "heretics," especially during the medieval period? Why, none other than: practicing orgies, incest, cannibalism, and worship of Satan.[14]

Cohn masterfully demonstrates how the Knights Templar were destroyed through calumnies that drew on the same archetype that we find recurring throughout the medieval period: the archetype of the inhuman secret society. Here is a quotation cited by Cohn from the order for the arrest of the Templars:

> A bitter thing, a thing to weep over, a thing horrible to think of and terrible to hear, a detestable crime, an abominable act, a fearful infamy, a thing altogether inhuman, or rather, foreign to all humanity has, thanks to the report of several trustworthy persons, reached our ears, smiting us with grievous astonishment and causing us to tremble with violent horror . . .[15]

In other words, the Knights Templar were described by the megalomaniacal King Philip the Fair (who expropriated their wealth and lands in order to fund his own schemes) as antihuman, as worshiping idols, demons, and Satan himself, anointing their idols with "the fat of roasted infants," and committing sodomy—in brief, Cohn shows, "the charges against the Templars were simply a variant of those which, as we have seen, had previously been brought against certain heretical groups, real or imaginary."[16] These same kinds of charges were again to emerge in the early modern period with still more victims, this time mostly women, in the great witch-hunt craze.

Cohn's conclusion is perhaps too sweeping. He concludes that

> what we have been examining is above all a fantasy at work in history (and incidentally, in the writing of history). It is fantasy, and nothing else, that provides the continuity in this story. Gatherings where babies or small children are ceremonially stabbed or squeezed to death, their blood drunk, their flesh devoured . . . belong to the world of fantasy. Orgies where one mates with one's neighbour in the dark, without troubling to establish whether that neighbour is male or female, a stranger or, on the contrary, one's own father or mother, son or daughter, belong to the world of fantasy.[17]

One might object that there is evidence of orgies, for instance, as a human phenomenon. But Cohn is certainly right that the archetype of the antihuman secret cabal "was cynically and consciously exploited to legitimate an exterminatory policy which had already been decided on," as in the case of the Knights Templar.[18] Furthermore, Cohn concludes, in the great witch-hunt of the early modern period, the same kind of victimizing fantasy was codified into the law, administered by bureaucratic officialdom—"and on the charge of committing [an] imaginary offence, many thousands of human beings were burned alive."

The point here is not that there was never anything like witchcraft or heresy but, rather, that the phenomenon of heretic-hunting and witch-hunting draws on an archetypal anticonspiratorial fantasy that has very deep roots, going right back to the very earliest period of Christianity, and that kept manifesting itself throughout European history. On this point, Cohn's case is indisputable.

What is perhaps most noteworthy of all—as one steps back from *Europe's Inner Demons* to consider the phenomenon of heretic-hunting more generally—is that the archetype manifests itself unconsciously, most of the time. In this regard, Philip the Fair's persecution of the Knights Templar is somewhat anomalous because it was so cynical. By and large, the phenomenon of heretic-hunting manifests itself with great earnestness: the persecuting officials, even many of the people, come to believe that they are in mortal danger from a tiny, secret "heretical" group, or from witches, or for that matter, from Jews, in Hitler's Germany, or from Trotskyites and "traitors" under Stalin's nightmarish reign, or even from Freemasons, imagined "Illuminati," and "occultists" in modern Europe or the United States. Probably it should not be surprising, but it still is, to find this phenomenon continuing recur unconsciously on the political left as well as on the right, and even in the work of an author such as Theodor Adorno.

10

Theodor Adorno and the "Occult"

Without doubt, one of the more influential authors of the mid-twentieth century is Theodor A. Adorno (1903–1969), whose work, especially as a central member of the "Frankfurt School," was instrumental in creating what became known as "cultural studies"—that is, the critical-theoretical analysis of contemporary culture. Underlying much of Adorno's work—from *The Authoritarian Personality* (1950) to *Minima Moralia* (1951) and to the kinds of cultural criticism represented in such posthumous collections in English as *The Culture Industry* (1991)—is his effort to understand and analyze the nature of National Socialism in the wake of Hitler. A significant theme in Adorno's writing, especially in the decade after World War II, was "irrationalism," especially as manifested in what he termed "the occult" or "occultism." But as we shall see, Adorno's attacks on what he believed to be "occultism" in fact represent an anti-esotericism of the left that is almost a mirror reflection of the Inquisitorial tendency that we often see operating on the political right.

Adorno believed that Nazism represented an eruption of antirational or irrational forces in society, and that by analyzing and combating "authoritarian irrationalism" in forms like popular astrology and "occultism," he also in some larger sense was combating what he believed to be contributing conditions for anti-Semitism and Nazi authoritarianism. After all, in the popular mind, many major figures within German National Socialism are associated with "occultism";

not only Hitler himself but also Heinrich Himmler, Rudolf Hess, and various other primary Nazi figures had some "occult" interests.[1] What is more, it is well established that Nazism emerged in an ambience that included figures and movements often loosely associated with "occultism," such as the Thule Society, various kinds of "Aryan" quasi-mythologies, in turn often bound up with racial theories, forms of antimodernism, neopaganism, vegetarianism, and other perspectives that, however disparate and even opposed to one another they might be, could be lumped together as "irrational" if not outright "occultism." One can see how Adorno, looking at the nightmare of Nazi totalitarianism and its persecution of Jews, arrived at his thesis that the enemy of the rational and humane must be irrational and inhumane—and that what one must do to prevent the reappearance of Nazism is to analyze and root out the irrational as it presents itself in modern societies. Hence Adorno wrote such works as "Theses against Occultism," or "The Stars Down to Earth," which bitterly attack and dismiss "occultism" as irrational and thus as symptomatic of the pathology that produces fascism.

Of course, there is an obvious question that doesn't seem to have occurred to Adorno himself, but that we are compelled to broach during our inquiry into Adorno's anti-occultism. Why is it Adorno didn't recognize that historically, "occultists" in Anglo-European history were far more likely to be among those persecuted *along with* Jews than to be themselves persecutors? Is Adorno, in his anti-occultism, engaged in the same kind of rhetorical sleight of hand that we see in such figures of the right as Voegelin and Schmitt—that is, a blaming of the victim? After all, at the very basis of Adorno's critique of "occultism" is the belief that it is "irrational" in binary opposition to that which is "rational"—yet such a belief is precisely the kind of dualism that we see underlying Inquisitional logic more generally. Ironically, Adorno objectifies and rejects "occultism" and "occultists" in a manner rather reminiscent of an anti-Semite objectifying and rejecting "the Jews" on the basis of gross overgeneralizations, caricatures, half-truths, logical fallacies, and outright lies.

Let us begin by looking at one of the most widely reprinted of Adorno's writings on occultism: his "Theses Against Occultism" (1946–1947), published in *Minima Moralia*, but also as a separate piece in *Telos* (1974), and again in *The Stars Down to Earth and Other Essays on the Irrational in Culture* (1994).[2] The first thing one notices about Adorno's remarks on "occultism" is their abruptness and abstractness. He begins, "The tendency to occultism is a symptom of regression in consciousness. Consciousness has lost the strength to think the absolute and to bear the conditional."[3] "Monotheism," he continues, "disintegrates into a second mythology." "Spirit dissociates itself into spirits, and in the process loses the ability to see that they do not exist," "society's veiled forces" "fool its victims with false prophecy," and "after millennia of enlightenment, panic once again breaks out over humanity, whose domination over nature, by turning into domination over man, surpasses all the horrors that man ever had to fear from nature."

Where should one begin to comment on Adorno's pronouncements? First, one cannot tell what he means by the term "occultism," which he never defines and which remains entirely nebulous. Apparently, he chiefly means here by "occultism," spiritualism, that is, phenomena of mediumship that became popular during the nineteenth and early twentieth centuries, and also various kinds of "fortune tellers." Underlying his assertions is an insight into the commodification of "the occult" that took place during the nineteenth and twentieth centuries: "a reborn animism denies the very alienation that it itself has generated and thrives on, [for which] it substitutes non-existing experience."[4] But one must at least ask: why is an "animist" or "occult" experience by definition "non-existing"? Merely because one says so? Assertion without evidence does not constitute an argument. Furthermore, the first paragraph of "Theses Against Occultism," which begins with the bald claim that "attraction to the occult is a symptom of the retrogression of consciousness," concludes with a giant leap to the idea that somehow the modern "domination of nature" has turned into "domination over man" (presumably totalitarianism). But how does one arrive at such a conclusion?

Adorno wants to make a "retrogression to magical thinking" responsible for totalitarianism, by which specifically he means Nazi totalitarianism. However, the link between these two—occultism and totalitarianism—is more of a fuzzy smooshing together of disparate, disconnected things. Hence in the third paragraph, Adorno claims that "the hypnosis exerted by occult objects resembles totalitarian terror: over time, they become one and the same."[5] Really? Why? How? Adorno's bizarre explanation: "the horoscope corresponds to the Central Office's directives to the citizens and the mystique of numbers prepares for administrative statistics and price fixing." "Ultimately," he concludes, "integration reveals itself as the ideology of disintegration into power groups exterminating each other. Whoever gets into it is lost." Into what? A tarot card reader is somehow akin to—what? Hitler's brownshirts? This is the kind of fallacious thinking and illogic that one would reject in a freshman college paper. How on earth do we arrive at some sort of link between the suppressed and marginalized "occult" in the form of astrology or Kabbalistic number mysticism on the one hand, and central office directives or administrative statistics? As to a "power group" "exterminating" anyone—isn't "the occult" typically associated with the *victims* of such efforts at extermination in the West? Witches, heretics, do these not represent the suppressed, the marginalized, the

98　THE NEW INQUISITIONS

objects of Inquisitional terror? Yet by Adorno's logic, they are somehow, inexplicably, to blame for the bureaucracies that persecute them.

One is frequently struck by how Adorno's rhetoric really is an unconscious transposition from anti-Semitism to anti-occultism. He refers to "occultists" as aligned with "shady asocial marginal phenomena," revealing "the forces of inner decay," as "diseased consciousness" for which "the refuse from the world of appearances becomes the *mundus intelligibilis*"; "occultism" is "barbarically insane" "crudeness," that appeals to "the decaying subject." The "occultist" [or "occultism"] "wants the world to conform to its [occultism's or the occultist's] own decay; this is why it has to do with props and bad wishes."[6] Adorno himself makes the connection: "like Fascism, the power of the occult is not just a pathos [*pathisch*]—the two being related by a model of thought as in the case of anti-Semitism."[7] But the connection is slightly different: the "model of thought" of anti-Semitism (i.e., making all manner of negative associations with Jews as "shady," "asocial," "marginal," and representing forces of "decay") is simply transposed by Adorno to attack "occultists" with exactly the same bitter hostility.

At this point, Adorno hauls out what he sees as more big guns, which he trains mostly on spiritualism. "Occultism," he announces, "is the metaphysics of the dopes." "Since the early days of spiritualism, the beyond has conveyed nothing more essential than the greetings from the deceased grandmother," he writes, acknowledging "the *lumen naturale* did go further than the trip to the grandmother." The allusion to the *lumen naturale* or "light of nature" here suggests a distinction between the complexities of traditional esotericism as manifested in seventeenth- or eighteenth-century alchemical texts, and the more superficial and banal forms of twentieth-century spiritualism that offer a commodified "occult" access to the dead. But this is not a distinction he is interested in pursuing; rather, "Theses Against Occultism" is, as its title would suggest, a diatribe largely free of subtle (or even unsubtle) distinctions. He is more interested in claiming that "occultists" "provide feeble-mindedness with a *Weltanschauung*," and that their "rotten tricks are nothing but the rotten existence which they brighten."[8]

Near the end of his attack on "occultism," Adorno offers a side trip into what he construes as comparative religion. He asserts that

> the great religions have either imposed silence concerning the salvation of the dead, or they taught the resurrection of the body. They are in earnest about the inseparability of the spiritual and the corporeal. There was no intention or anything "spiritual" which was not somehow grounded in bodily perception and, in turn, demanded bodily fulfillment. This is too crude for occultists, who fancy them-

selves above the idea of resurrection and who actually do not want salvation at all.[9]

What a strange passage! Usually, spiritualism is attacked as being crude because it insists too much on an extension of the physical world into the spiritual—but here all great religions are proposed to have insisted on bodily perception and bodily fulfillment, and "occultists" are claimed to be uninterested in these, or in the "inseparability of the spiritual and the corporeal"! As anyone with some knowledge of the vast and complex history of esotericism knows, these are all rather peculiar overgeneralizations that bear little or no relation to the actual history of esoteric currents, groups, or individuals.[10]

Adorno concludes his odd "Theses Against Occultism" by asserting that "the idea of the existence of the spirit [or of spirit] is "the most extreme height of bourgeois consciousness."[11] Here we are not very far at all from Marx's claim that religion is the opiate of the masses. But Adorno has a final target: Hegel. He thinks that "occultists" confuse spirit and the world of things as commodity, and that thus "the world spirit becomes the highest spirit, the guardian angel of the existing, the deranged." This, he continues, "is what the occultists live on: their mysticism is the *enfant terrible* of Hegel's mystical element. They push speculation to fraudulent bankruptcy."[12] "Occultists" objectify spirit, and in so doing (Adorno concludes), make possible the final assertion: "There is no Spirit."

Frankly, it is hard to write about "Theses Against Occultism" because the work is so full of confusion and overgeneralization mixed up with a disturbing bitterness that borders on a kind of nihilism. Although there are a few hints that Adorno is distinguishing between traditional currents of Western esotericism like alchemy and later movements like spiritualism, the fact is that he never defines what he means by "occultism" and as a result, the whole thing seems like a mean-spirited attack on what he might as well refer to as "those people." How is it that someone so attuned to the rhetoric of anti-Semitism could fail to recognize that his own rhetoric of anti-occultism so resembles it? There is little more effort to understand or to accurately depict "occultism" in Adorno's "Theses" than there is to understand or to accurately depict Jewish culture or Jews in "The Protocols of the Elders of Zion."

The strange reversal that, in effect, blames the victims of history for authoritarianism is also at work in the other often-reprinted work of anti-occultism by Adorno, an article entitled "The Stars Down to Earth: The Los Angeles Times Astrology Column."[13] To the extent that "The Stars Down to Earth" only analyzed the phenomenon of popular newspaper astrology columns, it may be rather interesting. But instead of straightforward analysis,

Adorno seriously takes a popular astrology listing in the *Los Angeles Times* as an example of "occultism," and furthermore earnestly analyzes the newspaper astrology listing as if its purported "occultism" in turn reveals latent Nazism in American society. In his view, the popular astrology listing represents "large-scale social phenomena involving irrational elements" bound up with "various mass movements spread all over the world in which people seem to act against their own rational interests of self-preservation."[14] In what we now can see is his typical style on this subject, he does not *arrive* at this conclusion but, rather, *begins* with it as his premise in the very first lines.

Throughout Adorno's article on the *Los Angeles Times* astrology column during the period 1952–1953, he uses the same kind of anti-occultist rhetoric that we saw in "Theses Against Occultism." Those who pay attention to astrology columns may be "psychotic" or exhibit "psychotic character structure;" astrologers and astrology are "nefarious;" the occult is "modern big time irrationality;" "the modern occultist movements, including astrology, are more or less artificial rehashes of old and by-gone superstitions" "discordant with today's universal state of enlightenment."[15] It is "pseudo-rationality" "the very same traits that play such a conspicuous role in totalitarian social movements."[16] Why? Because "astrological irrationality" represents "abstract authority." Thus "it is a moot point whether people who fall for astrology show" "a psychotic predisposition."[17] Adorno's particular contribution to anti-occultism is to claim that astrology is "an enlarged duplicate of an opaque and reified world.[18] In other words, an interest in astrology is symptomatic of the alienation inherent in modernity itself; but Adorno goes much further yet in his anti-occultist claims based on a single popular newspaper column.

Astrology, as represented by a popular newspaper column, resembles a "sect," and is thus "sinister" by nature because it "is indicative" of emerging "totalitarianism." How? "Just as those who can read the phony signs of the stars believe that they are in the know, the followers of totalitarian parties believe that their special panaceas are universally valid and feel justified in imposing them as a general rule," Adorno claims. In other words, because astrologers presumably believe in astrology, they "presage" nothing less than "the one-party state"![19] How did we get here? By huge, totally unsubstantiated leaps. One could as easily argue on the same premise that Adorno himself, by believing in his own unsubstantiated claims, presages a "one-party state" driven by ideology—say, a Marxist totalitarianism. Adorno coyly admits that astrology can serve "the function of a defense against psychosis," but still holds that astrology is bound up with mental illness, in particular with "paranoid tendencies" and "the retrogression of society as a whole," if not with outright psychosis. And he concludes with a reference to Leibniz's "profound contempt only for those activities of the mind which aimed at deception," chief among which is "astrology."[20]

Once again, one hardly knows where to begin. Perhaps the most striking aspect of Adorno's attack on "astrology" is his chosen subject: a newspaper astrology column. Such columns then, as now, have virtually nothing to do with astrology in any historically informed or complete sense.[21] Rather, "sun sign" columns consist in bland, abstract pronouncements meant to apply to huge swaths of the population: "beware of strangers today" is about as specific as the predictions get. Virtually no one takes them seriously. To take newspaper "sun signs" as synecdochic for "occultism" as a whole is a parody of academic or scholarly analysis; it conflates a popular simulacrum of "occultism" commodified into a newspaper product with all the complex variants and historical forms of esotericism simply by using the, broad, undefined label of "occultism." One can understand, given his interest in popular culture, why Adorno would choose to analyze a newspaper astrology column—what's peculiar is his use of that column to draw sweeping conclusions about "occultism" as a whole. In that, his work in many respects resembles that of fundamentalist Christians who also draw sweeping, dramatic conclusions from the thinnest of "evidence" from popular culture.

Yet how few scholars seem willing to criticize or even to question Adorno's anti-esotericism. Adorno's anti-occultist premises are transmitted through various scholarly works and accepted wholesale without much if any critical analysis. For instance, Daphna Canetti-Nisim, in her contribution to a collection entitled *Religious Fundamentalism and Political Extremism* (2004), accepts the basic idea that "an" [sic] "alternative religious tradition," comprised of such disparate currents as astrology, divination, spiritualism, and even Kabbalah, somehow predisposes people to support an authoritarian political system.[22] The mostly unspoken corollary to such a claim is, of course, that those who accept "an" alternative religious tradition (as if "occultism" were a single unified entity) ought to be placed under surveillance or perhaps better, gotten rid of— they are, just as the Inquisition saw them, "dangerous." Hence, once again, those who historically represent a marginalized viewpoint are not victims but, by the special jiu-jitsu of anti-esotericism, are *to blame* for authoritarianism!

The fallacy here is the same that we find in Voegelin's work, even if Voegelin and Adorno might seem to come from opposite ends of the political spectrum. Somehow, "Gnostics" or "occultists" are to blame for the emergence of totalitarianism—even if, as recent scholarship has amply demonstrated, in reality "occultists" were among the first victims of the Nazis, and were marked for immediate suppression, imprisonment, or even extermination.[23] If Voegelin's thesis that "Gnostics" were to blame for leftist or Marxist totalitarianism had some grain of truth, then why do we find that in fact influential leftist or Marxist authors are at least as anti-occultist (or, as the case may be, anti-Gnostic) as their counterparts on the right? Voegelin and Adorno actually proceed on the same basis: they simply make assertions or pronouncements about how "occultists" or "Gnostics" are to blame for totalitarianism, how they "set the stage" for it, or whatnot. But neither of them adduce any convincing evidence, and their subsequent followers then take for granted as proven what has merely been claimed without support.

There are two primary aspects of the inquisitorial instinct: the first is ideological, and the second, the practical implementation of that ideology. What we see in Adorno is essentially the same kind of ideological inquisitionalism that one sees in Voegelin: here is a political tendency one both fears and detests—in Adorno's case, Nazism; in Voegelin's case, Communism—and so one seeks an ideological-political scapegoat. "Occultism" or "Gnosticism" are ideal as scapegoats because they carry much historical baggage; they are freighted with centuries of opprobrium, yet they remain vague and indefinable, ideal for service as vehicles of contempt precisely because of their imprecision. "Everyone" knows that "occultism" (or "Gnosticism") is bad, even if "everyone" isn't entirely sure what is meant by the term. Both Adorno and Voegelin draw on this dynamic in order to construct an ideological scapegoat through an intellectual inquisition; but neither of them witnessed the practical consequences of scapegoating "occultists" or "Gnostics," for theirs was a purely intellectual exercise in witch-hunting.

What happens when an ideological inquisition becomes a basis for state policy? Let us take the case of Germany after 1933, in which as Corinna Treitel documents, "participants in the German occult movement faced a largely hostile state." They "continued their occult activities under constant threat of discovery and punishment"; they belonged "to a criminalized group in a brutal police state: they suffered intimidation, coercion, suppression, and—in extreme cases—murder."[24] It is true that a few "occultists" were affiliated with the Nazis, but take the case of "Hitler's prophet," professional astrologer and clairvoyant Erik Jan Hanussen. He published an astrological newsletter that predicted the triumph of National Socialism and was rumored to be an advisor to Hitler; but "a few days after the Reichstag fire [in 1933], 'Hitler's prophet' was arrested and summarily executed by three storm troopers just outside of Berlin."[25] Or take the case of Johannes Maria Verweyen, a professor of philosophy with interests in Freemasonry, vegetarianism, and poetry, as well as in the Theosophical Society of Blavatsky (which he renounced in 1934 to return to Catholicism). He was blacklisted by the Nazis in 1934, was driven from his chair in philosophy at the University of Bonn, was harassed and put under surveillance, was arrested in 1941, and, finally, died in the concentration camp of Bergen-Belsen in 1945.[26] Good idea to blame him for Nazism.

My point here is not that there were no occult influences on National Socialism—such influence is well documented, especially in a figure such as Heinrich Himmler. See, for example, the extensive research of Nicholas Goodrick-Clarke, notably *The Occult Roots of Nazism* (1985/1992).[27] Rather, in good part *because* of such influences (but also because National Socialism engaged a rhetoric of "progress"), the Nazis were inclined to persecute or eliminate occultists that might be perceived as a threat. This phenomenon is similar to what we see in the inquisitional archetype more generally: Communists purged fellow Communists; and as we shall see, in the early twenty-first century, American evangelical Christians often attacked other evangelical Christians more bitterly than anyone else.

I certainly sympathize with Adorno in his desire to determine exactly why and how totalitarianismism comes to power. Indeed, my own great-grandparents on my mother's side fled Germany to settle in the United States around 1930 in part because (we only recently discovered) my great-grandmother was Jewish, something she kept hidden from us her whole life. Although it may be rhetorically convenient to blame Nazism on "occultism," and certainly there were connections between the Nazi regime and occultism, it is also true that some occultists were right there in the concentration camps next to Jews, Gypsies, Poles, and others. What accounts for Adorno's bitter, derisive, and far from subtle anti-occultism, expressed in terms that echo the anti-occultist rhetoric of Nazi Germany? I think that for Adorno, as for Voegelin, and for all of us who have inherited the rhetorical constructs of "progress" and the "enlightenment," "the occult" makes for an easy target and scapegoat. "Occultists," particularly popular figures who write newspaper or tabloid astrology columns and the like, represent the "superstitious past," and so are often targeted for elimination by rightist and leftist ideologues who engage the language of "progress" toward a future utopia from which "backward" figures such as "occultists" are purged.

What I began to suspect, as I considered the case of Adorno in light of Carl Schmitt and Eric Voegelin, is that anti-occultism is a phenomenon in itself, one that appears on both the political left and right. The temptation toward ideological inquisitionism and political scapegoating seems to be very strong on both ends of the political spectrum, and the natural victim often seems to be "occultism." By engaging the rhetoric of anti-occultism, figures on both the left and the right were drawing (mostly unconsciously) on the inherited language and conceptual frameworks of their predecessors in the Inquisition and in the witch-hunts of the early modern era. Mostly, the rhetoric of anti-occultism remains intellectual. But when the rhetoric of anti-occultism is taken seriously by a police state, then the consequences—in terms of suppression, harassment, surveillance, imprisonment, and murder—are brutally evident, regardless of whether the state power is nominally of the left or of the right.

Thus, although Adorno's bitter attacks upon "occultists" at first glance may seem harmless, they exist in a larger context that is far from harmless, and that he surely should have known. How is it that he, or Voegelin, or Schmitt, could have overlooked this historical and rhetorical context of anti-occultism, let alone its human consequences when put into practice through witch-hunters, or grand inquisitor—or state police? One perhaps can understand, I suppose, why those on the right sympathetic to Roman Catholicism would consciously (as in the case of Schmitt) or unconsciously (as in the case of Voegelin) embrace the Inquisition as an intellectual and political model. By why would Adorno (even by implication) accept such a model, too, let alone anti-occultist rhetoric like that of the Nazis themselves?

The fact is, anti-occultism or anti-esotericism is woven deeply into the very fabric of twentieth-century thought both on the left and on the right. Both Communists and Nazis continued the prior Church tendency to persecute and obliterate those who were seen to embrace or embody "irrational" "occult" or "heretical" beliefs or practices. In his reaction against the mythological and irrational dimensions of National Socialism, Adorno was unconsciously reiterating the kind of rhetorical demonization that the Nazis engaged in! And in his crusade against irrationalism, Adorno was in fact overlooking the terrifying role that rationalist industrialism played within National Socialism—what were the gas chambers if not industrial chambers of death? These are sets of paradoxes worth noting. Such paradoxes came into being precisely because anti-occultism or anti-esotericism is so deeply embedded within the history of the West that it goes almost unrecognized even by its practitioners, and it goes almost totally unremarked on by commentators or analysts. Virtually no one on the left seems to have noted the unpleasant origins and implications of Adorno's anti-occultism—instead, one finds almost exclusively tacit or explicit endorsements. Of *course* one should be anti-occultist, goes the assumption. As Adorno himself would have acknowledged and appreciated, the more unrecognized such assumptions are, the more malign power they have.

But, one might reply to all this, surely the rhetoric of anti-occultism had ceased or at least lost its power by the end of the twentieth century. So one might think—but one would be wrong. Let us consider the case of Carl Raschke in relation to American evangelical Christianity.

II

Another Long, Strange Trip

One might think that the themes we've seen repeated from the eighteenth and nineteenth into the twentieth centuries—the secularization and politicization of Christian attitudes toward heresy—is limited to this earlier period, and that the late twentieth and early twenty-first centuries would not be subject to the same tendencies. After all, a deep skepticism toward political metanarratives is a major impetus for what became known as "postmodernism." Having seen the colossal failures represented by Leninism and Stalinism, not to mention National Socialism, one could expect that faith in such mass movements would have waned by the end of the bloody twentieth century. But one might forget that the original heresiophobic impulses of early institutional Christianity continue, sometimes in unexpected places, and that witch-hunts are not as far away as one might think.

That Old Bugaboo, "Gnosticism," Yet Again

The case of Carl Raschke, a professor of religious studies at the University of Denver, Colorado, is well worth considering. Raschke's work is akin to that of Georges Sorel, in that like Sorel, he seems to shift his fealty from one movement to the next without any clear underlying unity. He began his career with a book endorsing a more or less traditionalist view of American society: *The Bursting of New Wineskins: Reflections on Religion and Culture at the End of Affluence* (1978). In it, he defends "traditional culture" that, "in the past, sustained by grassroots associations and popular institutions, has actually been a bulwark against exploitation, while bureaucratic and totalitarian management has thrived on the formation of masses of rootless individuals."[1] He deplores "disorganized religion," and looks forward to a "resurgence of traditional life," to a "re-organization of religion" and a "rehabilitation of the common life" that reflects in a new way the medieval sense that "the order of religious meanings was intertwined with the order of society."[2] And he deplores the "new psycho-religiosity" of "mystical or semi-mystical moods."[3] Already in this first book, then, we see a nascent longing for a unified religiosecular state, and loathing for "psycho-religious" "heresy."

But it is in his next book, *The Interruption of Eternity: Modern Gnosticism and the Origins of the New Religious Consciousness* (1980), that Raschke unveils a much more explicit heresiophobic agenda. The genesis of the book, he writes in the preface, came during the emergence of new religious movements during the 1970s. During this period, he began "groping toward some clues," and concluded with some haste that "the different underground religious communities" and indeed, "key attitudes on the part of certain intellectuals" are none other than "Gnosticism." What does he mean by "Gnosticism?" Not anything historically grounded, but rather people who are opposed to the " 'progress' of the modern, industrial world," people who are "in revolt against the course of modern history and seek salvation within the sphere of the timeless."[4] Thus—even though Voegelin is not even in this book's index—we know at once that we are in the presence of yet another Voegelin-inspired inquisitor.

Sure enough, we soon find that Raschke is launching sweeping attacks hither and yon against "new Gnostics" who, he thinks, are engaged in a "revolt against history" and who refuse the notion of progress. Carlos Castaneda, the Marquis de Sade, Giordano Bruno, Louis-Claude de Saint-Martin, Franz Mesmer, these are all "Gnostics," just as are the Romantic poets (notably Blake, Byron, and Shelley), philosophers such as Fichte and Nietzsche, the poet Yeats, the novelist Herman Hesse, the psychologist C. G. Jung, not to mention the founder of Christian Science, Mary Baker Eddy.[5] He refers with distress to "American Gnostics," such as Whitman and Emerson, and claims that American "New Thought" was "America's pragmatic and simplified version of Gnosticism."[6] Once one defines "Gnosticism" broadly enough, why, one can find its adherents everywhere. The emergence of Asian religions in America, of hippies and of writers such as Alan Watts—all these too are somehow

"Gnostic" and thus to be feared.[7] Indeed, no less than all "the new religions constitute a Gnostic escape route for the masses of individuals in our society who, thrown out as the detritus of crumbling communal groups and institutions, including the family, are desperately looking for some kind of salvation by their own resources."[8] Gnostics, Gnostics everywhere!

What is it that so exercises Raschke about his peculiar constructed "Gnosticism"? He sees it as a "Gnostic flight by mind-magic into eternity," a seeking of "salvation in the timeless world."[9] Of course, one might think that concepts like "eternity," "salvation," and "timelessness" might have positive religious connotations—but evidently they don't if one is on the hunt for heresy everywhere. One is unsurprised to read Raschke's final claim that "the danger these days is that we are all becoming Gnostics of a sort."[10] By this time, it's become clear that in his mind, everyone already is a Gnostic, save perhaps him! Raschke represents a kind of militant secularist, whose attacks on what he styles "Gnosticism" also assert the primacy of "time," "history," and "linear progress," as though if we were distracted from "linear progress" by art, poetry, or religion, "history" might disappear. There is a strange, pervasive anxiety informing the whole of this book.

An Epidemic of Evil!

But that anxiety about "Gnostics" is nothing compared to the outright panic visible in Raschke's 1990 mass-market paperback *Painted Black*. This lurid little tome, its covers a tasteless safety-orange, "includes a shocking 8-page photo insert," and describes itself this way:

> **An Epidemic of Evil!** Carl A. Raschke, America's leading authority on subcultures of darkness, puts together a terrifying puzzle. What he discovers, piece by piece, is an alarming epidemic of violence that is sweeping the country. Fully documented, this landmark book clearly presents the chilling facts and cases behind an invisible wave of evil that holds our children by their minds and parents by their hearts. *Painted Black* reveals things you'd never believe could exist in your hometown . . . but do.[11]

Clearly this is a work of no little hysteria. Raschke's own preface is similar in tone: he claims to offer a "comprehensive" study of Satanism, which "is not a 'new religion' deserving the sort of latitudinarian tolerance or respect one would be expected to accord under the U.S. Constitution, say, to an emergent sect of South Pacific pantheists." For "Satanism is a sophisticated and highly effective motivational system for the spread of violence and cultural terrorism, all the while hiding behind the cloak of the First Amendment."[12]

The word "lurid" is the ideal description for this book, which lists numerous serial killings and ritual murders, and ties them together with figures such as Anton LaVey, tossing in the Marquis de Sade, not to mention Oscar Wilde, Charles Baudelaire, and Friedrich Nietzsche.[13] The photo spread includes the obligatory shot of Aleister Crowley, heavy metal musician Ozzy Osbourne, graffiti on a garage door in Denver, and a couple of photos from the notorious trial of the McMartin preschool case, in which (amid some hysteria) various members of the Buckey family were convicted of serial child abuse. Typical of the book is this:

> Item: Police in Britain were stifled in their efforts to come up with suspects in the serial gang rape of London women. Victims reported that one of the rapists had a telltale spider's web tattoo on his hand. Another sported a tattoo with the letters MAR. Both tattoos were insignia of the heavy metal group Marillion, which sings about rape and mayhem.[14]

Where to begin? The band Marillion was in fact one of the most literary and sophisticated of all British rock bands during this period, and hardly could be described as "heavy metal" in any meaningful sense. To describe their melancholy and complex lyrics as being about "rape and mayhem" would be akin to reducing the complexity and genius of, say, Ralph Waldo Emerson's essays to nothing but "Gnosticism"—but, of course, that's what Raschke did in his earlier book, so one should hardly be surprised by much of anything at this point. Thus, the fantasy game "Dungeons and Dragons" is, in Raschke's learned opinion, a horrifying initiation into "black magic," and so on.[15] It is scarcely possible to exaggerate the hysterical nature of this book, nor the number of errors in it (although some have tried at least to chronicle them).[16]

What distinguishes *Painted Black* from *The Interruption of Eternity*, aside from its bright orange paperback cover and its breathless sensationalism, is the fact that this is a real effort to awaken an American inquisition. Thus, he concludes by asserting that "Satanism" is becoming nothing less than a "major national problem."[17] And Raschke even goes so far as to liken the late twentieth century to the medieval period, when "there was a religious underground with striking affinity to today's counterculture."[18] He alludes to mass murderer Charles Manson, and then writes that "the claim of a corporate ancestry of [the medieval heresy] Catharism is far greater than a metaphor. It is the watershed of all modern systems of belief emphasizing the right of the human creature to revolt against the ultimate order of things."[19] Never mind that the Cathars were ascetic, harmless, and mostly massacred by the Church—suddenly they are nothing less than the ancestors of Manson and, well, narcotics traffickers and child molesters! Already, he writes with a hint of satisfaction, the furor over Satanism has "yielded a climate of fear in middle-class quarters where fear had never flourished before."[20] What we need, he implies, is a good old-fashioned Inquisition. The police and "specialists" like himself are on board—all they need is a little more widespread fear.

This is dangerous stuff indeed. With self-styled "experts" asserting the certainty of ritual child molestation in various day care centers, some people were falsely imprisoned during the very period when Raschke wrote this book—on the coaxed testimony of confused children and the lurid accusations of police and prosecutors on witch hunts.[21] Only later did questions arise. But the purpose of the justice system is not to provide a venue for witch-hunts—it is to provide a sober, informed, judicious analysis of the facts. It is surprising, given the hysterical tenor of Raschke's book, and of numerous other books and public pronouncements by "experts," that there weren't more Inquisitional forays and witch-hunts that dispensed with those troublesome niceties insisted upon by the American Constitution and its various amendments. Fortunately, Raschke's book didn't have the kind of impact he so clearly wanted: to fully awaken the medieval Inquisitorial spirit. But as we shall see, the 1980s and 1990s "Satanic panic" was bad enough.

Digital Revolution

Raschke's later works deserve some brief attention here. In 1996, he published a book on "postmodernity" that shows almost no trace of the harshly anti-gnostic arguments of his earlier books. Instead, it appears that in the intervening decade and a half, he became enamored of the trendiest notions of the period—the theoretical jargon, the focus on the body—and gave up on hunting for heretics everywhere.[22] And his subsequent book, *The Digital Revolution and the Coming of the Postmodern University* (2003), is a paean to an imagined wonderful aeon of a "hyperuniversity" emerging via the impersonal venue of computers. He decries the "inherent conservatism" of "residential university faculty," and extols "a reformation of the academy by undermining the hegemony of the 'knowledge specialist.'"[23] He celebrates the fall of the "Medieval walls of the academy," and imagines instead an "anti-authoritarian" "postmodern" era of "hypertextuality" and the end of the "privileges" of those who in the past were the conservators of higher learning.[24]

Are there the connections between the anti-heresiology of *The Interruption of Eternity* and *Painted Black,* Raschke's later celebration of "postmodernity," and what he imagines as the death of traditional higher education? One wonders. Certainly the times were not entirely conducive to an Inquisitor searching for the signs of heresy everywhere. But the times were in favor of those who embraced the latest fashionable concepts, such as "postmodernity," or "hyperuniversities." Little wonder that, having found little lasting support for his anti-heresiological campaigns, after the talk show circuit lost interest in him, he turned instead to embracing those currents that were least amenable to the conservation of the humanities and of traditions of academic knowledge. If so many of the great writers and intellectuals of the past were deluded "Gnostics," no doubt it would seem best to abandon the whole enterprise of academic tradition and to launch one's little boat onto the great, noisy, and shallow torrent of "the digital revolution and the postmodern university."

Hence, if there is one overarching conclusion we can draw here, it is this: whatever its flaws, the late-twentieth-century American political and social system did not encourage or support the worst consequences of anti-Gnosticism. What we see in the anti-gnosticism of Raschke or others in academia or, for that matter, in the anti-occultism of evangelical Christianity, is their relative impotence. Whereas in Nazi Germany and in Lenin's and Stalin's Soviet Union, the Grand Inquisitors had very real consequences, in the United States of the late twentieth century, even the more extreme forms of anti-heresiological rhetoric still did not have widespread consequences, let alone take thousands or even millions of victims. Although Raschke or various evangelical authors might see "Gnostics" or "heretics" behind every bush and in virtually every major intellectual since the seventeenth century, the secular American society that they deplored—with its plethora of new religious movements and its broad religious pluralism—still acted as a constraint against an American inquisition. But, as we will see, secular pluralism wasn't fully able to contain what became known as the American "Satanic panic."

12

High Weirdness in the American Hinterlands

By the early twenty-first century, it had become clear that there were, broadly speaking, two Americas. One was the inheritor of what we may term Enlightenment rationalism and liberalism in the older sense, carrying the connotations of liberality and the kind of generosity of spirit—and skepticism of religious zealotry—that characterized Thomas Jefferson especially but that was found liberally among the Founding Fathers more generally. This America was inclined toward pluralism, toward a secular state, and toward the long tradition of America as refuge from religious persecution elsewhere in the world. But for the second, newer America, this foundational American tradition was anathema—for the second America is marked by a literalist, fundamentalist doctrinalism, by a virulent hatred of "liberalism," and, most important for our purposes, by a persistent strain of what one must term a dispersed inquisitionalism.

Naturally, what I am sketching here is a broad but nonetheless widely recognized distinction, codified in the misleading characterization of the United States as composed of "red" and "blue" states—colors from the convenient designations of broadcast television networks for those states that apparently voted Democratic (blue) or Republican (red) in the presidential elections of 2000 and 2004. The blue states (notably New England, the Upper Midwest, and California) of course included a significant population that corresponded to what I term the "second America," and by the same token, the red states included their own lesser proportion of those who still corresponded to what I term the "first America," so the distinction between "red" and "blue" is actually somewhat misleading because it ignores the more important division between those Americans who are indebted more to the pluralist, Enlightenment vision of Jefferson, and those more inclined to espouse a literalist Christian fundamentalism.

Now, some may think that this distinction I am making here is perhaps overbroad, and no doubt it is, albeit less so than the division between "red" and "blue" states. Undoubtedly, there is a broad swath of the American population that belongs neither to "red" nor to "blue," and that is not particularly aligned with either the pluralist "first America" or with the fundamentalist "second America." It is too easy to overstate such divisions within the population as a whole. Still, I am willing to wager that much and perhaps all of what follows will come as a bit of a shock to many readers, especially those that belong to the "first America" of Jeffersonian rationalism, for what I am terming the "second America" has a deeply paranoiac strain of inquisitionalism that runs through it, of which many Americans remained entirely unaware. Although we cannot examine every instance of it, in surveying this unique strain of new American dispersed inquisitionalism we certainly can establish clearly its existence and nature.

The Satanic Panic of Late-Twentieth-Century America

We earlier noted the Satanic panic of the 1980s in America, to which Carl Raschke contributed a lurid tome and various pronouncements on talk shows of the time such as *Geraldo*. But it is time now to go more deeply into the history of the Satanic panic in America, and to follow a particularly interesting current within it—a current we may term "Illuminatiphobia." One is tempted to use the term "lineage" to describe this particular phenomenon, because it can be traced to specific interconnected individuals and works. The Satanic panic came to a head during the 1980s, but it had its beginnings in the 1970s, and in particular with a lurid best-selling book by Mike Warnke entitled *The Satan Seller* (1973).

Aptly named, *The Satan Seller* became a national best-selling Christian title from Logos International in 1973, at that point in American history when the hippie movement was fading away but also was feeding into Christianity through the "Jesus movement," as well as more broadly through ordinary social osmosis. As Jon Trott and Mike Hertenstein put it in their riveting exposé of Mike Warnke in 1992 entitled "Selling Satan: The Tragic History of Mike Warnke,"

A generation of Christians learned its basic concepts of Satanism and the occult from Mike Warnke's testimony in *The Satan Seller*. Based on his alleged satanic experiences, Warnke came to be recognized as a prominent authority on the occult, even advising law enforcement officers investigating occult crime. We believe *The Satan Seller* has been responsible, more than any other single volume in the Christian market, for promoting the current nationwide "Satanism scare."[1]

But when *The Satan Sellers* was published in 1973, and for a long time thereafter, Warnke's wild tales of his youthful involvement with a "Satanic brotherhood"—elaborated in his books and in his public talks, as well as in his appearances on various television shows—went unchallenged. Warnke claims that *The Satan Seller* sold three million copies; he claims to have been on the television shows *The 700 Club, The Oprah Winfrey Show, Larry King Live, Focus on the Family,* and *20/20*; and he continued as a nationally known Christian author, preacher, and public speaker into the twenty-first century, long after investigative reporting had revealed his tales of youthful "Satanism" to bear little or no relationship to the truth.

What is it about Warnke's stories of Satanism that continued to make him an attractive figure on the Christian evangelical circuits long after those stories had been thoroughly discredited—by Christian evangelical investigative reporters, no less? The answer, I think, is that Warnke's yarns disguised as memoir drew on archetypes that people *wanted* (indeed, still want) to believe.

Especially in the wake of the hippie movement and the most extreme excesses of the period, like the murders committed by the Manson Family, the late-twentieth-century evangelical movement in America emerges in part as a kind of reactionary social countermovement, one premised on the supposed widespread decadence of American society that evangelicals were to reject and redeem. What more aptly symbolizes that decadence than Warnke's tale of himself as a kind of youthful salesman of Satanism who "ascended in the satanic ranks to the position of high priest, with fifteen hundred followers in three cities. [In addition to beautiful women consorts] he had unlimited wealth and power at his disposal, provided by members of Satanism's highest echelon, the Illuminati."[2] The breathless rhetoric actually reveals this "Satanism" to bear a striking similarity to an American direct-marketing pyramidal corporate structure, with young Mike as an up-and-coming corporate salesman, albeit one who claims to have participated in ritual rape and murder, and to have met Charles Manson himself. What a redemption story to sell!

Because, of course, that is the real narrative of *The Satan Seller*: it sells a tale of a man's descent into depravity and of his subsequent redemption. The deeper the depravity, the more impressive is the redemption. Thus, it is perhaps not surprising that according to the investigative reporters Jon Trott and Mike Hertenstein, throughout his life, Warnke would not only fabricate stories but also then elaborate on them so as to make the bad worse. In a typical instance from early in his career, Karen Siegel recalls: "Mike liked to introduce me as a former hippie or drug addict—which I'd been, but I wasn't proud of. Then he started introducing me as a former prostitute, which I'd never been. I had to ask him to stop."[3] In any case, Warnke's "Satanism" redemption story was a tale that sold, and sold well.

One might think that once Warnke realized that his concocted story of "Satanism" was beginning to claim real victims via a public hysteria, he would have backpedaled, but such a narrative wouldn't be taking into account the money and fame that the "Satanic panic" brought him. By the mid-1980s, Warnke had appeared on the ABC network television show *20/20*, in a segment called "The Devil Worshippers," and he had developed a public persona as a consultant to police departments on "occult crime," as well as a "center" for refugees from an imagined international network of Satanists. The "center" reportedly consisted in a brick building, a director, and someone to answer the telephone. Warnke claimed fifty thousand calls a month, but the center's former director said it was more like 120. What the "Center" and the publicity did accomplish: bring in over $2 million a year to Warnke's non-profit organizations by 1988–1990. He and his wife of the time purchased various condominiums, horses, a former plantation estate that they termed a "parsonage," and so forth. Warnke was riding high, his profits buoyed whenever he told the story of "Jeffy" a boy whom "Satanic ritual abuse" had reduced to a "vegetable." His "center" would care for "Jeffy" if only Warnke's audience would cough up another "love offering."[4]

I have two friends who were professional counselors during the 1980s Satanic panic, one in the South, and one in the Upper Midwest. Both report that clients began showing up with fears that their children were getting involved in "the occult" or worse, in some organized Satanic group, and occasionally clients would come in with vague suspicions that they, too, had been victims of Satanic ritual abuse during childhood. Such notions had been spread widely, not only through sensationalistic, unsubstantiated books that appeared in the wake of Warnke's success with *The Satan Seller*—books such as Michelle Smith and Lawrence Pazder's *Michelle Remembers* (1980), or Lauren Statton's *Satan's Underground* (1988)—but also, they report, by way of Southern Baptist church networks and other evangelical church organizations.[5]

It took more than a decade for the Satanism scare to spread widely across

America and to begin to generate actual arrests and trials, which went on even as books highly critical of the phenomenon appeared. Wild claims were routinely made: thus, one book, *The Edge of Evil* (1989), asserted on good hearsay that forty to sixty thousand people were ritually murdered in the United States alone each year![6] Naturally, because such numbers are so insanely high compared to official numbers concerning people missing or murdered, there must be a national conspiracy to keep the real numbers hidden—or so the thinking went. Among the best books chronicling how and why this bizarre new inquisitional period emerged in the United States and England is Jeffrey Victor's *Satanic Panic* (1993). Victor shows how the rumor-panics—which popped up in communities across America during this period, mostly driven by wild evangelical claims dispersed through local church networks—reflected the age-old rhetoric of secret "Satanic" cults that practiced (what else?) kidnapping and ritual murder of children, exactly what Christians were accused of by Romans in late antiquity.[7]

It is incredible that only a decade before the end of the twentieth century, there was a full-blown "Satanist" witch-hunt generated in the American evangelical community. We look back on this period and at the sensational books and news stories, the "police consultants," the "Satanic ritual abuse" counselors, the hysteria that emerged mostly (although by no means exclusively) in the American Protestant community, but, most of all, at the way the hysteria manifested itself in the "secular arm" of the law enforcement system in England and in the United States, and we can hardly believe that all of this happened in a more or less technologically advanced, "modern" Western society at the end of the twentieth century![8] Yet a decade later, the panic had mostly subsided.

It is true that by the early twenty-first century, one could hardly find a book in Christian bookstores that alluded to the Satanic panic of only a scant decade earlier. And it is also true that at least some of that absence was a result of the efforts of courageous Christian authors such as the investigative reporters for *Cornerstone Magazine,* who cumulatively generated an awareness, at least among a significant number of evangelicals, that the Satanism scare of the 1980s and early 1990s was overwrought hysteria. This led to a widespread evangelical shift: a belief that a much greater danger was to be found in the "decadent mainstream culture"—that is, in what many perceived as social disorder of more mundane sorts. Thus, as is of course well known, we see the rise of the "evangelical right" to political power, and an emphasis on a religious social agenda during the late twentieth and earlier twenty-first centuries in the United States.

Illuminatiphobia

But this shift should not be read—as it often is—as tantamount to an abandonment or an overcoming of those fears that generated the Satanic panic of the 1980s and early 1990s. Rather, a too-little-acknowledged refocusing took place. At the same time that the "Satanic ritual abuse" hysteria was subsiding in the early 1990s, and at just the period when the "religious right" was turning its fairly newfound collective attention toward gaining political power, we see the fears of the religious right refocusing. The Satanic panic was really based more on fears concerning the personal or individual: that is, individual children or people were imagined as having been subjected to "Satanic ritual abuse." But the new fear, spread most widely by Pat Robertson in his book *The New World Order* (1991), was social and political, or collective rather than personal. The new fear was not of "Satanic ritual abuse," but, rather, of a shadowy secret order that wanted to control the world, create a single world government, and usher in the Antichrist. The new fear was of the "Illuminati."

"Illuminatiphobia" can be traced back to the same period and even some of the same books and authors that generated the Satanic panic. Mike Warnke, in his wild narrative *The Satan Seller*, claimed that he was admitted to the secret inner circle of Satanists—very wealthy and powerful men—and that this group was called the "Illuminati." Jon Trott and Mike Hertenstein wrote that, in 1967, when living in San Diego, Warnke paid a visit to the pastor of Scott Memorial Baptist Church. This pastor was none other than Tim LaHaye, who is mentioned in the acknowledgments of *The Satan Seller*, who much later was coauthor of the *Left Behind* series of books, and who will shortly play a significant role in our narrative. Typically, Warnke claimed that he brought up the term "Illuminati," but in fact,

> "The conversation really wasn't like he put it in his book," says Dr. LaHaye. "I brought up the term Illuminati first. I had been reading a book on the subject, and I tried testing him to see if he really knew anything about it. He didn't seem to have ever heard the word before."[9]

It is fascinating to see that these two themes—Satanic panic and Illuminatiphobia—can be traced back to Warnke and LaHaye in the California evangelical scene as early as the 1960s. But the time was not right for Illuminatiphobia to flourish: it remained mostly dormant through the 1970s and 1980s, whereas the Satanic panic waxed.

This is not to say that Illuminatiphobia didn't exist during this period—it did, among members of right-wing fringe groups such as the John Birch Society, and among followers of perennial presidential candidate Lyndon LaRouche, for instance. But this peculiar phenomenon was far from mainstream in the 1970s and 1980s: it mostly circulated in the evangelical community through tracts, pamphlets, and, curiously, through the same means that helped bring down the Shah of Iran in 1979: the surreptitious circulation of cassette tapes, in this case among evangelical church members across the United States. These cassette tapes consisted in talks by John Todd, a man in his late twenties who claimed that he had been raised as a witch, that "witches were conspiring to take over the world," and that the "Illuminati" had a secret plan to install one of their own as the American president (Jimmy Carter[!]) who then was sure to declare martial law, outlaw guns, and drive true Christians into the hills.[10]

Todd's cassette tape and traveling ministry against the "Illuminati," chiefly during 1976–1979, strongly encouraged Christian separatism and survivalism in the evangelical community. Todd himself, an enterprising fellow, in addition to tapes and a traveling ministry, reportedly sold dehydrated food to aspiring survivalists whom he encouraged with tales of the imminent domination of the world by the Illuminati. His views were strange from the start but grew weirder and weirder. Todd claimed that he had been initiated into something called the "Grand Druid Council," asserted to be second to the Rothschild family in the occult *cosa nostra*. As Michael Barkun points out in *A Culture of Conspiracy* (2003), the anti-Rothschild rhetoric clearly comes freighted with a long history of anti-Semitic conspiracy theory.[11] Todd claimed to have seen secret "Illuminati" documents that ordered the removal of President Nixon, the eventual election of President Jimmy Carter (said to be a pawn of the Illuminati and perhaps even the Antichrist!) and finally "world takeover" by the "Illuminati" in 1980.[12] By the late 1970s, Todd had taken to claiming that Ruth Carter Stapleton (President Carter's sister) was nothing less than the "most powerful witch in the world," and, further, that many prominent evangelical leaders in fact were in cahoots with the "Illluminati."[13]

At this point we touch on one of the most bizarre elements of the Illuminatiphobic paranoia: its inevitable tendency to accuse other evangelicals of being pawns of the Illuminati. The exposé book *The Todd Phenomenon* undoubtedly would not have been written had Todd stuck to marketing his Illuminatiphobia. But, instead, Todd inaugurated what was to become a familiar pattern in Illuminatiphobic circles: he began denouncing all the major evangelical leaders as pawns of the Illuminati or as outright members. Jerry Falwell, Bob Jones (founder of Bob Jones University), Billy Graham, Jim Bakker, the owners of Christian television—the list goes on and on of those whom Todd accused of having taken millions of dollars in money from the "Illuminati," and so forth. One can see why survivalism is an almost inevitable consequence of such views: if American society (even evangelical leadership) is the province of Lucifer and about to collapse into "revolution" or "Illuminati" domination, then it makes a certain weird sense to encourage survivalist enclaves in the American hinterlands. But what on earth accounts for the attacks on fellow evangelicals as "Illuminati"?

As it turns out, such attacks by American evangelicals on American evangelicals as "Illuminati" remained a common phenomenon into the early twenty-first century. Hicks and Lewis, authors of *The Todd Phenomenon* (1979), asserted that "what started out as a mere testimony of God's saving grace has grown into a full-blown inquisition."[14] This new inquisition of evangelicals by evangelicals continued, and is quite suited to new media. Just as Todd used cassette tapes to great effect in the 1970s, in the 2000s, the Illuminatiphobes seized on the Web and adapted Todd's rhetoric. Thus, Web sites such as cuttingedge.org or thewatcherfiles.com proliferated, proclaiming the guilt of every major evangelical leader as occultists or pawns of the "Illuminati." Those evangelicals who decry the "Illuminati" and propose a conspiracist, paranoiac worldview are bound to be accused of being "Illuminati" themselves. A simple Web search will reveal sites claiming, like Todd himself, that evangelical leader Pat Robertson is a member of (or a pawn of) the Illuminati.[15]

Now this is entertaining not least because Pat Robertson is arguably more responsible than anyone else in spreading Illuminatiphobia across the United States via his 1991 best-selling book *The New World Order*. *The New World Order* sold at least half a million copies and not only made a stir, but arguably contributed to the defeat of President George H. W. Bush in 1992. In fact, the book's title came explicitly from the phrase often uttered by Bush Sr. in speeches during the latter half of his presidency, and Robertson makes it quite clear that he thoroughly disapproves of any Bushian effort toward global United Nations initiatives, and, for that matter, of the multinational military coalition that Bush Sr. brought together for the First Gulf War.[16] Indeed, the "entire war," he thinks, may well have been a "setup," a result of an international conspiracy.

Very early in the book, Robertson comes right out and directly writes that a "single thread runs from the White House to the State Department to the Council on Foreign Relations to the Trilateral Commission to secret societies to extreme New Agers. There must be a new world order." To him, it does not matter particularly which political party is in power; "some other power" shapes United States public policy irrespective of which party is putatively in charge. Robertson continues: "Some authors and researches have pointed to the influence of the eighteenth-century elite group, the Illuminati"; others point to the "demonic" New Age religion. But in any case, "the events of public policy" are "planned"; they spring "from the depth of something that is evil, neither well intentioned nor benevolent."[17]

To his research associates' credit, Robertson's book is documented—it is not merely a farrago of wild, unsubstantiated assertions. For instance, he cites the historian Carroll Quigley's books *The Anglo-American Establishment* (1981) and *Tragedy and Hope* (1966), which emerge as sources fairly frequently in what we may loosely call the "conspiracy community." Quigley was a historian at Georgetown University, and is most remembered for discussing in print the history of connections between English wealth and aristocracy and an American ruling élite dominating the Council on Foreign Relations.[18] Quigley was actually a historian—albeit admittedly one whose major work cited by Robertson, *Tragedy and Hope,* is devoid of footnotes or sources—and the figures and groups Robertson discusses are also real. The question is what interpretation one lays upon those historical subjects.

In *The New World Order,* the interpretation is consistently conspiracist. Its method is to take facts, events, or figures that appear to be unrelated, and to weave together out of them an unfailingly sinister picture of secret powers and alliances, all out to institute a one-world bureaucratic power that will in turn prepare the way for the Antichrist. The Illuminati figure in Robertson's book as a convenient reference point, but Robertson is not quite as cavalier with the term as many other evangelicals have been. He refers, of course, to Adam Weishaupt and the founding of the Illuminati lodge on 1 May 1776, and discusses the diffusion of illuminist ideas through France and Germany. Weishaupt did exist, after all. But not surprisingly, Robertson ignores the profusion of other secret or semi-secret societies in Europe during this period—he ignores context and parallels—and instead hurries on to claim that Marx and Engels wrote their *Communist Manifesto* at the behest of secret societies whose origins were "German Illuminism."[19] He then hedges: "The Illuminist streams clearly flowed in Marxist Communism in the 1840s. Whether there was a meaningful confluence of these streams in Europe and elsewhere, remains to be seen."[20] In any case, Robertson concludes, the aims of those who seek a new world order are "1) the elimination of private property, 2) the elimination of national governments and national sovereignty, 3), the elimination of traditional Judeo-Christian theism, and 4) a world government controlled by an elite made up of those who are considered to be superior, or in the occultic sense, 'adepts' or 'illuminated.'"[21]

Later in the book, however, Robertson engages the more usual kinds of Illuminatiphobic rhetoric. He professes to know with unsubstantiated certainty that "Members of the Illuminati at the highest levels of the order were atheists and Satanists." Furthermore, "they made every effort to conceal their true purposes by the use of the name of Freemasonry."[22] Now we're off to the races. Soon we learn that Masonic initiation into the 32nd Degree consists in requiring that "the candidate therefore must strike back at [three] assassins which are, courtesy of the Illuminati, the government, organized religion, and private property."[23] As if this weren't enough, the ritual is said by Robertson to be "based on the cult of Amitabha Buddha [sic!]."[24] On occasion, reading such works is mind-bending. In toto, we have learned that "The New Age religions, the beliefs of the Illuminati, and illuminated Freemasonry all seem to move along parallel tracks with world Communism and world finance. Their appeals vary somewhat, but essentially they are all striving for the same frightening vision."[25]

What does Robertson propose to do, based on his paranoiac view of the world? Robertson lays out a clear agenda, beginning with the organization of the Christian Coalition, which will "build a significant database to use to communicate with those people who are regular voters." He predicts that Republicans will retake the Senate in 1992, and the House in 1996, and insists that an adequate presidential candidate will have to disavow "the Rockefeller-controlled Council on Foreign Relations and Trilateral Commission," and will have to regard the United Nations and globalism with a very suspicious eye.[26] In George W. Bush, of course, Robertson's agenda was largely fulfilled, and in fact, the final chapter of *The New World Order* reads for the most part like a broad blueprint for what actually had happened in the United States by 2004, with near one-party rule by Republicans.

In *The New World Order,* Robertson signaled the shift from the dispersed inquisition of the "Satanic panic" to the broader sociopolitical venue of an "epic struggle" between "people of faith and people of the humanistic-occultic sphere."[27] He was by no means alone in this shift, of course. Another important figure in it was Tim LaHaye, whom we first saw in 1967, informing the young Mike Warnke about the "Illluminati." LaHaye, like Robertson, has been a leading figure in the American evangelical world, and instrumental in the fusion between the Republican Party and Christian evangelical leaders. LaHaye went on to write or cowrite numerous books, including of course the phenomenally successful *Left Behind* series of apocalyptic novels that reportedly sold fifteen million copies in 2001 alone.[28]

The "Illuminati" play a more or less tangential role in the *Left Behind* series, but they appear explicitly in LaHaye's nonfiction book *The Rapture* (2002), where LaHaye writes that:

> I myself have been a 50-year student of the satanically inspired, centuries-old conspiracy to use government, education, and media to destroy every vestige of Christianity within our society and establish a new world order. Having read at least 50 books on the Illuminati, I am convinced that it exists and can be blamed for many of man's inhumane actions against his fellow man during the past 200 years.
>
> Dr. Adam Weishaupt, a professor at Goldestdat University, launched the Illuminati in Bavaria on May 1, 1776. For 30 years my wife and I have worked tirelessly to halt the effects of this conspiracy on the church, our government, media, and the public schools; so obviously I am not hostile to the conspiracy theory. An enormous amount of evidence proves that the secularization of our once Judeo-Christian society has not been an accident but is the result of the devilishly clever scheming carried on by this secret order.[29]

LaHaye goes on to make the connection, if possible, even more explicit:

> In fact, one reason the Illuminati conspirators are running far behind their schedule to usher in the new world order is that the Religious Right in the 1980s registered and got out the vote of a record number of evangelical Christians in the election of Ronald Reagan as president. His election didn't solve all our national problems; it wasn't intended to. But it lit the way for other Christians who could turn the conspirators back another decade.[30]

Here LaHaye, like Robertson, makes explicit that the ascent to political power of the Religious Right is to be seen as a manifestation of a global sociopolitical battle with none other than—the dreaded "Illuminati."

Another source for spreading Illuminatiphobia in evangelical circles is Larry Burkett's novel *The Illuminati* (1991). *The Illuminati* was published by Thomas Nelson Publishers in Nashville, a leading evangelical press, and reportedly sold at least 250,000 copies. Its chapter on the history of the Illuminati is quite entertaining, if you like that sort of thing. The novel baldly asserts that "the Druids" "changed their name to the Freemasons and adopted many of the same rituals and religious traditions practiced within the Christian Churches." "From the Freemasons, a small group of world leaders emerged, dedicated to the establishment of a worldwide order, known as the 'Illuminati.'"[31] The group, which "flourished from just after the time of Christ," was composed of political, religious, economic, academic, and military leaders, and had a hand in the founding of the United States.[32]

Burkett continues with this hallucinatory history lesson: "Now, nearly two hundred and fifty years after America had become a nation, the Society [the Illuminati] was stronger than ever, and its original purpose was becoming a reality: a one-world economic system, controlled and directed by this shadowy group of the most influential men (and now women) in the world."[33] Lenin, Hitler, and Mao had been members hand-picked to unify the world, but had failed, so a new "Leader" was no doubt on the way, Burkett wrote, perhaps via the sinister, Illuminati-controlled Council on Foreign Relations in the United States.[34] I mention Burkett's novel here because it underscores what we see in the works of Robertson and LaHaye as well as in the works of Texe Marrs (who claims to have sold two million books)—indeed, the script is almost identical.[35] There is an imaginary sinister sociopolitical power called the "Illuminati," they have immense power via organizations such as the Trilateral Commission and the Council on Foreign Relations, and only the American evangelical right can stop them.

The Christian Illuminati

What I find particularly fascinating is that LaHaye and other evangelicals went on to cofound a shadowy semisecret advisory group of their own: the Council for National Policy. Here is how one investigative reporter described this group:

> An elite group with only a few hundred members, the CNP meets three times a year, usually at posh hotels or resorts, going to extraordinary lengths to keep its agenda and membership secret. According to members willing to speak about it, however, the council unites right-wing billionaires with scores of conservative Christian activists and politicians, and these encounters have spawned countless campaigns and organizations. Its ranks have included prominent politicians such as Ed Meese and John Ashcroft, and among its members can be found an editor of the conservative *National Review*, leading televangelists such as Pat Robertson and Falwell, representatives of the Heritage Foundation and other key think tanks, and activists including Grover Norquist and Oliver North.
>
> Supported by moneybags such as Texas oilman Nelson Bunker Hunt, Amway founder Richard DeVos and beer magnate Joseph Coors, some in the group helped fund Oliver North's secret campaign to aid the Nicaraguan contra rebels during the 1980s and fi-

nanced the right-wing jihad against President Clinton in the 1990s. (The impeachment effort was reportedly conceived at a June 1997 meeting of the CNP in Montreal.) In addition, the group has funded an army of Christian organizers. Falwell says that in the past two decades, he has raised hundreds of millions of dollars for his ventures, including Liberty University, through the CNP. "My guess is that literally billions of dollars have been utilized through the Council for National Policy that would not otherwise have been available," he says. Bush attended a CNP meeting at the start of his presidential campaign in 1999 to seek support, and Defense Secretary Donald Rumsfeld took part in the group's gathering [in] April [2003] in Washington, D.C.[36]

In other words, what LaHaye and other leading evangelicals did was to create *the mirror image* of what they most feared—they created a Christian Illuminati.

The imaginary Illuminati are held to control vast wealth; the Christian Illuminati in fact have access to vast wealth through very real billionaires. The imaginary Illuminati are said to have enormous political power; the Christian Illuminati actually possess great political power. The imaginary Illuminati are said to see themselves as the "elect," or the "illuminated"; the Christian Illuminati see themselves as God's "anointed" and as "born again"—yes, illuminated. The imaginary Illuminati are said to be secretive and shadowy as they determined much of the course of United States policy behind the scenes; the Christian Illuminati are in fact secretive and shadowy as they determined much of the course of United States policy behind the scenes. The imaginary Illuminati are said to have the power to vet all the candidates for President; the Christian Illuminati actually *do* have the power to vet presidential candidates, as we see in the case of George W. Bush. Administration officials, Republican legislators, evangelical leaders—all converged in the secretive "Council for National Policy," its very name the mirror image of the Illuminatiphobe's hated "Council on Foreign Relations." Odd, no?

Not really. Recall the transformation that took place in Christianity: initially, Christians were subjected to brutal Roman persecution; yet later, institutional Roman Christianity subjected "heretics" to brutal persecution and death. It is perhaps not so surprising that American evangelical Christianity—having ginned up enough fear over an imaginary Illuminati as a paranoiac explanation for massive social changes in the United States and the world—would itself go on to create just such a group in reality. The psychological dynamics are clear and fairly well established. Jeffrey Victor, author of *Satanic Panic*, puts it this way:

> In conditions of shared social stress with complex, unclear, and ambiguous causes, people need a quick, easy explanation for their plight. The easiest solution is to blame scapegoats. In Western societies, the scapegoating process has traditionally been guided by the blueprint provided in a demonology, which attributes the causes of evil to a small, conspiratorial group seeking to undermine the moral order of society. . . . In the past, the demonology has been used in different times and places to scapegoat such groups as heretics, Jews, witches, Catholics, and Freemasons.[37]

Victor concludes: "The long history of accusations against heretics, Jews, and witches tells us nothing about heretics, Jews, and witches. However, *it tells us a lot about the mind-set of the claims-makers.*"[38] Exactly. Is it, then, really so surprising that the culmination of Illuminatiphobia is the creation of what amounts to a Christian Illuminati?

Neither the Satanic panic nor Illuminatiphobia have vanished from the American hinterlands, of course, as a brief search on the internet readily reveals. The Illuminati, it is said, secretly control the weather—better to blame the Illuminati than one's lawnmower's and automobile's emissions, after all, for global warming. The Illuminati are behind those sinister environmentalists, just as they are behind any efforts at international cooperation, and the Illuminati already have taken over all the main evangelical leaders, including Pat Robertson and Tim LaHaye, who are themselves occultists, for lo! look at the occult symbols on some of their book covers.[39] Here the conspiracy theories reveal again their recursive loop, as the "conspiracy" is widened to claim as "operatives" even the evangelical leaders who "expose" it.

Such is the rhetoric one finds on fringe Web sites generated from the American hinterlands: once a true believer has embarked on the course of paranoiac thinking, evidently he or she can never be suspicious enough. Indeed, one of the growing conspiracy theories is that the Illuminati is a name for—I am not kidding here—shapeshifting reptilians from the "fourth dimension" who take the form of world leaders like Bill Clinton or George Bush, who plot against humanity itself, and who don't shrink from sexual abuse of children! The Christian link? The shapeshifting reptilians are "verified" by Genesis, for after all, it was a serpent that tempted Adam and Eve.[40] Can a reptilian witch-hunt be far away? As Kurt Vonnegut might write: and so it goes.[41]

Yet another book that crops up frequently in such circles is the *The Gnostic Empire Strikes Back* by Peter Jones. In it, the author jumbles together "militant feminism," "Eastern religions," "homosexual rights," "nature worship," "political correctness," "New Age Gnosticism," and "mysticism" so as to stir up anxiety among fellow American evangelicals. Jones claims that a "pagan 'Gnostic' empire, personified by [Roman emperor] Julian [the Apostate] and so roundly defeated by the early church many centuries back, is now openly and brazenly striking back."[42] Hence, he recommends "Using, Not Blunting the Sword of the Lord" because virtually the whole of American society is become infested with "diabolical" influences.[43]

Clearly, the American appetite for paranoiac conspiracism is rather large. Indeed, Illuminatiphobia already existed in late-eighteenth- and early-nineteenth-century America, after the distribution of John Robison's *Proofs of a Conspiracy* (1798)—a book still cited by nearly all the Illuminatiphobes (including Pat Robertson). What I have called the "second America"—literalist, often paranoid, and prone to witch-hunts—has a long history of credulousness, of which the Satanic panic, Illuminatiphobia, and reptiliphobia for that matter are only relatively recent instances. All of this belongs to what the historian Richard Hofstadter labeled "The Paranoid Style in American Politics," a fashion that seems to retain its coterie of gullible aficionados in every era.[44] But these subterranean currents in American society almost always remain on the fringes of society, and I retain faith that what I earlier called the "first America" of Jeffersonian pluralism and common sense will continue to prevail.

But our investigation is not quite finished—it has another chapter. For LaHaye's Council for National Policy anointed candidate George W. Bush in 1999, and as it turned out, his administration went on to effectively bring together many of the themes in this book.[45]

13

The American State of Exception

It was long a commonplace, particularly during the nineteenth and especially the twentieth centuries, for American scholars to argue for what is sometimes termed the American exception. By this is meant in part the notion that the United States, with its representative government and its system of checks and balances, is ingeniously designed to avoid the dangers of authoritarian repression and a one-party state. And, of course, there is the larger notion that the United States is somehow an exceptional or, in the rhetoric echoed by Presidents Reagan and George W. Bush, a "chosen nation," with a singular destiny. Although such nationalist language is not all that uncommon—similar rhetoric is to be found in Russia, Germany, China, and many other nations—in the United States in the early twenty-first century, such rhetoric began to have consequences that are of particular interest for our argument here. Out of such rhetoric emerged an American state of exception, and with it, the disturbing outlines of inquisitorial behavior.

We will recall the juridical term "state of exception" from our earlier reference to Carl Schmitt's *Politische Theologie* (1922). It refers not to an exceptional nation blessed by God but to a suspension of law by authoritarian decree. According to Schmitt, as we have seen, a ruler or sovereign can be defined as one who decides on a state of exception. Thus, for example, upon assuming power, Hitler suspended the German constitutional protection of civil liberties—and as Giorgio Agamben points out, that state of exception prevailed throughout the entire period of the Third Reich.[1] Hence, Agamben continues, "modern totalitarianism can be defined as the establishment, by means of the state of exception, of a legal civil war that allows for the physical elimination not only of political adversaries but also of entire categories of citizens who for some reason cannot be integrated into the political system."[2] The "state of exception" is pivotal for understanding how some dimensions of a totalitarian state can emerge even within a constitutional republic.

In the wake of the events of September 11, 2001, the U.S. Congress passed what was known as the USA PATRIOT Act, which suspended at least some American civil liberties in order for federal authorities to investigate or pursue suspected terrorists within the United States. After the subsequent American invasion of Afghanistan, it eventually became clear that the United States also had imposed a state of exception on military prisoners whom it suspected of being terrorists or of knowing about terrorists or terrorist plots. This latter state of exception resulted in the creation of an entirely new class of prisoners, often accused Taliban members from Afghanistan, who were termed "enemy combatants," or "detainees," and who were not defined as prisoners of war under the Geneva Convention, nor accorded the rights of the accused under American law. In short, in the wake of September 11, 2001, the United States imposed what we may term a targeted or limited state of exception both internally (in the PATRIOT Act) and externally (in the establishment of "detainee" camps at Guantánamo and elsewhere around the globe).

The prisoners or "enemy combatants" held in camps like Guantánamo were subject to what in Nazi Germany was the basis for the Nazi state itself: *gewollte Ausnahmezustand,* or a "willed state of exception" (willed by administrative fiat). They had, effectively, no human rights—they existed in a no-man's land without citizen's rights, and so without judicial recourse, without the rights accorded to military prisoners under the Geneva Convention, and so without a military tribunal. As a result, there also was no time limit imposed on their imprisonment: held on an island military base, they might as well have been transported into outer space. How they were treated, or whether they were guilty or innocent is not under consideration here—what matters in terms of our case here is that these prisoners existed in a juridical "state of exception."

After the American invasion and occupation of Iraq in 2003, the same rationale was invoked for the suspension of the Geneva Convention so as to allow more "vigorous" interrogation of Iraqi prisoners. More and more documents became available under the American Freedom of Information Act that revealed Bush Jr. administration officials consciously sought to circumvent the Geneva Convention in the belief that torture of prisoners would be more effective not only in gaining information but also in showing American resolve to "do what it takes" and thus overcome Iraqi resistance.[3] These arguments in favor of a "state of exception" for Iraqi prisoners led as if inexorably to the scandals of prisoner torture and sexual abuse at Abu Ghraib, Guantánamo, and elsewhere. Such abuse of prisoners is a consequence of the abrogation of human rights, and of the consequent attitude that the prisoners (the enemies) are less than human.

Rendering to the Secular Arm

But there is a related example of the American "state of exception" in what the United States government euphemistically termed "extraordinary rendition." "Rendition" is a somewhat hazy term for a shadowy practice that, although it reportedly had its origins in the 1990s, became more and more common after September 11, 2001: the practice of spiriting American prisoners secretly away to foreign countries where they could be tortured or killed. As Jane Mayer put it,

> The extraordinary-rendition program bears little relation to the system of due process afforded suspects in crimes in America. Terrorism suspects in Europe, Africa, Asia, and the Middle East have often been abducted by hooded or masked American agents, then forced onto a Gulfstream V jet.... Upon arriving in foreign countries, rendered suspects often vanish. Detainees are not provided with lawyers, and many families are not informed of their whereabouts.[4]

"Detainees" are imprisoned, often in vile conditions in, for example, Egypt, and then tortured. Subsequently, some are released, whereas others simply disappeared, probably executed. "Rendition" is, of course, the secular equivalent of the common practice of the Inquisition throughout its history: "rendering" suspected heretics to the "secular arm" because the Church itself did not conduct torture and murder.

How was the Bush Jr. administration able to legally justify the "rendition" of uncharged, unconvicted, unrepresented individuals into the hands of torturers and murderers in foreign countries? John Yoo, Alberto Gonzales, and other Administration lawyers argued in the aftermath of the invasion of Afghanistan that it constituted a "failed state," and as such fell outside the Geneva Convention. A horrified State Department lawyer reportedly argued, "There is no such thing as a non-covered person under the Geneva Convention. It's nonsense. The protocols cover fighters in everything from world wars to local rebellions."⁵ But even as cogent rebuttals to this "state of exception" were being written, the decision had already been made. On 8 January 2002, George W. Bush chose to "suspend the Geneva Convention," despite the advice of State Department counsel that he could well be tried later for war crimes.

In a subsequent interview conducted nearly two years later, White House attorney John Yoo remained adamant in defense of a "state of exception." "Why is it so hard for people to understand that there is a category of behavior not covered by the legal system?" he said. "What were pirates? They weren't fighting on behalf of any nation. What were slave traders? Historically, there were people so bad that they were not given protection of the laws. There were no specific provisions for their trial, or imprisonment. If you were an illegal combatant, you didn't deserve the protection of the laws of war."⁶ Furthermore, according to Yoo, Congress doesn't have the power to "tie the President's hands in regard to torture as an interrogation technique." He continued, "It's the core of the Commander-in-Chief function. They can't prevent the President from ordering torture."⁷ Torture and murder—the suspension of all human rights—are thus claimed to be the prerogative of American executive fiat alone, with no checks and balances from Congress or from the judiciary. Yoo crafted the Bush Jr. administration memo of 9 January 2002, which asserted that neither the federal War Crimes Act nor the Geneva Convention—that is, neither American nor international law—constrains the imperial presidency.⁸ There is no clearer instance of a "state of exception" than rendition.

There are alleged to be more than 150 such cases, but the true numbers can't be known because of government secrecy. The former British ambassador to Uzbekistan said that he knew of three such cases of rendition to Uzbekistan, where individuals were tortured and sometimes murdered by boiling water.⁹ The chief problem faced by the CIA and other government organizations that resort to "rendition" is that once they have shipped someone secretly to another foreign country and the individual has been tortured, then what? If the individual turns out to be innocent, then they have created another enemy, and if guilty, they cannot draw on what he says in a court of law because of all their previous illegal actions to extract the testimony. Thus, some former agents say, they have created a "nightmare," an "abomination" that makes it virtually impossible to get convictions through testimony even in a military tribunal, let alone a court of law.

Given this history of "rendition" under his administration, it is ironic that, in the inaugural address for his second term, George W. Bush spoke forcefully about how the United States stands for "liberty" and against "tyranny" the world over. It is particularly dissonant to hear the following words in that inauguration speech:

We have seen our vulnerability and we have seen its deepest source. For as long as whole regions of the world simmer in resentment and tyranny—prone to ideologies that feed hatred and excuse murder—violence will gather, and multiply in destructive power, and cross the most defended borders, and raise a mortal threat. There is only one force of history that can break the reign of hatred and resentment, and expose the pretensions of tyrants, and reward the hopes of the decent and tolerant, and that is the force of human freedom.[10]

One is uncertain how one "simmers in tyranny." But whose ideologies, exactly, "feed hatred and excuse murder"? Would the answer not be both al-Qaeda, on the one hand, and the Bush Jr. administration, on the other?

But the most famous lines from this speech are also the most sweeping, for they call for nothing less than the mission of exceptional America to rid the entire world of tyranny. The speechwriters of George W. Bush write, and he reads, "So it is the policy of the United States to seek and support the growth of democratic movements and institutions in every nation and culture, with the ultimate goal of ending tyranny in our world." This is an admirable goal, for who favors tyranny except the tyrant? Yet the latent Jacobinism of the sentence, its vast revolutionary scope, drew a skeptical reaction even from the main speechwriter for Bush Sr., who remarked on her "disquiet" in the *Wall Street Journal*.[11] The line calls the United States to action in "every nation and culture"—presumably, then, in Communist China and in Pakistan, too, where authoritarian regimes are propped up by American dollars through trade or through direct aid.

Declaration of an exceptionalist America, in this case, follows in the wake of the declared state of exception. What makes this rhetoric so disquieting is any knowledge of the "state of exception" as enacted by the very same administration. With such knowledge, a line such as this one takes on a peculiar double quality: "The rulers of outlaw regimes can know that we still believe as Abraham Lincoln did: "Those who deny freedom to others deserve it not for themselves; and, under the rule of a just God, cannot long retain it." Of course, the freedom denied to those subjected to the "state of exception" is justified because they are, in the simple phrasing of Carl Schmitt, "enemies," not "friends." Yet, what if some of them are not enemies, only bystanders? And in any case, whose is the "outlaw regime"? Echoing Dostoevsky's *The Possessed*, George W. Bush proclaims "we have lit a fire as well—a fire in the minds of men."[12] He did not know, and his speechwriters evidently did not care, that he was citing Dostoevsky's depiction of Bolshevik revolutionaries whom the great Russian writer saw as possessed.

I do not intend to argue, here, what has been pointed out by various conservative and libertarian critics—that the behavior of the Republicans in power in Washington, D.C., resembled fascism more than a little.[13] Rather, I'll leave such comparisons for others, or perhaps for another time. On the face of it, the call for America to rid the entire world of tyranny and to establish freedom everywhere is well and good. Yet such rhetoric overlooks the gulags and secret prisons around the globe where (under the auspices of the very same administration!) men are imprisoned and where some, through secular "rendition," are tortured and murdered. To "go abroad, in search of monsters to destroy" may sound thrilling, but surely there was a reason that John Adams and George Washington so famously warned against such foreign adventures. Would Washington really have approved of "rendition"?

Such policies were defended on the editorial pages of the *Wall Street Journal*, on the general principle I suppose that diminishing or abrogating individual human rights is a small price to pay in order to maintain a stable business environment. Thus, the editors wrote that "The Pentagon could close Guantánamo tomorrow, and the critics would quickly find other antiterror policies to deplore: military commissions, or the 'rendition' of terror suspects to third countries, or interrogation techniques, or something else." Not that there's anything there Americans ought to deplore. They continued: "Someone in the Administration ought to point out that these measures are designed to prevent the next terror attack—which, if it ever comes, could prompt a bipartisan crackdown on civil liberties that would make Guantánamo look like summer camp."[14] A crackdown on *whose* civil liberties? American citizens? Criminalized dissent and internal gulags suddenly seem not so totally far-fetched.

Consider the following, taken from a partisan Republican weblog called—and here again I am not kidding—"Moonbat Central." An ardent high school teacher named Michael Calderon published a blog entry that included the following speculation concerning what might happen if terrorists set off a low-yield nuclear weapon in the United States. He writes:

> Expect heavily armed and infuriated conservatives to launch a cleansing war against the traitors. The armed will mow down the mostly unarmed segments, especially those elements that devoted forty-plus years to anti-American hatred to destroy this country. Should the likes of Noam Chomsky, Howard Zinn, Michael Parenti, Michael Moore, Ward Churchill, Dennis [sic] Raimondo, et al. act out their sedition in a just-nuked America, expect their bodies to be found shot full of holes. Expect gun battles at banks, food stores,

ATMs, gas stations, and outside hospitals. Leftist professors will be strung up. It will be every man, woman, and child for themselves.[15]

What a charming vision of an American future—so full of good will toward all. My point is that rancorous scapegoating like this would have to be more widespread among the populace in order to "justify" gulags and criminalized dissent.

It is all too easy to demonize others: the twentieth century, if it taught us anything, should have taught us that. Hence, it is at least worth noting the intellectual origins of these very real early-twenty-first-century American policies and apparent objectives, as well the rhetoric that accompanies and seeks to defend such policies. The intellectual genealogy we have considered throughout this book—from Tertullian's heresiology, through the establishment of the Inquisition, through the eighteenth-century and nineteenth-century calls for an authoritarian state, right through to the secular inquisitions of communism and fascism—does have a certain relevance not only for understanding the history of the Bush Jr. administration but also more broadly for how some elements of totalitarianism can appear within what at least appears to be a constitutional republic or a parliamentary democracy.

I do not doubt that those who defend "rendition," and torture, just as those who institute such policies, are initially at least, perhaps motivated by good intentions. They are convinced of their own rectitude, certain that their vision of the world is the right and only one, that its light must fill every cranny, that they must light a fire in the minds of men, and perhaps along the way must burn a heretic or two, or a thousand, or a million. Why? Because just around the corner is a secular millennium. But to reach that millennium, as Vice President Richard Cheney memorably put it, on a Sunday morning talk show called *Meet the Press*, the government needed to "work through, sort of, the dark side." "And so," he continued, "it's going to be vital for us to use any means at our disposal, basically, to achieve our objective."[16] To reach the imagined secular millennium, to reach the true communist state, to reach the Third Reich, to reach utopia, even, apparently, to selectively eliminate tyranny, we must "work through, sort of, the dark side." Isn't that, in the end, what they all say?

14

Berdyaev's Insight

When we consider more broadly the theme of inquisitorial antignosticism or heresiophobia, we cannot help but wonder why it is that this phenomenon emerges in some countries and not in others, at one time, and not at another. What is it that conduces to a Grand Inquisitor? A relatively pluralistic and secular United States in the last third of the twentieth century would appear not to have been conducive to a grand inquisition, but much the same could have been said of the Weimar Republic in Germany just prior to the onslaught of National Socialism or, for that matter, of the Silver Age of Russia just prior to the onslaught of Communism. Indeed, there are quite a few parallels between these periods: all three of them were characterized by what we might call religious creativity, by all manner of new religious movements and religious experimentation, and by a relatively liberal but ineffective state notable for the corruption it tolerated or encouraged. We would do well to study carefully the past emergences of the Inquisitorial totalitarian state so that, as the title of the 1935 American novel had it, *It Can't Happen Here*.

The totalitarian state emerges as the bastion of certainty after a period of prolonged and intense uncertainty—it presents the illusion of total authority, and of global answers. It imposes an extreme form of order that is, fundamentally, disorder. And it can only enforce that disorder through an inquisitorial apparatus of spies, informers, secret police, torture, imprisonment, and murder. The pattern is depressingly similar: we have seen it again and again, in the

Soviet gulags and the Nazi concentration camps, in the Communist Chinese prisons and in countless other, lesser-known venues. The totalitarian secular state always ends up manifesting itself in religious persecution. Why? The truth is the reverse of what so many anti-gnostics have argued. The danger always comes, not from those who fear history—and still less from those who critique "progress"—but from those who fear religious and intellectual freedom, and who want to enforce on everyone the primacy a literal, historicist perspective bereft of any hint of transcendence.

It is extremely interesting to see how the currents of anti-gnosticism and heresiophobia recur again and again on both the nominal "left" and the nominal "right." Once seen in light of heretic-hunting, totalitarian "right" and totalitarian "left" reveal themselves as fundamentally similar. Among the analysts of this dynamic, only one stands out as the most perceptive: the great Russian religious philosopher Nicholas Berdyaev (1874–1948). Berdyaev had been a central figure in the Russian Silver Age of great religious and creative ferment during the late nineteenth and early twentieth centuries—and he was also a witness to the ascent to power in Russia of the Communists. From his vantage point of exile in France, living among Russian expatriates like himself, and informed by his long and deep study of mysticism and of the dynamics of heretic-hunting, he was able to diagnose the inquisitional pathology better than anyone since the prophetic Dostoevsky, whose figure of the Grand Inquisitor we discussed in our introduction.

Dostoevsky Revisited

After all, before Nicholas Berdyaev—who was witness to the horrors of the Bolshevik revolution and its aftermath, and its most penetrating critic—it was Fyodor Dostoevsky who, already in the nineteenth century, foresaw and warned against a Communist revolution. Dostoevsky saw that at the heart of the Communist endeavor was not "the labor question" but "before all things the atheistic question, the question of the tower of Babel built without God, not to mount to Heaven from earth but to set up Heaven on earth."[1] Dostoevsky wrote that "French socialism is nothing but a compulsory communion of mankind— an idea which dates back to ancient Rome and which was fully conserved in Catholicism. Thus, the idea of the liberation of the human spirit from Catholicism became vested there precisely in the narrowest Catholic forms borrowed from the very heart of its spirit, from its letter, from its materialism, from its despotism."[2] And the export of French socialism with Communism into Russia was thus bound, in his view, to create a fanatical atheistic despotism.

Dostoevsky believed that Roman Catholicism as an institutional, temporal power, represented a form of Christianity as old as Tertullian and Irenaeus, one that had abandoned spiritual impulse for earthly power. Because (in his view) Roman Catholicism focused on earthly or juridical authority, it had lost its spiritual authority, and its natural successor was to be an outright atheist socialist despotism. The new socialist or Communist despots would be like the Grand Inquisitor in *The Brothers Karamazov*, and would take on themselves the "burden" of enforcing upon the whole of society what they deem best for it. Of course, in the process, like the inquisitors, they would have to hunt down and destroy "heretics" and impose a rigid dogmatic unity on society—they would have to suppress freedom of conscience or freedom of thought—but that would be only for the benefit of others. Thus the terrible new regime would have at its head antireligious ascetics, fanatics devoted to the new earthly kingdom. What Dostoevsky could not have foreseen was how many millions would die under the new inquisitors of Communism.

But was Dostoevsky right in his fundamental insight: that Communism had its origin in some aspects of Roman Catholicism? One eyewitness to the onslaught of Russian Communism who thought so was Nicholas Berdyaev. Berdyaev had written already in 1917 that "Dostoevsky prophetically foresaw the demonic aspect of the Russian Revolution in *The Devils* (*Besy*), [and recognized] the demonic metaphysics of revolution in *The Brothers Karamazov*."[3] Yet Berdyaev did not focus exclusively on Catholicism: for him what matters is the *phenomenon itself*—how the fanaticism of heretic-hunting comes into being, and what it signifies. Thus, in Berdyaev's view, it is not so important whether Communism has part of its origin in Catholicism—what matters, rather, is the underlying dynamic of heretic-hunting itself. In this lies Berdyaev's great insight.

Berdyaev on Inquisitional Psychopathology

The root of the Inquisition, Berdyaev realized, was fanaticism: the obsessive reduction of the whole manifold world to one thing. He observed that:

> A believing, an unselfish, an intellectual man can become a fanatic, and commit the greatest of cruelties. To devote oneself without reservations to God or to an idea, substituting for God, whilst ignoring man, is to transform a man into a means and a weapon for the glory of God or for the realisation of the idea, and it means to become a fanatic—wild-eyed and even a monster.[4]

This was the origin of the Inquisition, and Berdyaev has perhaps the best understanding of the psychological dynamics driving the Inquisition of any author I have read. He continues:

> The inquisitors of old were perfectly convinced that the cruel things done by them, the beatings, the burnings on the bonfires and other things,—they were convinced that this was a manifestation of their love for mankind. They contended against perdition for the sake of salvation, they guarded souls from the allure of the heresies, which threatened with perdition. Better be it to subject one to the brief sufferings in the earthly life than the perishing of many in eternity. Torquemada was a non-avaricious and unselfish man, he wanted nothing for himself, he devoted himself entirely to his idea, his faith; in torturing people, he made his service to God, he did everything exclusively for the glory of God, and in him there was even a soft spot, he felt malice and hostility towards no one, and he was of his kind a "fine" man. I am convinced, that such a "fine" man, convinced in his faith and unselfish, was also Dzerzhinsky, who in his youth was a passionately believing Catholic and indeed wanted to be a monk. This is an interesting psychological problem.[5]

It is an interesting psychological problem, not least because as Berdyaev points out, the same dynamic is at work in the Communist dictatorships.

Fanatics require enemies, and if enemies do not exist already, then the fanatics will manufacture them. Thus develops an atmosphere of witch hunting. Berdyaev rightly held that the Russian revolution represented a kind of demonic collectivism and fanaticism:

> The terrible fact is that the human person for [Russians] is drowning in a primitive collectivism, and this is nowise a point of excellence, nor a sign of our greatness. It makes absolutely no difference whether this all-engulfing collectivism is that of the "Black Hundreds" or of the "Bolsheviks." The Russian land lives under the power of a pagan khlysty-like element. In this element, every face is submerged, for it is incompatible with personal worthiness and personal responsibility. This demonic element can pull forth from its bosom no true face, save only the likes of Rasputin and Lenin. The Russian "Bolshevik Revolution" is a dreadful worldwide *reactionary* phenomenon, just as reactionary in its spirit as "Rasputinism" or as the Black Hundred khlystyism.[6]

Hence, too, the collectivist fanaticism that marked the Moscow "trials" of various Communists, which, Berdyaev observed, "are very reminiscent of witchcraft trials. In both the one and the other, the accused confesses to having criminal dealings with the devil. The human psyche changes little."[7] The basis for the collective psychosis of fanatical persecutors is always the same.

The fanatical persecutor becomes obsessed with the need for absolute, inhuman fidelity to one thing, be it the Church or the State. The persecutor does not begin as a persecutor, in general but, rather, as one who sees enemies of the collective everywhere. Imagining these enemies, who are seen as "of the devil," then turns the persecutor into a devil himself, and as Berdyaev puts it, he who "sees all around the snares of the devil . . . is always the one who himself persecutes, torments and executes."[8] He who senses enemies everywhere, becomes himself the greatest of enemies to others by becoming a persecutor—who all the while believes that what he does is actually for the good of the whole and for the good of others. Thus, the persecutor often takes on an unctuous sense of self-righteousness. And, as Berdyaev points out, this fanaticism of the persecutor easily passes over into the political sphere, where "against the powers of the devil there is always created an inquisition or a committee of the common salvation, an omnipotent secret police, a Cheka. These dreadful institutions are always created out of fear of the devil. But the devil has always proved himself to be the stronger, for he penetrates into these institutions and guides them."[9]

It does not even particularly matter, Berdyaev writes, what the nature of the projected enemy is. For a Communist, the enemy might well be other Communists who are insufficiently fanatical, or the enemy might be fascist—all that matters is that the world becomes divided into "I" and "not-I." Thus, Berdyaev writes, "having allowed himself to come under the obsessive grip of the idea of a worldwide peril and worldwide conspiracy of Masons, of Jews, of Jesuits, of Bolsheviks, or of an occult society of killers,—such a man ceases to believe in the power of God, in the power of truth, and he trusts only in his own coercions, cruelties and murderings. Such a man is, in essence, an object of psychopathology."[10] We see this pathology emerging as an intellectual tendency in the works of Maistre and of Donoso Cortés, of Sorel, Maurras, Schmitt, and Voegelin, but it becomes actualized in the regimes of Lenin, Stalin, and Hitler. Ideas—particularly ideas of extirpating imagined "enemies" of the collective—can have lethal consequences.

The modern pathology of fanatical persecution (under whichever regime, "right" or "left") is significantly different than that found in medieval Catholic societies, whether under the auspices of the Inquisition or not. Medieval Catholic society, Berdyaev writes, was pervaded by a common deep faith that offered at least a basis for some degree of tolerance, whereas modern society this common basis is gone, replaced by a cold, militaristic secularism. For the modern ideologue, the world is starkly and totally divided into those who are intellectually right (us) and transgressors (them). Communists, fascists, religious fundamentalists, the religiously "orthodox," all of these are unwilling to dispute or argue, but instead cast their opponents as "the enemy." From this dynamic arises the persecutorial mindset.

Driving the persecutor or Inquisitor is pride, exactly as Dostoevsky recognized and showed with the figure of the Grand Inquisitor. By embracing a rigid ideology, whatever it is, the ideologue now is able to convince himself that he is the possessor of the truth. He is part of the "inner circle," the elite group who are called to take on themselves the burden of policing society, of "improving" the human world. Ordinary people, they don't understand, and so must be coerced, sometimes even tortured or killed "for their own good," so the Inquisitor says to himself. The ideology provides the ego with the illusion of stability and authority—"I know the truth, and must enforce it upon you." But underlying all of this is a great uncertainty, an anxiety that the ideology and the persecutions and the trappings of power only serve to mask.

Totalitarianism of the Left and of the Right

During the mid-twentieth century, it was commonplace for communists and fascists to each accuse the other of being totalitarian, and to defend their own group's authoritarianism as merely a regrettable lapse, but not at all representative of its very nature. As a result, relatively few scholars regarded communism and fascism as different versions of the same fundamental phenomenon of totalitarianism. And, indeed, as late as the early twenty-first century, one sees scholars struggling with the implacable truth that both communism and fascism are variant forms of totalitarianism, that both commit crimes against humanity itself. Why is it so difficult to regard totalitarianism in terms of its dynamics? The answer is ideology.

Consider, for instance, scholars in a collection of articles on Stalinism and Nazism. In a case study of Romania, a Romanian author acknowledges that of course "Nazism was a criminal system against humanity, denounced worldwide." But, she continues, "Communism also was and still remains a criminal regime against humanity. If the entire world today condemns Nazism to the point of continuing the search for those who served it, it is impossible to explain why the same thing is not being undertaken with regard to Communism."[11] Yet it proves extremely difficult for even the author of this particular article to "accept a parallel between the two types of totalitarianism."[12] Obviously, there were social and organizational differences between Stalinism and Nazism—that isn't the point.

The point is rather that those on the right tend to vilify communism, whereas those on the left vilify fascism, instead of recognizing that the fundamental phenomenon in both cases is ideocracy. Ideocracy—or rule based on the enforcement of ideology through an apparatus of centralized state terror—describes both communism and fascism. Both have a rigid state ideology that, while hostile to the various forms of organized religion, itself bestows a quasi-religious certainty on its adherents. And it does not matter if those adherents "really" believe the ideology—it suffices only that they fervently *pretend* to believe it, just as Czeslaw Milosz pointed out in *The Captive Mind*. But the worst are those Eric Hoffer termed the "true believers," those who identify wholly with the ideocracy and thereby inflate their egos with it—they become the fanatical adherents, the informers and the murderers.

Yet behind the murdering functionaries are those who generate the ideology itself. Thus, it is revealing that a scholar of political science devoted to what he deems "political realism," concludes that despite their apparent differences, ultimately Lenin and Schmitt have a great deal in common. Both are "contemptuous, genuinely heartless, and, at times, genuinely cynical."[13] Politics, from this perspective "behind" both left and right, is simply a matter of violence in the service of domination. Thus, "those who apply substantial force to their fellows get compliance, and from that compliance they draw the multiple advantages of money, goods, deference, and access to pleasures denied to less powerful people."[14] In short, underlying all politics of both the "left" and the "right" is only the struggle for domination through violence-based power, and so, according to this view, political theorists should abandon moral or philosophical evaluations of politics, thus becoming merely the explainers of totalizing power.[15] Such a "realist view" leads, of course, directly to the gulag, the torture chamber, and the mass grave.

In the end, it is true that designations such as "right" or "left," "fascist" or "communist" or, for that matter, "corporatist" are not anywhere near as important as what underlies them: that is, the degree to which a regime manifests the fundamental characteristics of a totalitarian ideocracy. These are the dynamics whose origins are to be found in the Inquisition, but that were refined, industrialized, and brutalized further in the twentieth century: the dynamics of the secret police and informants, of surveillance and of constant fear; of secret trials and of the absence of *habeas corpus* protections or other civil liberties or human rights; of indefinite detention of dissenters or "heretics" in gulags or concentration camps; and, finally, the dynamics of industrialized murder of millions, whether through mass starvation or outright slaughter (murder even if it is given the juridical patina of the cold word *execution*). What is it that makes all this inhumanity possible?

The Betrayal of Humanity

When we look back at the emergence of totalitarianism in the twentieth century, we cannot help but be struck—just as Nicholas Berdyaev was struck—by how similar are the dynamics of religious fanaticism and political fanaticism. Both for the religious adherent and for the political devotee, the ego becomes inflated by the sense of certainty: "I" become infallible by way of identifying with a particular fixed set of dogmas and with the division of humanity into friends and enemies, us and them. "Our" side is always right; "their" side is of the devil, so fundamentally wrong that one can only detest them. Once one acquiesces in such a view, one is well on the way to becoming a persecutor, be it religious or political.

Key to this transformation into a persecutor is a set of doctrines that one holds to be absolute or universal truth: thus everyone else is made into an unbeliever, or a traitor. Initially, these doctrines might be attractive as a set of convictions that conveniently explain the world as it is; but the more pervasive the political or religious system and the more charged it is with an atmosphere of fear, the more adherents feel they have to prove that they are more certain than others, that they are the real guardians of truth. It is only a short step from this to the belief that one's duty is to impose the doctrines on everyone else, and that such an imposition is for "their own good," or for the "good of society." From this point, it is not far to persecuting the recalcitrant and, in the frenzy of persecution, only a small further step to rationalize even mass murder under the guise of "the greater good."

Not always visible in this process is that it entails becoming inhuman. By definition, the doctrines become more important than other people or indeed, than the world: gradually, one becomes a functionary in an insane system, insane because it is divorced from fundamental humanity, from basic human kindness. Some people go along with an insane system because they don't have the courage to resist, but many become convinced by it. These are true believers who don't see what they are becoming, often because they have been rewarded with "promotion" and "responsibility" to enforce "the truth" upon others. And it is much easier to see the mote in others' eyes than to see what is lodged in one's own. There are always apologists for an inhuman system: there are apologists for the Inquisition, apologists for Stalin, no doubt apologists for Pol Pot. But the apologists cannot explain away the torture chambers, the bonfires, and the mass graves, the outward signs of total inhumanity in the name of "purifying" humanity.

The totalitarian system is predicated upon paranoia and division. Other people are projected to be "the enemy," and therefore, in the name of the system, must be ferreted out and exterminated. Thus the basic goodness of human life—love of family, love of locale, love of friends and neighbors, love of one's religion—is tainted and finally ruined by ever-growing terror. No one knows any longer whom to trust. The Inquisition at least was relatively limited in scope, but, in the twentieth century, the advent of totalitarianism expanded paranoia society-wide, and made possible the objectification and extermination of whole groups of people: peasants, Jews, gypsies, intellectuals, "class traitors," and on and on.

Really, the totalitarian systems of the twentieth century represent a kind of collective psychosis. Whether gradually or suddenly, reason and common human decency are no longer possible in such a system: there is only a pervasive atmosphere of terror, and a projection of "the enemy," imagined to be "in our midst." Thus society turns on itself, urged on by the ruling authorities. The effect of such a collective psychosis is to strengthen the power of the authorities, and in particular of the figurehead leader, who becomes the one thing stable in society as an infernal incarnation of the doctrines. Even in the early twenty-first century, some Russians were still nostalgic for the "man of steel," Stalin.[16] True believers in such a system (fanatics) find in it an easy identity—what they believe to be truth itself, even though it is in fact a conglomeration of lies—and so they are willing, indeed, eager and proud to betray not only their basic humanity but even life itself.

It Can Happen Here

How is it that some countries escape totalitarianism, whereas others fall prey to it? Although some conservative critics of Roosevelt's administration claimed that the New Deal constituted *de facto* fascism in the United States, in reality the United States clearly did not become totalitarian during the twentieth century.[17] Nor, for that matter, did England, or Switzerland, or many other countries, even if they shared some common cultural features with Germany, Italy, or Russia. How is it that Cambodia fell prey to a Pol Pot, whereas some other

Far Eastern nations did not? In the end, the answer lies with the presence of particular charismatic figures—or with a small cadre—who seized and consolidated power.

Of course, there are a variety of other factors to consider. Chief among them is the existence of a governmental system of checks and balances. As long as there is a balance of power among opposing political parties and between branches of government—and so long as there is genuine freedom of the press—it is unlikely that totalitarianism could take hold in a society. But it is possible, as the case of Germany certainly shows. The Weimar Republic included all of these political dimensions, albeit in a form eroded by economic collapse and by what we might call parliamentary paralysis. Yet as soon as a National Socialist party took power, it systematically began eliminating its competition as well as a critical press. The existence of checks and balances only works as long as political opposition and genuine dissent is possible.

What underlies the ascent to power of Lenin and later Stalin, as well as Hitler and even to a lesser extent Mussolini—not to mention Mao or Pol Pot—is violence. There is no intrinsic reason why such an ascent to power could not be accomplished in the United States or any other country—it is a matter of a confluence of factors. There must be a central ideology of secular or religious millennialism that encourages believers to imagine that by killing people today, a better future lies just around the corner. It helps also if there is a preceding socioeconomic disaster, so that people are predisposed to, on the one hand, look for scapegoats, and on the other, to imagine a better future if only the scapegoats were removed. But there also must be a charismatic ideologue to act as the movement's impetus and center.

Thus every totalitarian regime has had its dictator, with whom the regime is virtually synonymous. Hitler, Stalin, Pol Pot, Mao, Kim Jong Il: it is the cult of the "strong man," of the "great leader" who becomes the focal point of the entire system. One could speculate that an hierarchic structure with a single man at its center is somehow necessary so that the impersonal and horrific can be "normalized" and imagined as service to the father-figure of the dictator. A totalitarian leader draws on the ancient instinct to follow the wise man, but the instinct is perverted, so that the society moves inexorably toward the rationalization of monstrosities and horrors. The totalitarian "great leader" is a secular caricature of a combined religious leader, a pope, and a monarch, a king. But whereas ideally the latter are governed by an overarching religious ethos that constrains them to protect subjects, the dictator in a totalitarian system is under no such constraints—indeed, quite the opposite. Totalitarian power accrues primarily from scapegoating and from violence.

And so, it can happen here. What is more, it is in the nature of things that, once a totalitarian state takes hold, it is extremely difficult to dislodge it. "Dislodging" such a state requires a vantage point from outside it, and the very nature of the totalitarian state makes dissent a crime—indeed, a form of heresy. Not for nothing did Maistre refer to the dangers of "la secte" to his imagined total state—and not for nothing did Lenin, immediately upon seizing power, target competing religious groups and traditions in Russia. In the totalitarian state, exactly as Milosz pointed out, dissent is *heresy*—and nothing is so feared by authoritarians as freedom of choice, authentic freedom. Totalitarianism can take hold anywhere that fanatical ideologues can take sufficient power to prevent freedom of choice or expression. As the Inquisition had it, so, too, say the totalitarians: one is free to choose, as long as one doesn't even breathe aloud, let alone acknowledge the alternative choices. But that, of course, is not freedom at all.

15

Conclusion

Disorder as Order

Without doubt, one of the most important tasks for intellectual historians is to investigate and come to understand the phenomenon of ideocracy and its origins. As we have seen, Catholic Inquisitions provided an archetypal predecessor for one of the fundamentally new political developments of modernity: totalitarianism. But was there a direct intellectual line to be traced from the Inquisitions to the modern totalitarian state? Clearly, we can see how, by figures such as Maistre and Donoso Cortés, the Inquisitions were tied in with an authoritarian state and with the notion that order has to be enforced when revolution becomes a real threat. And we can see how, from these earlier figures, there is a line through Georges Sorel and others directly into both fascism and communism. But I believe that the archetypal dimensions of the Inquisition are more important than the specific intellectual lines through which the inquisitional mentality was transmitted into modernity.

When we look at the history of totalitarian states, we see that they resemble one another in archetypal ways: secret police, propaganda, requiring enemies, punishing dissent, and so forth. I believe that is because there is an archetypal phenomenon here that manifests itself according to different circumstances. Thus, we find some modern Catholics defending the Inquisitions, even the murder of Giordano Bruno, at the same time that we find a Catholic bishop asserting that modern European secularism is in danger of turning into an anti-Catholic Inquisition![1] The point is that the inquisitional phenomenon transcends ordinary political or religious distinctions: it is an archetype of its own, one that manifests in Protestant witch trials and in the McCarthy hearings in the United States during the 1950s, as well as in the Gestapo and in the Cheka.

Central to the dynamics of this phenomenon is an insider-outsider dynamic based on a constructed "orthodoxy." This "orthodoxy," be it political or religious, is constructed around a literalist faith that requires dissenters or heretics in order to define itself. We see exactly this phenomenon in Islamic radicalism of the Takfiri or al-Qaeda varieties of Wahhabism: these radical groups, entirely a modern invention, enjoin *jihad* against all who do not hold their own rigid and literalist politicoreligious faith. They are the insiders: everyone else is outside, sometimes even Sufis [mystics] of the same religious tradition. Theirs is a this-worldly faith in the sense that their fury is trained on those whom they see as infidels and opponents in this world.

Under consideration here is fanaticism of a form with which we ought to be familiar by now. Like communism, or fascism, it seeks to impose on the whole of society a single vision, ultimately a secular millennialist view of society that demands compliance. Rather than looking inward, as the Sufis enjoin, and seeking to reform oneself, the fanatic looks outward and believes that if only he were successful in reforming others, if only order could be enforced on all in society—then what? Here it becomes a bit hazy: then society would be molded into a millennialist unity in which the strictest moralism would rule. But all of this is *external;* it is in the end the objectified society of the inquisitor in which freedom is removed "for your own good."

In such a society, criminals seize power and impose institutionalized disorder. Imposing extreme order results, not in order but in the ultimate disorder in which the best are persecuted by the worst. A clinical psychologist told me of his long experience as a court psychologist in a major Midwestern American city, and of what many criminals told him during interviews. Over and over, they spoke of the rush of delusory power that they felt as they committed a crime: they felt a sense of invulnerability that derived from the commission of the crime, but that blinded them to the consequences of their acts. The same phenomenon is at work when totalitarians seize power: they commit crimes on far greater scales than any petty criminal, and they no doubt also feel the rush of illicit power as they commit, not just crimes, but crimes against humanity itself.

Such crimes against humanity always are fortified by rationalizations and justifications: it is for the good of the people; it is for the enforcement of the doctrines of the state; it is so that we can establish the coming secular or religious millennium. Furthermore, such crimes are often even regularized in "handbooks," inquisitorial guidebooks that accompany "tribunals" and "hearings" that provide occasions for more or less elaborate self-justifications. But when we penetrate through to the core of these crimes, something else is at work. Just as the order of totalitarianism is always disorder, so, too, the logic of the state in these state crimes is always ultimately illogic. No, there is something else at work in the gas chambers of the Nazis and the mass murders of Stalin or Pol Pot.

An "antimetaphysical" position became *de rigeur* in academic philosophy during the late twentieth century: at least in part in reaction to the horrors of totalitarianism, many scholars sought false refuge in the notion that one should take no metaphysical or meta-narrative position at all, assuming that such positions were to blame for the lunatic meta-narratives of secular millennialism. But if one rejects all metaphysical assertions, one then has no basis from which to critique totalitarianism or social criminality other than a strictly social one. Thus, one social position is placed against another, and the inhumanity of totalitarianism is relativized: there is no room for a concept of evil.

Böhme's Metaphysics of Evil

At this point, we might turn to the writings of Jacob Böhme (1575–1624), whose work may offer us some insight into how the inquisitorial mind operates. During the most creative part of his life, Böhme had been persecuted by a local Protestant pastor, so he had witnessed the phenomenon firsthand. In his *Six Theosophic Points,* Böhme explains how every human being has an inner choice between wrath and love. If we "withdraw into the dark fire of the source of anguish," then we exist inwardly in "fear and enmity, each form of life being hostile to the other." By contrast, "God's kingdom is found only in the bright clear light in freedom, in love and gentleness, for that is the property of the white clear light."[2] We can incarnate one or the other.

According to Böhme, both the dark world of wrath and the light world of love are accessible to us on earth—indeed, they both can be seen manifesting in visible nature.[3] We are given the freedom to manifest either one. When we "burn with wrath, envy, falsehood, lying, and deceit," then we live in or manifest "the dark world's fire."[4] And if so, then we are not really human but, rather, are demonic beings in human form.[5] According to Böhme, "the more evil and hostile a creature is in the dark world, the greater is its might. As the powerful tyrants of this world often exhibit their power in malignity, that men must fear them . . . just so is this a characteristic of those in the dark world."[6]

As a result, Böhme writes, tyrants and those who incarnate the dark world make this visible realm a "murderous den of the devil." For those who incarnate the dark world pretend to be human, but in fact are not. They "do the butchery, and increase God's wrath, and kindle the dark world in this outer world."[7] Thus there are two species of man on earth: there are those who serve God in humility and who, like Christ, are persecuted; and there is a species that "calls itself men, walks also in human form, but [in fact is] evil beasts."[8] Those people who incarnate the dark world might claim to be holy and even wear clerical garb, but this is only a disguise: what matters is what they are like inwardly. Full of suppressed fury, cold inhumanity, and arrogance, they vaunt themselves over others and like nothing better than to demonstrate their power over others by inspiring terror and spreading hell on earth.

It is no doubt easy for some readers to dismiss Böhme's perspective, but it does offer an eschatological and metaphysical context for understanding the phenomenon of totalitarianism. Certainly when we look at the atrocities perpetrated by the various totalitarian states—the industrialized murders committed by the Nazis, the horrific abuses of and murders of Tibetan Buddhists under Chinese Communism, the butchery by Stalin's secret police, the monstrous regime of the Cambodian Pol Pot, whose minions actually acted out hellish scenes with themselves cast as demons—is it really so hard to believe that human life really can be seen as a struggle between two sides, one meek and humble, the other tyrannical and grasping for the power over life and death? Perhaps such a view seems too dualistic, and yet one wonders whether it would seem so farfetched to the hundred million or hundred fifty million victims of these totalitarian regimes.

Ideocracy's Consequences

One thing we learn when we consider more broadly our authors here: ideocracy has consequences. In context, we can understand why Maistre or Donoso Cortés endorsed the imposition of order as exemplified in the authoritarian state, modeled partly on Catholicism and its inquisitions. Given the horrors of the French Revolution, and the likelihood of future revolutions, they believed that only an authoritarian enforcement of order could protect social and individual security and stability. What they did not, what they could not expect were the totalitarian regimes of the twentieth century that did enforce a kind of centralized state order—but at a terrible, nightmarish cost. Our nineteenth-century authors did provide an initial intellectual framework for the modern ideocratic state, but they did not anticipate how extreme an ideocratic state might become, nor, in the end, would they likely have countenanced what such states did in fact become.

The same cannot be said for all of our twentieth-century figures. Sorel was serially infatuated by the latest form of secular millennialism, and by the idea of revolutionary violence: endorsing violence, he was thus far more culpable when later communists and fascists indeed unleashed violence on their victims. Figures such as Lenin, Stalin, Hitler, Mao, and Pol Pot: they unleashed the madness of ideocratic violence in the name of secular millennialism, and they are utterly culpable; if we might find something redeeming in the work of their intellectual predecessors, ultimately we can find nothing redeeming in those directly responsible for so many millions of victims.

But what of twentieth-century authors such as Carl Schmitt, Eric Voegelin, or Theodor Adorno? Of course, Schmitt was somewhat culpable in the Nazi regime, regardless of his occasional prescient politicosocial insights. Yet Adorno was a bitter opponent of Nazism, and detested Schmitt: why include a chapter on him? And Voegelin was a vigorous opponent of communism, who certainly did not endorse ideocratic regimes: indeed, the intellectual framework that he provided served well to diagnose the ideocratic, pathological dimensions of the "political religions" inspiring twenty-first-century terrorism.[9] But when we consider these authors together, we see how the dynamics of heresiophobic victimization continues right through the modern period, even among authors who were horrified by the advent of totalitarianism in its various forms.

Heresy and History

All of these authors in various ways continued heretic-hunting traditions that can be traced back not only to the Catholic inquisitions but even further to the origins of institutional "orthodox" Christianity in late antiquity. Voegelin's and Voegelinians' sweeping condemnations of "Gnosticism" have their direct antecedents in the anti-heresiological rhetoric of Church Fathers such as Tertullian—as does the work of Carl Schmitt, who also provides a further link between the inquisitions and the fascist state. Even Adorno, with his vitriolic attacks on American "occultism" and likening of occultists to fascists, unwittingly continued the kind of persecutory anti-occultist rhetoric that one finds in Nazi Germany, and that reflects long-standing Western currents of anti-occultism. It is not that these authors are responsible for totalitarian states—it is that their writing reveals the same victimizing dynamics that are clearly at work in totalitarian states.

Behind all of these works and figures, stretching all the way back to late antiquity, is a long-standing Christian emphasis on time or history and a rejection of "heresy," conceived as timeless gnosis. The conflict between "orthodoxy" and Gnosticism was between those who insisted on a strictly historical interpretation of religious doctrine, and those who insisted that religious truth has a transcendent, ahistorical dimension. Orthodoxy, as rooted in the works of Tertullian, Irenaeus, and Epiphanius, lays great emphasis on the historical birth and life of Christ, whereas Gnosticism laid more emphasis on Christ's transcendent, mystical, or gnostic significance beyond history or time.

The origins of totalitarianism are to be found in this rejection of transcendence and in an insistence that meaning is found only inside a historically bounded horizon. Of course, even among the Church Fathers one finds a Clement of Alexandria, who insisted on the possibility, indeed, the necessity of an orthodox gnosis, and historically Catholicism (more or less uneasily) included gnostics like Meister Eckhart or Marguerite of Porete, even if its inquisitions sometimes burned them at the stake. But with the advent of what we could call militant secularism in the twentieth century, religion itself became the enemy: in the secular ideocracy, religious faith is seen as a threat to the total hegemony of the state. Thus, Lenin said that when he heard the word "religion," he reached for his revolver. And thus, too, Chinese Communists continued to ceaselessly and bitterly persecute Tibetans and Tibetan Buddhist religious leaders, even half a century after Communism had achieved total authority over occupied Tibet, and had almost totally extirpated Tibetan culture and religious tradition.

The phenomenon of the Catholic inquisitions could be seen as archetypal for secular millennialism, in that underlying them was the belief that the Church had to eliminate its dissenters in this world, within history, in order to better achieve the unified church state. And when we look at the phenomena of fascism and communism in the twentieth century, we also see various efforts to achieve a kind of unified, totalized, quasi-religious church state in this world, within history. Driving the totalitarian state is a millennialist vision that "justifies" the elimination of dissenters or "heretics" today so as to achieve an ideal state tomorrow, or the day after tomorrow—but always within history, here on earth. And this ideopathology (a pathological insistence on a rigid ideology that results in many victims) is more broadly found than we might want to acknowledge.

The Ubiquity of Ideopathology

It is alarming to realize how little has been written as an effort to explain the ideopathological origins and nature of totalitarianism. After all, the pathological, genocidal state is arguably the most distinctive contribution to history of the twentieth century. What I have argued here is that the modern totalitarian state emerges out of an intellectual lineage that is traceable directly back to early modern defenses of the Catholic Inquisitions, and that has branches on both the "left" and the "right." That this is so, however, ought not to be read as therefore asserting that modern totalitarianism can be blamed on Roman Catholicism. Rather, what we have seen is that a particular kind of human quasi-religious pathology—which we can see in Calvin's Geneva with the burning of Michael Servetus, just as in the Inquisition-imposed murder of the Nolan genius Giordano Bruno—is visible in modern "secularity" in a wide array of authors and movements on both the so-called left and right. Those who wish to assert a hegemonic ideocracy require heretics and heresy-hunting, whether their ideocracy is religious or secular. Secular heretic-burning, projected in a mass, industrialized way, is genocide.

In *The Pathology of Man,* Steven Bartlett extensively investigates the phenomenon of human aggression and genocide, focusing on the case of National Socialist Germany, and working from a psychological perspective. He concludes from his research that very few people in a genocidal state will resist—only in the range of 0.5 percent.[10] Bartlett notes that although various participants in genocide—including Nazi soldiers and physicians—could have refused to participate without significant consequences to themselves, very few did so. Only a very small number of people seem to have the intellectual courage and capacity to stand against genocidal social forces. Here I will cite Bartlett at length:

> People capable of resisting human evil, as in the mass killings of the Holocaust, are, to varying degrees, then, "marginal individuals:" Their experience of the world allows for some measure of disengagement from prevailing ideas and values; they are more able than most to stand emotionally alone, without the crutch of group agreement; they may feel a certain amount of repugnance toward violence that harms innocent people and perhaps toward collectivism itself; they are more resistant to the emotional attractions of conformity, the gratifications of hatred, power over others, divisiveness, destruc-

tiveness and its adrenaline-producing capacity; and the list could be lengthened.[11]

The vast majority of people, Bartlett concluded, will go along with and even wholeheartedly participate in genocide, whereas very few will be capable of the intellectual independence that characterizes resistance. Very few people will be capable of this kind of *haerein* or heresy, that is to say, very few will be capable of the individual choice to separate from the genocidal state or populace. But Bartlett's pessimistic conclusions go much further.

Bartlett's thesis, in *The Pathology of Man*, is that genocide and ecocide are not deviations from normal human society, but rather are particular expressions of "normal" modern human society, which is inherently pathological. His research demonstrates that "normal people engage in genocide [and terrorism], killing other normal people for a variety of reasons. Certainly the human normality of genocide is a fact we would rather not acknowledge, even as psychologists."[12] He continues that "A historian once asked what needed to happen to the German people in order for them to accept a government intent upon mass murder. 'Unfortunately,' he concluded, '*nothing needed to happen.* In nations across the world, people accept government crime.'" In other words, "*Nothing needs to happen* in order for psychologically normal, average, everyday people to accept and comply with a callous and cruel government intent upon a program of systematic dehumanization and murder of the members of another group or nation."[13] Thus, when psychiatrist Douglas Kelley returned from the Nuremberg trials after World War II, he came back convinced that even in the "democratic conditions that prevail in the United States," one might well see "a re-enactment of genocidal atrocities perpetrated against a dehumanized enemy."[14] "I am convinced that there is little in America to-day which could prevent the establishment of a Nazi-like state," Kelley wrote morosely.

At the core of Bartlett's argument is this: that although contemporary psychological and sociocultural models more or less unquestioningly counterpose "normal" and "pathological" as opposite categories, a careful and unbiased analysis reveals that in fact not only are "the perpetrators of human evil" "often psychologically normal people," but, what is more, to be "normal" is in fact to *be* pathological in the sense that, by and large, it is "normal" people who are inexorably destructive both to the natural world and to their own species.[15] Seen from this very broad perspective, what we have been discussing in this book—the particular pathology represented by the Inquisitions of modern totalitarianism—is not something limited only to Nazi Germany or to Pol Pot's Cambodia, nor even to the various intellectual lineages we have traced but, rather, strikingly exemplifies much more extensive and deeply rooted basic human pathology. Ours, he writes, is the tragedy of a species that has become pathogenic toward itself and toward other forms of life that share the planet, that is "able to become conscious of its own dysfunctions," but because its members are "so amply rewarded by those very dysfunctions, ignores and denies them."[16] Thus, Bartlett is pessimistic even about the warning represented by his own conclusions, for he holds that not only is "normal" modern society deeply pathological, but, what is more, this pathology itself will keep most people from heeding his analysis and warnings.

What then does he propose? Bartlett systematically lists and discards as impractical the various secular possibilities for overcoming mass human pathologies. Argument won't work because most people won't listen; psychiatry won't work on large populations (and its effects on individuals is at best ambiguous); social reform itself tends to be subverted and become pathological; and public condemnation and ridicule of human pathological behavior—for example, ridicule of behavior including self-centeredness, glorification of violence, the "gratifications of hatred," "overweening desecration of the world's ecology"—is highly "unlikely." Yet, if none of these methods will work to overcome human pathogenicity, are we left with outright pessimism and nothing else? So it would seem. But we have not yet looked at the other side of the fence.

Mysticism and Plato's Cave

Throughout this book, we have focused on the phenomenon of heretic-hunting and inquisitionalism in modern secular political philosophy and institutions. Along the way, we necessarily had to analyze, on occasion, how political philosophers on both the "left" and on the "right" have tended to denigrate mystics or gnostics very much in the tradition of the Inquisitions. It even became somewhat fashionable in some circles, more or less following Eric Voegelin, to denounce all secular millennialist political movements and figures as being somehow "gnostic." As we have seen, such attempts derive from profound confusion over what "gnostic" means, and from an almost total ignorance of the rapidly expanding scholarly understanding of gnosticism, mysticism, and Western esoteric traditions.[17] We have already discussed such confusions in detail, and there is no need to reconsider them here. Rather, I would like to conclude by at least alluding to a foray into exactly the opposite—that is, into the question of what gnosis might offer in the way of healing the kinds of pathologies discussed in this book.

After all, what might be the positive political ramifications of mysticism or gnosis? This is a subject totally unexplored in scholarship—not unexpectedly, given the massive weight of centuries of heresiophobia and victimization. Only a handful of authors in the past several centuries explored the territory on either side of this book's subject. On the one side is arrayed the force of the inquisitors, the heresy-hunters, religious and secular, who seek to enforce order and in fact generate what I have called the order of disorder, but that could just as well be called (after Dante) the order of Dis. But what about the other side? What are the political or psychological implications of mysticism or gnosticism? Surely there are some, after all. Here is much too vast a territory for us to begin to cover here, but we could at least begin to suggest the lay of the land.

For inquisitionalism is always based upon dualism—it requires an *other* who can be blamed, attacked, killed. By contrast, mysticism is based upon the mystic's transcendence of dualism, on the union or reunion of the human with the human, natural, and divine. Here I am using the terms "mystic" and "mysticism" purely for convenience's sake, and by them am referring to those who follow not an outward path that requires the domination of others or of the natural world but an inward path that culminates in a joyous transcendence of self-and-other, that is to say, in an *overcoming* of dualism.[18] It is at least possible that convincing solutions to human pathology are invisible to Bartlett because he is looking in the wrong place. Perhaps the question of how to heal humanity of its pathologies is to be answered not by outward imposition of any ideology or ideocracy but only by inward reflection and transformation.[19] In this regard, it may be revealing that even Bartlett, for all his pessimism about humanity, concludes his massive study by quoting the great Christian mystic Thomas Traherne, who urged his readers—in the face of all the human folly and brutality in the world—to become healers, physicians of humanity.

There is a great deal more that we could write about this subject here, but it is better only to offer intimations of an almost wholly unexplored inner continent, outlines of which are already visible in some of my various other works.[20] Even mentioning the existence of what we may call an inner, hidden continent or destination sometimes has been criminalized as heresy, especially in the West, but for all that, in each generation there seem to emerge at least a few more who tell us that they have made their way to it, and, like the one who escaped from the Cave in Plato's allegory, have come back to tell their stories to us disbelievers who still dwell in darkness. It is no doubt "normal" to disbelieve and even, as Plato tells us, to attack and even kill those who claim to have been outside the Cave. But the perennial question remains: what if those who say that they have been outside the Cave are right? What if the "heretic" was right all along?

With such questions in mind, we end our inquiry—at least for now.

Notes

CHAPTER 1

1. One such figure is Thomas Fleming, editor of the American political magazine *Chronicles*, whose editorial columns sometimes ramble off into angry denunciations of St. Clement of Alexandria (whom Fleming sees as a kind of vegetarian hippie).

2. See Tertullian, *Against the Valentinians*, in *The Ante-Nicene Fathers*, vol. III.

3. See Jaroslaw Piekalkiewicz and Alfred W. Penn, *Politics of Ideocracy* (Albany, N.Y.: SUNY Press, 1995).

4. From Benito Mussolini, "Dottrina," in *Political Quarterly* 4 (July 1933):341–356, here quoted with minor grammatical corrections of the translation.

5. See Czeslaw Milosz, *Captive Mind* (New York: Harper, 1953), p. 58.

6. Ibid., p. 60.

7. Ibid., pp. 198–199.

8. Ibid., p. 208.

9. Ibid., pp. 209–210.

10. Ibid., p. 213.

11. Ibid., p. 214.

12. Ibid., p. 219.

13. See Fyodor Dostoevsky, ch. 5, "The Grand Inquisitor," in *The Brothers Karamazov* (New York: Random House, 1985), p. 267.

CHAPTER 2

1. See, for example, the collection sponsored by the Vatican, Agostino Borromeo, et al., eds., *Minutes of the International Symposium "The Inquisition"* (Rome: Vatican, 2004).

2. See, for various broad overviews of the history of the inquisition, Elphege Vacandard, *The Inquisition: A Critical and Historical Study of the Coercive Power of the Church*, B. Conway, trans. (London: Longman, 1915), or Edward Burman, *The Inquisition: The Hammer of Heresy* (Wellingborough: Thorsons, 1984). Another such study is Guy Mathelié-Guinlet, *L'inquisition: Tribunal de la foi* (Paris: Aubéron, 2000). See also more recent academic works like Joseph Pérez, *The Spanish Inquisition* (New Haven, Conn.: Yale University Press, 2005), and Irene Silverblatt, *Modern Inquisitions: Peru and the Colonial Origins of the Civilized World* (Durham, N.C.: Duke University Press, 2004). Also of interest is John H. Arnold, *Inquisition and Power: Catharism and the Confessing Subject in Medieval Languedoc* (Philadelphia: University of Pennsylvania Press, 2001).

3. See Henry Charles Lea, *Superstition and Force* (Philadelphia: Lea, 1892), 485. Lea is also the author of *The History of the Inquisition of the Middle Ages*, 3 vols. (New York: Macmillan, 1908), and of *A History of the Inquisition in Spain*, 3 vols. (New York: Macmillan, 1906–1907).

4. See, on confession, John H. Arnold, *Inquisition and Power: Catharism and the Confessing Subject in Medieval Languedoc* (Philadelphia: University of Pennsylvania Press, 2001), pp. 90ff.

5. Bartolomé Bennassar, "Patterns of the Inquisitorial Mind as the Basis for a Pedagogy of Fear," in Angel Alcalá, ed., *The Spanish Inquisition and the Inquisitorial Mind* (Boulder, Colo.: Social Science Monographs, 1987), p. 177.

6. Ibid.

7. Ibid., p. 178.

8. Ibid.

9. Ibid.

10. Ibid., p. 180.

11. Ibid.

12. Jaime Contreras, *El Santi Oficio de la Inquisición de Galicia* (Madrid, 1982), p. 149, cited in Bennassar, p. 181.

13. See Henry Ansgar Kelly, *Inquisitions and Other Trial Procedures in the West* (Aldershot: Ashgate, 2001), p. 417.

14. Bennassar, p. 181.

15. Ibid., p. 183.

16. Ibid.

17. John Tedeschi, *The Prosecution of Heresy* (Binghamton, N.Y.: Medieval and Renaissance Texts & Studies, 1991), pp. 132–133.

CHAPTER 3

1. See Jean-Louis Darcel, "Maistre, Mentor of the Prince," in Richard Lebrun, ed., *Joseph de Maistre, Life, Thought, and Influence* (Montreal: McGill, 2001), p. 127. On Saint-Martin, see p. 123. See also Franck Lafage, *Le comte Joseph de Maistre* (Paris: L'Harmattan, 1998), pp. 145–150.

2. See Robert Triomphe, *Joseph de Maistre: Etude sur la vie et sur la doctrine d'un materialiste mystique* (Geneva: 1968), and see also on the related topic Antoine Faivre, "Maistre and Willermoz," in R. Lebrun, ed., *Maistre Studies* (Lanham, Md.: University Press of America, 1988), pp. 100–125.

3. See Joseph de Maistre, *Letters to a Russian Gentleman on the Spanish Inquisition*, A. M. Dawson, trans. (London: Dolman, 1851), pp. 19–22.

4. Ibid., p. 33.

5. See Bartolomé Bennassar, "Patterns of the Inquisitorial Mind as the Basis for a Pedagogy of Fear," in Angel Alcalá, ed., *Inquisitión española y mentalidad inquisitorial* (Barcelona: Ariel, 1984), trans. as *The Spanish Inquisition and the Inquisitorial Mind* (Boulder, Colo.: Social Science Monographs, 1987), pp. 178–179.

6. Ibid., p. 38.

7. Ibid.

8. This is the argument throughout Letter IV, pp. 38ff.

9. See *Réflexions sur le protestantisme dans ses rapports avec la souveraineté*, in *Oeuvres completes* (Lyons: Vitte et Perrussel, 1884–1993), vol. 8, p. 493.

10. See Richard LeBrun, *Throne and Altar: The Political and Religious Thought of Joseph de Maistre* (Ottawa: University of Ottawa Press, 1965), pp. 152–154.

11. See Maistre, *On the Origins of Sovereignty*, in *Against Rousseau*, R. Lebrun, trans. (Montreal: McGill-Queen's University Press, 1996), p. 163.

12. Ibid., p. 142. See also *The Works of Joseph de Maistre*, J. Lively, ed. (New York: Macmillan, 1965), p. 114.

13. Lively, ed., *Works of Joseph de Maistre*, p. 135.

14. See Émile Faguet, *Politiques et moralists du dix-neuvième siècle*, I (Paris: 1899), p. 1, cited by Isaiah Berlin in *The Crooked Timber of Humanity* (New York: Knopf, 1991), p. 94. See also Samuel Rocheblave, "Étude sur Joseph de Maistre," *Revue d'histoire et de philosophie religieuses* 2 (1922):312.

15. Berlin, *Crooked Timber*, p. 119.

16. Ibid., p. 125.

17. Maistre, *Oeuvres*, I, p. 376, cited in Berlin, *Crooked Timber*, p. 126.

18. Berlin, *Crooked Timber*, p. 126.

19. Ibid.

20. Lebrun, ed. *Joseph de Maistre's Life, Thought*, pp. 286–287.

21. Ibid., p. 288.

22. See Stephen Holmes, *The Anatomy of Antiliberalism* (Cambridge, Mass.: Harvard University Press, 1993), pp. 7, 36.

23. See Graeme Garrard, "Joseph de Maistre and Carl Schmitt," in Lebrun, ed., pp. 221–222.

24. Ibid., pp. 236–238.

CHAPTER 4

1. See John T. Graham, *Donoso Cortés: Utopian Romanticist and Political Realist* (Columbia: University of Missouri Press, 1974), pp. 19ff.
2. See Jeffrey Johnson, ed., *The Selected Works of Juan Donoso Cortés* (Westport, Conn.: Greenwood, 2000), p. 46; "Speech on Dictatorship," from *Obras completas de Don Juan Donoso Cortés*, 2 vols., J. Juretschke, ed. (Madrid: Bibliotec de Autores Cristianos, 1946). See also Bela Menszer, ed., *Catholic Political Thought: 1789–1848* (South Bend, Ind.: University of Notre Dame Press, 1962).
3. Ibid., p. 44.
4. Ibid., p. 53.
5. Ibid., p. 55.
6. Ibid., p. 57.
7. Ibid., p. 56.
8. See Graham, *Donoso Cortés*, pp. 302–308.
9. Ibid., p. 302.
10. Ibid., p. 303.
11. Ibid., p. 304.
12. Johnson, *Selected Works*, p. 72.
13. Ibid.
14. See his letter to the editor of *El Heraldo*, 15 April 1852, in *Selected Works*, p. 95.
15. Ibid., pp. 97–98.
16. See "Letter to Cardinal Fornari on the Errors of Our Times," in ibid., pp. 102–103.
17. See Donoso Cortés, *Essays on Catholicism, Liberalism, and Socialism*, W. McDonald, trans. (Dublin: W. Kelly, 1874), p. 201, and Juan Donoso Cortés, *Ensayo sobre el catolicismo, el liberalismo y el socialismo*, J. Gómez, ed. (Barcelona: Planeta, 1985).
18. *Essays*, pp. 37–44; *Ensayo*, pp. 25–29.
19. *Essays*, p. 42; *Ensayo*, p. 29.
20. See Carl Schmitt, "The Unknown Donoso Cortés," in *Telos* 125 (Fall 2002): 84–85.
21. Ibid., p. 86.
22. See, for example, Carl Schmitt, "Donoso Cortés in Berlin (1849)" in *Telos* 125 (Fall 2002):99.

CHAPTER 5

1. Wyndham Lewis, *The Art of Being Ruled* (London: 1926), p. 128.
2. Sorel's emphasis on the salutary value of violence as a revolutionary means manifested itself in a new form in the celebration of the violence of war in Nazi-era figures such as Ernst Jünger. In both cases, violence was seen as having a quasi-mystical revelatory power, though in Sorel that power was instrumental in bringing about an imagined coming workers' utopia, whereas in Jünger and related similar celebrants of war, heroism in war was a kind of existential act in itself.

3. See, on the Mafia and Sorel's work, Michael Freund, *Georges Sorel: Der revolutionäre Konservatismus* (Frankfurt: Klostermann, 1932), pp. 63–64.

4. See Sorel, "Le caractère religieux du socialisme," published in *Mouvement socialiste* (November, 1906), and republished in *Matériaux d'une théorie du prolétariat* (Paris: Riviére, 1919, 1923), translated version in *Hermeneutics and the Sciences: From Georges Sorel, Vol. 2*, John Stanley, ed. (New Brunswick, N.J.: Transaction, 1989), pp. 67–98.

5. *From Georges Sorel, Vol. 2*, p. 36.

6. Ibid., p. 41.

7. Ibid., "The Religious Character of Socialism," p. 79.

8. Ibid.

9. Ibid.

10. Ibid., p. 80.

11. Ibid., p. 81.

12. Ibid., "Marxism and Social Science," p. 186, from Sorel, *Saggi di critica del Marxismo* (Milano-Palermo: Sandron, 1903), pp. 169–188.

13. Georges Sorel, *Reflections on Violence*, T. E. Hulme, trans. (Glencoe: Free Press, 1950), p. 125.

14. Ibid.

15. Ibid., pp. 124–125.

16. Ibid., p. 132.

17. See Sorel, *Reflections on Violence*, p. 285. It is clear, because he cites him, that Sorel knew Maistre's work first hand. Furthermore, the conclusion to *Reflections on Violence* is quite Maistrean.

18. Ibid., p. 298.

19. Ibid., p. 300.

20. Ibid., p. 28.

21. See Jack Roth, *The Cult of Violence* (Berkeley: University of California Press, 1980), pp. 223–224.

22. Ibid., p. 161.

23. See Sorel, *Reflections*, pp. 303ff.

24. Richard Vernon, *Commitment and Change: Georges Sorel and the Idea of Revolution* (Toronto: University of Toronto Press, 1978), p. 69.

25. See Jules Renard, *Journal, 1887–1910* (Paris: Gallimard, 1960), II:1203, cited in Michael Curtis, *Three Against the Third Republic* (Princeton: Princeton University Press, 1959), p. 57.

26. See Charles Maurras, *Au signe de Flore* (Paris: 1931), p. 9.

27. Charles Maurras, *Barbarie et poésie* (Paris: 1925), p. iii.

28. Charles Maurras, *L'Allée des philosophes* (Paris: 1924), p. 256.

29. Charles Maurras, *La Démocratie religieuse* (Paris: 1926), pp. 219, 343.

30. Ibid., pp. 195, 341.

31. See "Intermède philosophique: les solutions de la question juive," *La Gazette de France*, 7 January 1899, cited in William Buthman, *The Rise of Integral Nationalism in France* (New York: Columbia University Press, 1939), p. 232.

32. See "Sagesse! Sagesse!" in *La Gazette de France*, 9 Feb. 1899; and "M. Joseph

Reinach, *La Gazette de France*, 30 April 1899, cited in Buthman, *Rise of Integral Nationalism*, p. 232.

33. See Charles Maurras, *Oeuvres Capitales* (Paris: Flammarion, 1954), ii:33–34.

34. Charles Maurras, *Le Pape, la Guerre, et la Paix* (Paris: Nouvelle Librairie, 1917), esp. pp. 57–59.

35. On Maurras and occultism, see Maurras, *Music Within Me*, Count Potocki, trans. (London: Right Review, 1946), p. 3.

36. See Eugen Weber, *Action Française: Royalism and Reaction in Twentieth-Century France* (Stanford: Stanford University Press, 1962), p. 220.

37. Michel Winock, *Nationalism, Anti-Semitism, and Fascism in France* (Stanford: Stanford University Press, 1998), p. 183.

38. Ibid.

39. Ibid.

40. See Weber, *Action Française*, p. 363.

41. See Charles Maurras, *La Contre-Révolution Spontanée* (Paris: Lardanchet, 1943), pp. 99–102.

42. Charles Maurras, *La Démocratie Religieuse* (Paris: Nouvelle Librairie, 1921), pp. 204–207.

43. See Winock, *Nationalism*, pp. 155–157.

CHAPTER 6

1. See Jan-Werner Müller, *A Dangerous Mind: Carl Schmitt in Post-War European Thought* (New Haven, Conn.: Yale University Press, 2003), p. 7.

2. Ibid., p. 205.

3. See Carl Schmitt and G. Schwab, trans., *The Leviathan in the State Theory of Thomas Hobbes* (Westport, Conn.: Greenwood, 1996), p. 26.

4. See Hugh Urban, "Religion and Secrecy in the Bush Administration: The Gentleman, the Prince, and the Simulacrum," in *Esoterica* VII (2005):1–38.

5. See Leo Strauss, *Persecution and the Art of Writing* (Chicago: University of Chicago Press, 1952), p. 17; Leo Strauss, "Farabi's Plato," *Louis Ginzberg Jubilee Volume* (New York: American Academy for Jewish Research, 1945), pp. 357–393, 384.

6. Schmitt, *Leviathan*, p. 3.

7. Ibid., p. 29.

8. Ibid., p. 60.

9. Ibid., p. 62.

10. Ibid., pp. 96–97.

11. See Heinrich Meier, *Carl Schmitt and Leo Strauss: The Hidden Dialogue* (Chicago: University of Chicago Press, 1995), p. 59, citing *The Concept of the Political* (1933 ed.), III:9.

12. See Schmitt, *Politische Theologie II* (Berlin: Duncker und Humblot, 1970), p. 103, to wit: "Für eine Besinnung auf die theologischen Möglichkeiten spezifisch justischen Denkens ist *Tertullian* der Prototyp."

13. Heinrich Meier, *The Lesson of Carl Schmitt* (Chicago: University of Chicago Press, 1998), p. 92.

14. See Meier, *Lesson of Carl Schmitt*, p. 94, citing Tertullian, *De praescriptione haereticorum*, VII:9–13: "Quid ergo Athenis et Hierosolymis? Quid academiae et ecclesiae? Quid haereticis et Christianis?"

15. Schmitt, PTII, *Politische Theologie II*, p. 120: "Der gnostische Dualismus setzt einen Gott der Liebe, einen welt-fremden Gott, als den Erlöser-Gott gegen den gerechten Gott, den Herrn und Schöpfer dieser bösen Welt . . . [einer Art gefährlichen Kalten Krieges]."

16. Ibid., p. 122.

17. See A. Roberts and J. Donaldson, eds., *Ante-Nicene Fathers* (Edinburgh: T & T Clark, 1989), III:521.

18. Ibid., III:643.

19. See Tertullian's treatise "Scorpiace," *De praescriptione haereticorum*, III:633–648.

20. Here we might remark that Western forms of Christianity are strikingly different in this respect from those in the Eastern Church, where mysticism remained (however uneasily at times) incorporated into orthodoxy itself and not imagined as inherently inimical to orthodoxy.

21. See Carl Schmitt, *The Nomos of the Earth in the International Law of the Jus Publicum Europaeum*, G. L. Ulmen, trans. (New York: Telos, 2003), pp. 59–60.

22. Ibid., p. 60.

23. Carl Schmitt, G. Schwab, trans., *The Concept of the Political* (New Brunswick, N.J.: Rutgers, 1976), p. 51.

24. Ibid., p. 64.

25. Ibid., p. 65.

26. Ibid., p. 67.

27. I write "supposedly" dualist and "reputedly" held the world to be evil because these accusations, repeated by Tertullian and several other ante-Nicene Fathers, are hardly borne out as characteristics of all the works we see in the Nag Hammadi library, the collection of actual Gnostic writings discovered in 1945.

28. Ibid., p. 29.

29. See Luciano Pellicani, *Revolutionary Apocalypse: Ideological Roots of Terrorism* (Westport, Conn.: Praeger, 2003), p. xi. I wholeheartedly agree with Pellicani's basic thesis that "The expansion on a planetary scale of a new form of chiliasm that substituted transcendence with absolute immanence and paradise with a classless and stateless society is the most extraordinary and shattering historical-cultural phenomenon of the secular age." But this "new form of chiliasm" has nothing whatever to do with Gnosticism as an actual historical phenomenon. One cannot find a single instance in late antiquity among the Gnostics themselves for such a phenomenon—but if one were to refer instead to "the destructive calling of *modern* secular millennialist revolution" that seeks to "purify the existing through a policy of mass terror and annihilation," Pellicani's thesis would no longer be subject to the criticism of an anachronistic misuse of terms. Later in the book, Pellicani discusses the cases of the Pol Pot regime and of Communist China—both of which illustrate his larger thesis well. But neither of these have anything whatever to do with the phenomenon of Gnosticism in any historically meaningful sense. Even Voegelin himself expressed

doubts about attempting to apply "Gnosticism" to the case of Communist Russia—let alone to Cambodia!

30. See Carl Schmitt, "Das Judentum in der deutschen Rechtswissenschaft," in "Die deutsche Rechtswissenschaft im Kampf gegen den jüdischen Geist," in *Deutsche Juristen-Zeitung*, 41 (15 October 1936), 20:1193–1199, cited in Gopal Balakrishnan, *The Enemy: An Intellectual Portrait of Carl Schmitt* (London: Verso, 2000), p. 206. See also Schmitt's lecture "Die deutsche Rechtswissenschaft im Kampf gegen den jüdischen Geist," in *Die Judentum in der Rechtswissenschaft* (Berlin: Deutscher Recht-Verlag, 1936), a brief volume that contains Schmitt's assertions of Jews as "parasitic," adding "für uns" a "Jewish author has no authority." See in particular pp. 29–30. See also Bernd Rüthers, *Carl Schmitt im Dritten Reich*, 2nd ed. (Munich: Beck, 1990).

31. See "Können wir uns vor Justizirrtum schützen?" *Der Angriff*, 1 September 1936, cited in Andreas Koenen, *Der Fall Carl Schmitt* (Darmstadt: Wissenschaftliche, 1995), p. 703; see also Balakrishnan, *The Enemy*, pp. 202–203.

CHAPTER 7

1. See Arto Luukkanen, *The Party of Unbelief: The Religious Policy of the Bolshevik Party, 1917–1929* (Helsinki: Finnish Historical Society, 1994), pp. 42–43.
2. See Nicholas Berdyaev, *The Russian Revolution* (Ann Arbor: University of Michigan Press, 1966).
3. See Lev D. Trotsky, *The Young Lenin* (Devon, U.K.: Newton Abbas, 1972), p. 95.
4. Luukkanen, *Party of Unbelief*, p. 55.
5. Robert Wesson, *Lenin's Legacy: The Story of the CPSU* (Stanford: Hoover Institute, 1978), pp. 21–22.
6. Ibid., p. 99, citing Vladimir Lenin, *Collected Works* (London: Lawrence & Wishart, 1960), vol. 31, p. 353.
7. Ibid., p. 80.
8. See Vladimir Lenin, *On the United States of America* (Moscow: Progress, 1967), p. 364.
9. Ibid., p. 365.
10. Wesson, *Lenin's Legacy*, p. 21.
11. Ibid., p. 23.
12. See V. I. Lenin, *The Proletarian Revolution and the Renegade Kautsky* (New York: International Publishers, 1934), p. 19, citing Friedrich Engels, "Über das Autoritätsprinzip," *Neue Zeit* (1913–1914) I:39. See also Robert Service, *A History of Twentieth-Century Russia* (New York: Penguin, 1997), pp. 107–108.
13. John Reshetar, *A Concise History of the Communist Party of the Soviet Union* (New York: Praeger, 1965), p. 212. See Lewis Siegelbaum, *Soviet State and Society between Revolutions, 1918–1929* (Cambridge: Cambridge University Press, 1992), pp. 53–54.
14. Luukkannen, *Party of Unbelief*, pp. 64–65. See also Siegelbaum, *Soviet State and Society*, pp. 156–165.
15. See Aleksandr Solzhenitsyn, *The Gulag Archipelago 1918–1956* (New York: Harper & Row, 1974).

16. See Luukkanen, *Party of Unbelief,* pp. 80, 85. See also Dmitry Pospielovsky, *Soviet Antireligious Campaigns and Persecutions* (London: Macmillan, 1988), pp. 5–11.

17. See Robert C. Tucker, *Stalin in Power: The Revolution From Above 1928–1941* (New York: Norton, 1990), pp. 102ff. See also Joshua Rubenstein and Vladimir Naumov, eds., *Stalin's Secret Pogrom: The Postwar Inquisition of the Jewish Anti-Fascist Committee* (New Haven, Conn.: Yale University Press, 2001), and Oleg Khlevnyuk, "The Objectives of the Great Terror, 1937–1938," in Julian Cooper et al., eds., *Soviet History, 1917–1953* (London: Macmillan, 1995), pp. 158–176.

18. See Nicolas Werth, "Strategies of Violence in the Stalinist USSR," in H. Rousso, ed., *Stalinism and Nazism* (Lincoln: University of Nebraska Press, 2004), pp. 73–75.

19. Ibid., p. 73.
20. Ibid., pp. 84–85.
21. Ibid., p. 86.

CHAPTER 8

1. See Wouter Hanegraaff, "On the Construction of 'Esoteric Traditions' " in Antoine Faivre and Wouter Hanegraaff, eds., *Western Esotericism and the Science of Religion* (Leuven: Peeters, 1998), pp. 11–62. This article confirms my thesis here concerning Voegelin. See page 36, where Hanegraaff quotes Hans Blumenberg, who in *Säkulisierung und Selbstbehautptung* (Frankfurt: Surhkamp, 1985), p. 144, writes that "When someone says that modernity would be better labeled 'the Gnostic era,' he recalls to memory the enemy from the beginning [*der Urfiend*] who did not come from outside but sat at the very root of Christianity's origin." Hanegraaff adds "That is well-formulated," and concludes that "heresiological propaganda" did not cease with the Enlightenment, but continued in secular form in "conspiracy" or "disease" interpretations of esotericism like Voegelin's.

2. I will note here at the outset the conventional and useful scholarly distinction between the *generic* terms gnosis (direct realization of spiritual truth for oneself) and gnostic (those who realize spiritual truth or union, a term that can apply not only to Christians but also more broadly, to, for instance, Muslims and Buddhists), and the *specific* terms Gnosticism and Gnostic, which are generally taken to refer to the Christian religious currents of late antiquity that later became demonized by what came to be known as orthodox Christianity. Although Voegelinism uses capitalized and non-capitalized forms of these terms indifferently, I have endeavored to keep to common usage. When in doubt, however, I use lowercase forms such as "gnosis" and "gnosticism."

3. Eric Voegelin, *Science, Politics and Gnosticism* (Chicago: Regnery, 1958), p. 11.
4. Ibid., p. 12.
5. Ibid.
6. Ibid., p. 30.
7. Ibid., p. 30.
8. Ibid., p. 43.

9. See Gregor Sebba, "History, Modernity, and Gnosticism," in *The Philosophy of Order: Essays on History, Consciousness and Politics*, Peter Opitz and Gregor Sebba, eds. (Stuttgart: Klett, 1981), p. 190.

10. Eric Voegelin, *The New Science of Politics* (Chicago: University of Chicago Press, 1952), p. 134.

11. Ibid., pp. 134–135.

12. It is worth noting here that Philip J. Lee took up Voegelin's argument in a book entitled *Against the Protestant Gnostics* (New York: Oxford University Press, 1987), in which he makes giant Voegelinian claims about how "gnostic" Calvinism is, how the Founding Fathers of the United States make (in the sardonic summary of Culianu) "awesome gnostics," and how modern Protestantism has to purge itself of this growing menace.

13. Eric Voegelin, "Ersatz Religion" in *Science, Politics, and Gnosticism*, p. 83.

14. See Ioan P. Culianu, "The Gnostic Revenge: Gnosticism and Romantic Literature," in *Gnosis und Politik* (Munich: W. Fink, 1984), p. 290, in which he bemusedly remarks on his "enlightenment," his realization that neoplatonism, the entire Reformation, "Communism," "Nazism," "liberalism, existentialism and psychoanalysis were gnostic too, modern biology was gnostic," "science" is gnostic; Marx, Freud, and Jung were gnostic; "all things and their opposite are equally gnostic." One should note that although Culianu does not directly say so, this sarcastic list is in fact primarily referring to Voegelin's ascriptions to "gnosticism."

15. Ibid., p. 100.

16. See *The Philosophy of Order*, p. 452.

17. Ibid., p. 456.

18. On this subject, see Arthur Versluis, *Wisdom's Children: A Christian Esoteric Tradition* (Albany, N.Y.: SUNY Press: 1999), esp. ch. XVIII, "Theosophy and Gnosticism."

19. See, for instance, Alain de Benoist, *L'Europe Païenne* (Paris: Seghers, 1980); *Comment peut-on être païenne?* (Paris: Albin Michel, 1981). See also his dialogue with Thomas Molnar entitled *L'Éclipse du sacré* (Paris: La Table Ronde, 1986), esp. pp. 129–177. See also Deuteronomy 13.12–16.

20. Ferdinand Christian Baur, *Die christliche Gnosis, oder die christliche Religions-Philosophia in ihrer geschichtlichen Entwicklung* (Tübingen: 1835), pp. 21ff.

21. See Gregor Sebba, "History, Modernity, and Gnosticism," in *Philosophy of Order*, p. 192.

22. Ibid., pp. 195ff.

23. Stephen McKnight, "Voegelin's Challenge to Modernity's Claim to be Scientific and Secular," in *The Politics of the Soul*, Glenn Hughs, ed. (Lanham, Md.: Rowman & Littlefield, 1999), p. 186.

24. See Stephen McKnight, "Gnosticism and Modernity: Voegelin's Reconsiderations in 1971," 2001 APSA Panel Paper, downloaded as a pdf file from http://www.pro.harvard.edu/papers/091/091007/McKnightSt.pdf.

I took the liberty of correcting some grammatical errors in the transcription, but the meaning is unaltered. See also Stefan Rossbach, " 'Gnosis' in Eric Voegelin's Philosophy," downloaded as a pdf file from http://www.pro.harvard.edu/papers/091/091007/RossbachSt.pdf.

25. Ibid., p. 202.
26. See *The Philosophy of Order*, p. 241.
27. Stefan Rossbach, *Gnostic Wars: The Cold War in the Contest of a History of Western Spirituality* (Edinburgh: Edinburgh University Press, 1999), p. 230.
28. Stephen McKnight, "Gnosticism and Modernity."

I took the liberty of correcting some grammatical errors in the transcription, but the meaning is unaltered. Voegelin's remark cited is on page 2.

29. Cyril O'Regan, *Gnostic Apocalypse: Jacob Böhme's Haunted Narrative* (Albany, N.Y.: SUNY Press, 2002), pp. 1, 231, 299.
30. See Versluis, *Wisdom's Children*. See also Antoine Faivre, *Theosophy, Imagination, Tradition*, C. Rhone, trans. (Albany, N.Y.: SUNY Press, 2000).
31. O'Regan, *Gnostic Apocalypse*, p. 24.
32. Ibid., p. 23.
33. Ibid., p. 212.
34. Ibid., p. 213.
35. Ibid., p. 14.
36. See Catherine Tumber, *American Feminism and the Birth of New Age Spirituality: Searching for the Higher Self, 1875–1915* (Lanham, Md.: Rowman & Littlefield, 2002), pp. 2–3.
37. Ibid., p. 174.
38. Ibid., pp. 174–175.

CHAPTER 9

1. Joseph McCarthy died in 1957.
2. See Norman Cohn, *Pursuit of the Millennium* (London: Secker, 1957), p. xiii.
3. Ibid., p. xiv.
4. Ibid., p. 306.
5. Ibid., p. 307.
6. Ibid., pp. 179–185.
7. Ibid., p. 184; the phrase "Goded with God" was that of Ann Bathurst, in her journal entry of 25 December 1692, where she exclaimed "in the fullness I say, *I am Goded with God,* he has filled and how else can I utter myself when I am filled with him? He speaks, not I: for I am no more I." See Arthur Versluis, ed., *Wisdom's Book: The Sophia Anthology* (St. Paul, Minn.: Paragon House, 2000), p. 165.
8. Cohn, *Pursuit*, p. 185.
9. Ibid., p. 186.
10. Ibid., pp. 179, 259, 304–305.
11. Ibid., p. 314.
12. See Norman Cohn, *Europe's Inner Demons: An Enquiry Inspired by the Great Witch-hunt* (New York: Basic, 1975), p. xiv.
13. Ibid., p. xi.

14. Ibid., especially pages 1–59, wherein Cohn treats the "demonization of medieval heretics," focusing in particular on the transformation of the Waldensians into "Luciferians."
15. Ibid., p. 85.
16. Ibid., p. 88.
17. Ibid., p. 258.
18. Ibid., pp. 258–259.

CHAPTER 10

1. See Nicholas Goodrick-Clarke, *The Occult Roots of Nazism* (New York: New York University Press, 1985) and *Black Sun: Aryan Cults, Esoteric Nazism, and the Politics of Identity* (New York: New York University Press, 2001). See also Corinna Treitel, *A Science for the Soul: Occultism and the Genesis of the German Modern* (Baltimore: Johns Hopkins University Press, 2004), especially her chapter "The Spectrum of Nazi Responses," pp. 210–242.
2. See Theodor Adorno, *Minima Moralia: Reflections from Damaged Life* (Frankfurt: Suhrkamp, 1951/London: Verso, 1974), pp. 238–244; *Telos* 19 (1974):7–13; and Stephen Crook, ed., *The Stars Down to Earth and other Essays on the Irrational in Culture* (London: Routledge, 1994), pp. 128–134.
3. See the *Telos* translation, p. 7; *Minima Moralia*, p. 238. Of these two, the *Telos* translation is significantly superior.
4. *Telos* translation, p. 7.
5. Ibid., p. 8.
6. Ibid.
7. Ibid., p. 9.
8. Ibid., p. 10.
9. Ibid.
10. See, for instance, Antoine Faivre's *Access to Western Esotericism* (Albany, N.Y.: SUNY Press, 1994), or Jean-Paul Corsetti's *Histoire de l'ésotérisme et des sciences occultes*, (Paris: Larousse, 1993), or the first half of my own *Restoring Paradise* (Albany, N.Y.: SUNY Press, 2004), or my forthcoming *Magic and Mysticism: An Introduction to Western Esotericism*.
11. Ibid., p. 11.
12. Ibid, p. 12.
13. See Theodor Adorno, "The Stars Down to Earth: The Los Angeles Times Astrology Column," *Telos* 19 (1974):13–90; see also Crook, ed., *The Stars Down to Earth*.
14. Ibid., p. 13.
15. Ibid., pp. 14–15.
16. Ibid., p. 16.
17. Ibid., p. 27.
18. Ibid., p. 85.
19. Ibid., p. 89.
20. Ibid., p. 90.
21. See, for example, Patrick Curry, *Prophecy and Power: Astrology in Early Mod-

ern England (Princeton: Princeton University Press, 1989). For another, much more limited but still historically informed account, see Arthur Versluis, *The Esoteric Origins of the American Renaissance* (New York: Oxford University Press, 2001), especially the discussion of astrological almanacs in early American life.

22. See Daphna Canetti-Nisim, "Two Religious Meaning Systems, One Political Belief System: Religiosity, Alternative Religiosity, and Political Extremism," in Leonard Weinberg and Ami Pedhzur, *Religious Fundamentalism and Political Extremism* (London: Frank Cass, 2004), pp. 35–54.

23. See Treitel, *A Science for the Soul*, pp. 210–242.

24. Ibid., p. 231.

25. Ibid., p. 233.

26. Ibid., p. 235.

27. For more on Nazism and occultism, see Nicholas Goodrick-Clarke, *The Occult Roots of Nazism: Secret Aryan Cults and Their Influence on Nazi Ideology* (New York: New York University Press, 1992 ed.), and *Black Sun: Aryan Cults, Esoteric Nazism, and the Politics of Identity* (New York: New York University Press, 2003 ed.). See also Joscelyn Godwin, *Arktos: The Polar Myth in Science, Symbolism, and Nazi Survival* (Grand Rapids, Mich.: Phanes, 1993).

CHAPTER II

1. See Carl Raschke, *The Bursting of New Wineskins: Reflections on Religion and Culture at the End of Affluence* (Pittsburgh: Pickwick, 1978), p. 93.

2. Ibid., p. 109.

3. Ibid., p. 73.

4. Carl Raschke, *The Interruption of Eternity: Modern Gnosticism and the Origins of the New Religious Consciousness* (Chicago: Nelson, 1980), p. xi.

5. Ibid., pp. 23–35, 146–157, 188–189, and so forth.

6. Ibid., p. 184.

7. Ibid., p. 218.

8. Ibid., p. 236.

9. Ibid., p. 242.

10. Ibid., p. 243.

11. See Carl Raschke, *Painted Black: From Drug Killings to Heavy Metal—The Alarming True Story of How Satanism Is Terrorizing Our Communities* (New York: Harper, 1990), back cover.

12. Ibid., p. xiii.

13. Ibid., p. 117.

14. Ibid., p. 268.

15. Ibid., pp. 293–332.

16. See, for a careful analysis of some of the errors in Raschke's book, http://www.witchvox.com/whs/kerr_experts_2a.html, "Raschke Paints Things Black," written by Detective Constable Charles A Ennis of the Vancouver Police Department, Youth Services Unit.

17. Raschke, *Painted Black*, p. 411.

18. Ibid., p. 399.

19. Ibid., p. 400.

20. Ibid., p. 406.

21. Raschke's book has a bibliography that includes many relevant news articles and books of the 1980s during the height of the day care "ritual abuse" witch-hunts. What it doesn't acknowledge, save in passing, are the books and articles of the prescient doubters. The False Memory Syndrome Foundation Newsletter and the Justice Committee (San Diego, Calif.) have documented thousands of cases of false memory syndrome and subsequent false accusations. See, for various views, C. Ronald Huff, Arye Rattner and Edward Sagarin, *Convicted But Innocent* (Thousand Oaks, Calif.: Sage, 1996); Mark Pendergast, *Victims of Memory* (Hinesburg, Vt.: Upper Access, 1995); or Jeffrey S. Victor, *Satanic Panic* (Chicago: Open Court Press, 1993).

22. See Carl Raschke, *Fire and Roses: Postmodernity and the Thought of the Body* (Albany, N.Y.: SUNY Press, 1996).

23. Carl Raschke, *The Digital Revolution and the Coming of the Postmodern University* (London: Routledge, 2003), pp. 72–73.

24. Ibid., p. 86.

CHAPTER 12

1. See Jon Trott and Mike Hertenstein, "Selling Satan: The Tragic History of Mike Warnke," *Cornerstone Magazine* 21 (1992)98, available from http://www.cornerstonemag.com/features/iss098/sellingsatan.htm.

2. Trott and Hertenstein, "Selling Satan."

3. Trott and Hertenstein, "Selling Satan."

4. All of these rather nauseating details, and many more, are to be found both in the Trott and Hertenstein *Cornerstone Magazine* article, and in their subsequent book.

5. See Michelle Smith and Lawrence Pazder, *Michelle Remembers* (New York: Congdon & Lattes, 1980), Lauren Stratford's *Satan's Underground* (Eugene, Oreg.: Harvest House, 1988; Gretna, La.: Pelican, 1991). Other books in the genre include Judith Spencer, *Suffer the Child* (New York: Simon & Schuster, 1989), and Robert S. Mayer's *Satan's Children* (New York: G.P. Putnam's Sons, 1991). On the phenomenon itself, see James T. Richardson, Joel Best, and David G. Bromley, *The Satanism Scare* (New York: Aldine de Gruyter, 1991).

6. See the purported text of a "restricted" bulletin issued by a Lt. Larry Jones of the Boise, Idaho, police department on "cult activity," *File 18 Newsletter* (2 May 1986), Boise, Idaho, reproduced at http://www.skepticfiles.org. The "facts" in the newsletter are also drawn upon by Jerry Johnston, *The Edge of Evil* (Dallas: Word, 1989), p. 4, quoting a Dr. Al Carlisle of the Utah Prison System who claims fifty to sixty thousand ritual murders a year in the United States. One could trace exactly how such notions were passed on in a sort of game of "telephone" between "cult experts" and police departments—cumulatively contributing to if not outright producing the hysteria—but such an effort is beyond our current scope.

7. Jeffrey Victor, *Satanic Panic: The Creation of a Contemporary Legend* (LaSalle, Ill.: Open Court, 1993), esp. pp. 273ff.

8. See Victor, esp. Chapter Four, "Rumor Panics Across the Country," and Chapter Six.

9. See Jon Trott and Mike Hertenstein, "Selling Satan."

10. See Darryl E. Hicks and David A. Lewis, *The Todd Phenomenon: Fact or Phantasy* (Harrison, Ark.: New Leaf, 1979). This strange little volume does document John Todd's tapes and activities, and it is quite helpful as a primary source in itself. Its authors are primarily bent on character assassination of Todd after his intemperate attacks on Billy Graham and other prominent evangelicals as secretly being in cahoots with the "Illuminati," but the work is ambiguous about whether the "Illuminati" conspiracy really exists.

11. See Michael Barkun, *A Culture of Conspiracy: Apocalyptic Visions in Contemporary America* (Berkeley: University of California Press, 2003), pp. 51–52.

12. Ibid., pp. 61–62.

13. Ibid., p. 121.

14. Ibid., p. 4.

15. See, for instance, the articles on http://www.thecuttingedge.org. A case in point is this quotation from a section of the Web site devoted to connections between Rev. Moon and the evangelical leadership:

> We have already spoken of "disinformation agents," a term commonly used in the intelligence field to describe an agent who is sown in the target country and is designed to look like, act like, and sound like a normal citizen or patriot of that country. Such agents will provide 75–90 percent good information to their target in order to build up credibility and believability, but during the time of the most critical moment, they will provide disinformation that is designed to make the target country lose the battle or the war.
>
> It seems to me that these Evangelical Christian leaders who have tight ties to the Illuminati or to Rev. Sun Moon may be considered disinformation specialists. This means they will provide good solid Christian information, perhaps to the 95 percent level, in order to establish rapport and trust among their followers. However, at the right moment, or for the *right issue*, they will "toe the line"—take the position—the Illuminati wants them to take.

See http://www.cuttingedge.org/news/n1818.cfm, and don't miss the elaborate thesis of "Illuminati" weather control at http://www.cuttingedge.org/articles/weather.cfm.

16. See Pat Robertson, *The New World Order* (Dallas: Word, 1991), pp. 9–10.

17. Ibid., pp. 6, 8.

18. See Carroll Quigley, *The Anglo-American Establishment* (New York: Books in Focus, 1981), and *Tragedy and Hope: A History of the World in Our Time* (New York: Macmillan, 1966); for how conspiracism can be based on Quigley, see Robertson, *New World Order*, pp. 111–113.

19. Robertson, *New World Order*, p. 69.

20. Ibid., p. 70.

21. Ibid., p. 71.

22. Ibid., p. 183.

23. Ibid., p. 185.

24. Amitabha is a bodhisattva of compassion, but Robertson somehow manages to confuse him with assassins.

25. Robertson, *New World Order*.

26. Ibid., p. 261.

27. Ibid., p. 268.

28. See Robert Dreyfuss, "Reverend Doomsday: For Tim LaHaye, the Apocalypse is Now," *Rolling Stone* (February, 2004) at http://www.rollingstone.com/features/nationalaffairs/featuregen.asp?pid=2771.

29. See Tim LaHaye, *The Rapture* (Eugene, Ore.: Harvest House, 2002), p. 208.

30. Ibid., p. 217.

31. See Larry Burkett, *The Illuminati* (Nashville: Thomas Nelson, 1991), p. 18.

32. Ibid., pp. 18–19.

33. Ibid., p. 19.

34. Ibid., p. 20.

35. I also will note here the books and Web site(s) of Texe Marrs, especially *Circle of Intrigue: The Hidden Inner Circle of the Global Illuminati Conspiracy* (Austin: Rivercrest, 2000), and http://www.texemarrs.com. Marrs's book cover proclaims that he taught political science at the University of Texas, Austin, and his books do have some endnote documentation. But they are shot through with a paranoiac outlook that converts everything into a manifestation of worldwide conspiracy—the devil is everywhere! A closer look at Marrs's Web site reveals a pronounced anti-Semitism that is more subdued in *Circle of Intrigue*—his Web site even has a predictable link to the "Protocols of the Elders of Zion." Marrs, like many Illuminatiphobes, found it easy to see George Bush Sr. as one of the Illuminati, but were more reticent about the "born-again" George Bush Jr., even though he, too, was a member of Skull and Bones, and so on. By 2005, Marrs's newsletter *Power of Prophecy* included the thesis that George W. Bush was a front man for the sinister Jews who were in fact in charge of his administration and policies. Given that the Bush Jr. administration oversaw the PATRIOT Act and various other abrogations of American civil liberties, and further given that administration's obsession with secrecy—both of which would have earned any Democratic administration much Illuminatiphobic vitriol—it is noteworthy how many Illuminatiphobes refrained from criticizing George W. Bush, particularly in his first term.

36. See Robert Dreyfuss, "Reverend Doomsday."

37. See Jeffrey Victor, *Satanic Panic*, p. 304.

38. Ibid., p. 290.

39. The reader is invited to peruse http://www.thecuttingedge.org, http://www.thewatcherfiles.com, http://www.tribwatch.com, and http://www.savethemales.ca, as well as, for what will be by then a welcome change of pace, http://www.answers.org or http://www.pfo.org.

40. See the increasingly bizarre books of David Icke, the most industrious proselyte for the reptilian theory, in particular, *The Biggest Secret* (Scottsdale, Ariz.: Bridge of Love, 1999), and *Children of the Matrix: How an Interdimensional Race Has Con-

trolled the World for Thousands of Years—and Still Does (Wildwood, Mo.: Bridge of Love, 2001). Here is a sample:

> Then there are the experiences of Cathy O'Brien, the mind controlled slave of the United States government for more than 25 years, which she details in her astonishing book, *Trance-Formation Of America*, written with Mark Phillips. She was sexually abused as a child and as an adult by a stream of famous people named in her book. Among them were the US Presidents, Gerald Ford, Bill Clinton and, most appallingly, George [H. W.] Bush, a major player in the Brotherhood, as my books and others have long exposed. It was Bush, a paedophile and serial killer, who regularly abused and raped Cathy's daughter, Kelly O'Brien, as a toddler before her mother's courageous exposure of these staggering events forced the authorities to remove Kelly from the mind control programme known as Project Monarch. Cathy writes in *Trance-Formation Of America* of how George [H. W.] Bush was sitting in front of her in his office in Washington D.C. when, he opened a book at a page depicting lizard-like aliens from a far off, deep space place. Bush then claimed to be an "alien" himself and appeared, before her eyes, to transform "like a chameleon" into a reptile.

See, for more if you can take it, http://www.geocities.com/Area51/Shadowlands/6583/eto42.html; http://www.greatdreams.com/thelie.htm; http://www.thereptilianagenda.com; and, of course, Sherry Shriner's http://www.thewatcherfiles.com, which actually has sections with titles such as "Spiritual Warfare Prayers to Stop Abductions and Close Portals and Entrances in Your Home." See also, for an example of how this could become a "reptilian" witch-hunt, "Murdering Masonic Reptilian Shape-shifters" at http://www.reptilianagenda.com/exp/e022401a.shtml.

41. It is worth noting here that although in the United States, witch-hunts typically have emanated from the Christian right, in Sweden in 2005 one saw a flurry of accusations concerning extreme feminist groups, including a national women's shelter group called ROKS. A controversial documentary called "The Gender Wars" broadcast on Swedish national television outlined how various prominent feminist groups and authors were propagating an extremely antimale ideology, to such a degree that the director of ROKS, Ireen von Wachenfeldt, was filmed in an interview endorsing Valerie Solanas's outrageous 1960s-era *The Scum Manifesto* (which recently had been translated and published in a new Swedish edition) asserting that men are "animals" and "walking dildos." She was later forced to resign. A prominent Swedish feminist academic, Eva Lundgren, was put under review by her university. See, for various aspects of the controversy, Andy Butterworth, "SVT Releases Unedited 'Men are Animals' Interview" (27 May 2005), http://www.thelocal.se/article.php?ID=1505&date=20050527; Andy Butterworth, "Controversial Women's Shelter Chairwoman Resigns," (6 July 2005), http://www.thelocal.se/article.php?ID=1710&date=20050706&PHPSESSID=37bb1ed2b69bcb035a2f73be7a0a9a24; and Paul O'Mahoney, "If in Doubt, Attack the Messenger," *Stockholm Speculator* (29 May 2005), http://www.spectator.se/stambord/index.php?author=2.

Most relevant for our interests: some major feminist figures associated with ROKS were alleged to have said that Sweden's male population included members of secret Satanic cults that victimized women. One polemical Swedish author summarized the most incendiary charges: "Many young women who have been in contact with ROKS have been brainwashed into believing that Satanist sects are out to kill them; individual women have even been forced to live in small cabins in our neighbor country Norway in order to avoid the imaginary sects. Many other women have been brainwashed by ROKS into believing that they have been exposed to sexual abuse during their childhood." See Nima Sanandaji, "Tax-hungry Swedish Feminists" (8 July 2005), http://www.lewrockwell.com/orig6/sanandaji2.html. Although closer investigation reveals that some of the more exaggerated claims about these feminist groups were later critiqued and in some cases retracted, the fact remains that the archetype of the "Satanic panic" in this strange episode evidently did perhaps partially manifest in Sweden not on the Christian right but on the feminist left.

42. See Peter Jones, *The Gnostic Empire Strikes Back: An Old Heresy for the New Age* (Phillipsburg, N.J.: P&R, 1992 ed.), p. 14.

43. Ibid., p. 99.

44. See Richard Hofstadter, *The Paranoid Style in American Politics and Other Essays* (New York: Knopf, 1965).

45. I might in passing note that the Illuminatiphobic theorists on, for instance, http://www.thecuttingedge.org, bear some striking resemblances to the Bush Jr. administration in their opposition to international accords like the Kyoto Treaty, their disdain for environmentalism, and a number of other areas. Further study of parallels might be instructive.

CHAPTER 13

1. See Giorgio Agamben, *State of Exception* (Chicago: University of Chicago Press, 2005), p. 2.

2. Ibid.

3. See Karen Greenberg and Joshua Dratel, eds., *The Torture Papers: The Road to Abu Ghraib* (Cambridge: Cambridge University Press, 2005).

4. See Jane Mayer, "Outsourcing Torture" in *The New Yorker* (14 February 2005), http://www.newyorker.com/fact/content/?050214fa_fact6.

5. Ibid.

6. Ibid.

7. Yoo is a primary advocate for an imperial presidency, as discussed in Paul Barrett, "A Young Lawyer Helps Chart Shift in Foreign Policy," *The Wall Street Journal* (12 September 2005), p. 1. Yoo defends presidential prerogatives at length in his book *The Powers of War and Peace* (Chicago: University of Chicago Press, 2005). To quote Barrett: "his claim is that American law permits the president to go to almost any lengths in the name of fighting terrorism."

8. See Paul Barrett, "A Young Lawyer," p. A12.

9. Ibid.

10. "Text of Bush's Inaugural Speech," 20 January 2005, AP version.

11. See Peggy Noonan, "Way Too Much God: Was President's Speech a Case of 'Mission Inebriation'?" in *The Wall Street Journal* (21 January 2005), http://www.opinionjournal.com/columnists/pnoonan/?id=110006184.

12. Interesting, the connection to Dostoevsky was recognized and pointed out by Justin Raimondo in "Radical Son," *The American Conservative* (28 February 2005), pp. 7–9.

13. See Llewellyn Rockwell, "The Reality of Red-State Fascism," on *LewRockwell.com* (31 December 2004), http://www.lewrockwell.com/rockwell/red-state-fascism.html. See also Steven LaTulippe, "The Ugly Mutation of American Conservatism" (13 January 2005), http://www.lewrockwell.com/latulippe/latulippe40.html See also Patrick Buchanan, "The Anti-Conservatives," in *The American Conservative* (28 February 2005), pp. 13–14, in which he writes about John Adams's comment that "America goes not abroad, in search of monsters to destroy." For the intellectual background of the Bush Jr. administration and handlers, see Hugh Urban, "Religion and Secrecy in the Bush Administration: The Gentleman, the Prince, and the Simulacrum," *Esoterica* VII (2005):1–38.

14. See "The Koranic Excesses," *Wall Street Journal* (6 June 2005), p. A10.

15. See Michael Calderon, "Is New Orleans a Prelude to Al-Qaeda's American Hiroshima?" (2 September 2005), http://moonbatcentral.com/wordpress/?p=1069.

16. See Mayer, "Outsourcing Torture."

CHAPTER 14

1. See Fyodor Dostoevsky, *The Brothers Karamazov* (New York: Random House, 1985), p. 26.

2. Fyodor Dostoevsky, *Diary of a Writer*, 2 vols. (New York: Scribner's, 1949) [January 1877]2: 563; see also *Diary* [November 1877] 2:906. See Denis Discherl, *Dostoevsky and the Catholic Church* (Chicago: Loyola, 1986), p. 97.

3. Nicholas Berdyaev, "The Ruin of Russian Illusions," GIBEL' RUSSKIKH ILLIUZII, originally published in the journal *Russkaya Mysl* (September–October 1917), pp. 101–107, republished in Vol. 4 of *Collected Works*, "Dukhovnye osnovy russkoi revoliutsii (Stat'i 1917–18)" ("Spiritual Grounds of the Russian Revolution [Articles 1917–18]," [Paris: YMCA, 1990]), pp. 113–122. Translated by Father S. Janos, http://www.berdyaev.com/berdiaev/berd_lib/1917_280.html.

4. Nicholas Berdyaev, "Concerning Fanaticism, Orthodoxy, and Truth," O PHANATIZME, ORTODOKSII I ISTINE, in *Russkie zapiski* (1937) 1:180–191, translated by Father S. Janos, http://www.berdyaev.com/berdiaev/berd_lib/1937_430.html.

5. Ibid.

6. See Berdyaev, "The Ruin of Russian Illusions," lightly edited for clarity.

7. See Berdyaev, "Concerning Fanaticism, Orthodoxy, and Truth."

8. Ibid.

9. Ibid.

10. Ibid.

11. See Roxana Iordache, "L'Autre Holocauste," *Romania Libera*, 27 April 1993, cited by Alexandra Laignel-Lavastine, in "Fascism and Communism in Romania," *Sta-*

linism and Nazism (Lincoln: University of Nebraska Press, 2004), pp. 173–174. In France, for instance, Raymond Aron has argued against the view of Stalinism and Nazism as equivalent, whereas Alain Besançon has argued in favor of it. See, on Italian Fascism as a "heresy of the left," the special issue of *Telos* (133, Winter 2006) devoted to this question.

12. Laignel-Lavastine, "Fascism and Communism," p. 183.

13. See Eckard Bolsinger, *The Autonomy of the Political: Carl Schmitt's and Lenin's Political Realism* (Westport, Conn.: Greenwood, 2001), p. 178.

14. Ibid., p. 180.

15. Ibid., p. 183.

16. Alexander Dugin, for example, drew on this nostalgia for Stalin in some of his writings early in the twenty-first century. See the collection of Dugin's writings at http://www.arctogaia.com.ru.

17. See, for instance, John T. Flynn, *As We Go Marching* (New York: Doubleday, 1944).

CHAPTER 15

1. Cardinal Renato Martino spoke about the possibility in Europe of a "lay Inquisition" that criminalized Catholicism or Christianity. See John L. Allen, *The Word From Rome* (12 November 2004), http://www.nationalcatholicreporter.org/word/word111204.htm. Yet at the same time, apologists such as Robert Lockwood sought to minimize the Inquisition, even going so far as to attempt to justify the burning of Giordano Bruno. See Robert Lockwood, "History and Myth: The Inquisition" (August 2000), http://www.catholicleague.org/research/inquisition.html.

2. See Jacob Böhme, *Six Theosophic Points* (Ann Arbor: University of Michigan Press, 1958), III.iv.20–21.

3. Ibid., IV.vi.1.

4. Ibid., V.vii.34.

5. Ibid., V.vii.40.

6. Ibid., VI.ix.15.

7. Ibid., VI.x.8.

8. Ibid., VI.x.10.

9. See Barry Cooper, *New Political Religions* (Columbia: University of Missouri Press, 2004), a Voegelinian analysis of terrorism that reveals some genuine insights into the phenomenon. One might note that Cooper never once, in this Voegelinian study, misuses the word "gnostic" in Voegelinian fashion: unlike dogmatic Voegelinians, he knows better.

10. See Steven Bartlett, *The Pathology of Man: A Study of Human Evil* (Springfield: C.C. Thomas, 2005), p. 182.

11. Ibid., p. 184.

12. Ibid.

13. Ibid., p. 185.

14. Ibid.

15. Ibid., p. 314.

16. Ibid., p. 322.

17. See, for example, the scholarly journals *ARIES* and *Esoterica*, the numerous books in this field, including the introduction to it in my own *Restoring Paradise: Western Esotericism, Literature, Art, and Consciousness* (Albany, N.Y.: SUNY Press, 2004), as well as the massive *Dictionary of Gnosis and Western Esotericism*, W. Hanegraaff, ed. (Leiden: Brill, 2005).

18. In this regard, Bartlett points out that surveys conducted after World War II showed that the higher an individual's emphasis on aesthetic dimensions of life, the more that individual was likely to be resistant to fascism. By contrast, those who fervently had endorsed fascism rated politics highest and aesthetics lowest. Aesthetic transcendence through art and music is, of course, also partial transcendence of self-other or subject-object dualism. It is not surprising that those seduced by totalitarianisms would have little use for aesthetics, something verified, for instance, by the lifeless concrete architecture produced by Soviet Communism.

19. Some will, of course, immediately retort that a figure like Julius Evola (1898–1974), a well-known esoteric author who was associated with Italian Fascism, and to a lesser extent with German National Socialism, "proves" a connection between the esoteric and totalitarianism. But Evola was far from being a mystic or gnostic. He insisted not on the transcendence of self-other dualism, but on an adamantine, enduring self as the goal of various kinds of esotericism, even mistakenly attributing such a view to Buddhism in his extremely misleading book *The Doctrine of Awakening*. Evola was an ingenious writer, no doubt of that, but he is hardly a solid peg on which to hang a theory that gnostics or mystics are somehow to blame for modern totalitarianism.

20. Here I am thinking, in particular, of my trilogy of works on Christian theosophy—*Wisdom's Children: A Christian Esoteric Tradition* (Albany, N.Y.: SUNY Press, 1999), *Wisdom's Book: The Sophia Anthology* (St. Paul, Minn.: Paragon House, 2000), and *Theosophia: Hidden Dimensions of Christianity* (Hudson, N.Y.: Lindisfarne, 1994)—as well as *Awakening the Contemplative Spirit* (St. Paul, Minn.: New Grail, 2004). *Wisdom's Children* and *Awakening the Contemplative Spirit* offer some initial considerations of subjects alluded to here.

Selected Bibliography

Adorno, Theodor. *Ästhetische Theorie* (Frankfurt: Suhrkamp, 1970).
———. *Kulturkritik und Gesellschaft* (Frankfurt: Suhrkamp, 1977).
———. *Minima Moralia: Reflexionen aus d. beschädigten Leben* (Frankfurt: Suhrkamp, 1980).
———. *Minima Moralia: Reflections from Damaged Life* (Frankfurt: Suhrkamp, 1951/London: Verso, 1974).
———. "The Stars Down to Earth: The Los Angeles Times Astrology Column," *Telos* 19 (1974):13–90.
Adorno, Theodor, et al. *The Authoritarian Personality* (New York: Harper, 1950).
———. "Theses Against Occultism," *Telos*, 19 (Spring 1974):7–13.
Agamben, Giorgio. *State of Exception* (Chicago: University of Chicago Press, 2005).
Alcalá, Angel, ed. *Inquisión española y mentalidad inquisitorial* (Barcelona: Ariel, 1984), translated as *The Spanish Inquisition and the Inquisitorial Mind* (Boulder, Colo.: Social Science, 1987).
Arnold, John H.. *Inquisition and Power: Catharism and the Confessing Subject* (Philadelphia: University of Pennsylvania Press, 2001).
Baader, Franz von. *Sämmtliche Werke,* Franz Hoffman, ed., 16 vols., 1851–1860 (Leipzig: Scientia Verlag Aalen, 1987).
Balakrishnan, Gopal. *The Enemy: An Intellectual Portrait of Carl Schmitt* (London: Verso, 2000).
Barkun, Michael. *A Culture of Conspiracy: Apocalyptic Visions in Contemporary America* (Berkeley: University of California Press, 2003).
Barrès, Maurice. *Le Culte du moi* (Paris: Plon, 1966/1922).
———. *Les Déracinés* (Paris: Plon, 1922).

180 SELECTED BIBLIOGRAPHY

———. *The Faith of France*, Elisabeth Marbury, trans. (Boston: Houghton, 1918).
———. *La République ou le Roi: correspondance inedite de Maurice Barrès et Charles Maurras* (Paris: Plon, 1970).
Bartlett, Paul. "A Young Lawyer Helps Chart Shift in Foreign Policy," *Wall Street Journal*, 12 September 2005, 1A.
Bartlett, Steven. *The Pathology of Man: A Study of Human Evil* (Springfield, Ill.: C. C. Thomas, 2005).
Baur, Ferdinand Christian. *Die christliche Gnosis, oder die christliche Religions-Philosophie in ihrer geschichtlichen Entwicklung* (Tübingen: 1835).
Bell, Daniel. *The Coming of Post-Industrial Society* (New York: Basic, 1973).
Benoist, Alain de. *Comment peut-on être païenne?* (Paris: Albin Michel, 1981).
———. *L'Europe Païenne* (Paris: Seghers, 1980).
Benoist, Alain de, and Thomas Molnar. *L'Éclipse du sacré* (Paris: La Table Ronde, 1986).
Berdyaev, Nicholas. *Dostoievski* (London: Sheed & Ward, 1934).
———. *The Russian Revolution* (Ann Arbor: University of Michigan Press, 1966).
Berlin, Isaiah. *The Crooked Timber of Humanity* (New York: Knopf, 1991).
Blumenberg, Hans. *Säkulisierung und Selbstbehautptung* (Frankfurt: Surhkamp, 1985).
Böhme, Jacob. *Six Theosophic Points* (Ann Arbor: University of Michigan Press, 1958).
———. *Sämtliche Schriften* (Stuttgart: Fromanns, 1960).
Bolsinger, Eckard. *The Autonomy of the Political: Carl Schmitt's and Lenin's Political Realism* (Westport, Conn.: Greenwood, 2001).
Borromeo, Agostino, et al. eds. *Minutes of the International Symposium 'The Inquisition'* (Rome: Vatican, 2004).
Burkett, Larry, *The Illuminati* (Nashville: Thomas Nelson, 1991).
Burman, Edward. *The Inquisition: Hammer of Heresy* (Wellingborough: Thorsons, 1984).
Buthman, William. *The Rise of Integral Nationalism in France* (New York: Columbia University Press, 1939).
Canetti-Nisim, Daphna. "Two Religious Meaning Systems, One Political Belief System: Religiosity, Alternative Religiosity, and Political Extremism," in Leonard Weinberg and Ami Pedhzur, *Religious Fundamentalism and Political Extremism* (London: Frank Cass, 2004), pp. 35–54.
Cohn, Norman. *Europe's Inner Demons: An Enquiry Inspired by the Great Witch-hunt* (New York: Basic, 1975).
———. *Pursuit of the Millennium* (London: Secker, 1957).
Contreras, Jaime. *El Santi Oficio de la Inquisición de Galicia* (Madrid, 1982).
Cooper, Barry. *New Political Religions* (Columbia: University of Missouri Press, 2004).
Corsetti, Jean-Paul. *Histoire de l'ésotérisme et des sciences occultes* (Paris: Larousse, 1993).
Cortés, Juan Donoso. *Ensayo sobre el catolicismo, el liberalismo y el socialismo*, ed. J. Gómez (Barcelona: Planeta, 1985).
———. *Essays on Catholicism, Liberalism, and Socialism*, W. McDonald, trans. (Dublin: W. Kelly, 1874).
Crook, Stephen, ed. *The Stars Down to Earth and other Essays on the Irrational in Culture* (London: Routledge, 1994).

Curry, Patrick. *Prophecy and Power: Astrology in Early Modern England* (Princeton: Princeton University Press, 1989).
Curtis, Michael. *Three Against the Third Republic* (Princeton: Princeton University Press, 1959).
Dirscherl, Denis. *Dostoevsky and the Catholic Church* (Chicago: Loyola, 1986).
Dostoevsky, Fyodor. "The Grand Inquisitor," ch. 5 in *The Brothers Karamazov* (New York: Random House, 1985 ed.).
———. *Diary of a Writer*, 2 vols. (New York: Scribner's, 1949).
Dreyfuss, Robert. "Reverend Doomsday: For Tim LaHaye, the Apocalypse is Now," *Rolling Stone* (February 2004) at http://www.rollingstone.com/features/nationalaffairs/featuregen.asp?pid=2771.
Faguet, Émile. *Politiques et moralists du dix-neuvième siècle* (Paris: 1899).
Faivre, Antoine. *Access to Western Esotericism* (Albany: SUNY Press, 1994).
Faivre, Antoine, and Wouter Hanegraaff, eds. *Western Esotericism and the Science of Religion* (Leuven: Peeters, 1998).
Flynn, John T. *As We Go Marching* (New York: Doubleday, 1944).
Freund, Michael. *Georges Sorel: Der revolutionäre Konservatismus* (Frankfurt: Klostermann, 1932).
Godwin, Joscelyn. *Arktos: The Polar Myth in Science, Symbolism, and Nazi Survival* (Grand Rapids, Mich.: Phanes, 1993).
Goodrick-Clarke, Nicholas. *The Occult Roots of Nazism: Secret Aryan Cults and Their Influence on Nazi Ideology* (New York: New York University Press, 1992 ed.).
———. *Black Sun: Aryan Cults, Esoteric Nazism, and the Politics of Identity* (New York: New York University Press, 2003 ed.).
Graham, John T. *Donoso Cortés: Utopian Romanticist and Political Realist* (Columbia: University of Missouri Press, 1974).
Greenberg, Karen, and Joshua Dratel, eds. *The Torture Papers: The Road to Abu Ghraib* (Cambridge: Cambridge University Press, 2005).
Guénon, René. *The Crisis of the Modern World*, Arthur Osborne, trans. (London: Luzac, 1942).
———. *La règne de la quantité et les signes des temps* (Paris: Gallimard, 1945).
Gunn, Judith. *Dostoyevsky: Dreamer and Prophet* (Oxford: Lion, 1990).
Hanegraaff, Wouter. *New Age Religion and Western Thought* (Leiden: Brill, 1996).
Hanegraaff, Wouter et al., eds. *Dictionary of Gnosis and Western Esotericism* (Leiden: Brill, 2005).
Hicks, Darryl E., and David A. Lewis. *The Todd Phenomenon: Fact or Phantasy* (Harrison, Ark.: New Leaf, 1979).
Hofstadter, Richard. *The Paranoid Style in American Politics and Other Essays* (New York: Knopf, 1965).
Holmes, Stephen. *The Anatomy of Antiliberalism* (Cambridge, Mass.: Harvard University Press, 1993).
Huff, C. Ronald Arye Rattner, and Edward Sagarin. *Convicted But Innocent* (Thousand Oaks, Calif.: Sage, 1996).
Hughs, Glenn, ed. *The Politics of the Soul* (Lanham, Md.: Rowman & Littlefield, 1999).

Icke, David. *The Biggest Secret* (Scottsdale, Ariz.: Bridge of Love, 1999).

———. *Children of the Matrix: How an Interdimensional Race Has Controlled the World for Thousands of Years—and Still Does* (Wildwood, Mo.: Bridge of Love, 2001).

Johnson, Jeffrey, ed. *The Selected Works of Juan Donoso Cortés* (Westport, Conn.: Greenwood, 2000).

Jones, Peter. *The Gnostic Empire Strikes Back: An Old Heresy for the New Age* (Phillipsburg, N.J.: Presbyterian and Reformed, 1992).

Juretschke, J., ed. *Obras Completas de Don Juan Donoso Cortés*, 2 vols. (Madrid: Bibliotec de Autores Cristianos, 1946).

Kelly, Henry Ansgar. *Inquisitions and Other Trial Procedures in the Medieval West* (Aldershot: Ashgate, 2001).

Khlevnyuk, Oleg. "The Objectives of the Great Terror, 1937–1938," in Julian Cooper et al., eds., *Soviet History, 1917–1953* (London: Macmillan, 1995), pp. 158–176.

Koenen, Andreas. *Der Fall Carl Schmitt* (Darmstadt: Wissenschaftliche, 1995).

Lafage, Franck. *Le comte Joseph de Maistre* (Paris: L'Harmattan, 1998).

LaHaye, Tim. *The Rapture* (Eugene, Ore.: Harvest House, 2002).

Lea, Henry Charles. *The History of the Inquisition of the Middle Ages*, 3 vols. (New York: Macmillan, 1908).

———. *A History of the Inquisition in Spain*, 3 vols. (New York: Macmillan, 1906–1907).

———. *Superstition and Force* (Philadelphia: Lea, 1892).

Lebrun, Richard. *Throne and Altar: The Political and Religious Thought of Joseph de Maistre* (Ottawa: University of Ottawa Press, 1965).

Lebrun, Richard, trans. *Against Rousseau* (Montreal: McGill-Queen's University Press, 1996),

Lebrun, Richard, ed. *Joseph de Maistre, Life, Thought, and Influence* (Montreal: McGill University Press, 2001).

Lee, Philip J. *Against the Protestant Gnostics* (New York: Oxford University Press, 1987).

Lenin, Vladimir. *Collected Works* (London: Lawrence & Wishart, 1960).

———. *On the United States of America*, C. Leteizen, ed. (Moscow: Progress, 1967).

Lewis, Wyndham. *The Art of Being Ruled* (London, 1926).

Lukacs, John. *A New Republic: A History of the United States in the Twentieth Century* (New Haven, Conn.: Yale University Press, 2004).

Luukkanen, Arto. *The Party of Unbelief: The Religious Policy of the Bolshevik Party* (Helsinki: Finnish Historical Society, 1994)

Maistre, Joseph de. *Letters to a Russian Gentleman on the Spanish Inquisition*, A. M. Dawson, trans. (London: Dolman, 1851).

———. *Oeuvres completes* (Lyons: Vitte et Perrussel, 1884–1993).

———. *The Works of Joseph de Maistre*, J. Lively, ed. (New York: Macmillan, 1965).

Mann, Michael. *Fascists* (Cambridge: Cambridge University Press, 2004).

Menszer, Bela, ed. *Catholic Political Thought: 1789–1848*, (South Bend, Ind.: University of Notre Dame Press, 1962).

Marrs, Texe. *Circle of Intrigue: The Hidden Inner Circle of the Global Illuminati Conspiracy* (Austin: Rivercrest, 2000).

Mathelié-Guinlet, Guy. *L'Inquisition, Tribunal de la foi* (Bordeaux: Aubéron, 2000).

Maurras, Charles. *L'Allée des philosophes* (Paris: 1924).

---. *Au signe de Flore* (Paris: 1931).
---. *Barbarie et poésie* (Paris: 1925).
---. *De la Colère a la Justice* (Genève: Milieu du Monde, 1942).
---. *La Contre-Révolution Spontanée* (Paris: Lardanchet, 1943),
---. *La Démocratie religieuse* (Paris: Nouvelle Librairie, 1926).
---. *Music Within Me*, Count Potocki, trans. (London: Right Review, 1946).
---. *Oeuvres Capitales* (Paris: Flammarion, 1954).
---. *Le Pape, la Guerre, et la Paix* (Paris: Nouvelle Librairie, 1917).
---. *Petit Manuel De l'Enquête sur la Monarchie* (Versailles: Oeuvvres Politiques, 1928).
---. *Principes* (Paris: Cité des Livres, 1931).
---. *Réflexiones sur la Révolution de 1789* (Paris: Les Iles D'Or, 1948).
Maurras, Charles, and Maurice Barrès. *La République ou Le Roi* (Paris: Plon, 1970).
Mayer, Jane. "Outsourcing Torture," in *The New Yorker* (14 February 2005). Available at: http://www.newyorker.com/fact/content/?050214fa_fact6.
Mayer, Robert S. *Satan's Children* (New York: G. P. Putnam's Sons, 1991).
McKnight, Stephen. "Gnosticism and Modernity: Voegelin's Reconsiderations in 1971," 2001 APSA Panel Paper, downloaded as a pdf file from http://www.pro.harvard.edu/papers/091/091007/McKnightSt.pdf.
Meier, Heinrich. *Carl Schmitt and Leo Strauss: The Hidden Dialogue* (Chicago: University of Chicago Press, 1995).
---. *The Lesson of Carl Schmitt* (Chicago: University of Chicago Press, 1998).
Merleau-Ponty, Maurice, and J. O'Neill, trans. *Humanism and Terror: An Essay on the Communist Problem* (Boston: Beacon, 1969).
Milosz, Czeslaw. *Captive Mind* (New York: Harper, 1953).
Müller, Jan-Werner. *A Dangerous Mind: Carl Schmitt in Post-War European Thought* (New Haven, Conn.: Yale University Press, 2003).
Mussolini, Benito. "Dottrina," in *Political Quarterly* 4 (July 1933):341–356.
Nguyen, Victor. *Aux Origines de L'Action Française* (Paris: Fayard, 1991).
Opitz, Peter, and Gregor Sebba, eds. *The Philosophy of Order: Essays on History, Consciousness and Politics* (Stuttgart: Klett, 1981).
O'Regan, Cyril. *Gnostic Apocalypse: Jacob Böhme's Haunted Narrative* (Albany: SUNY Press, 2002).
Pellicani, Luciano. *Revolutionary Apocalypse: Ideological Roots of Terrorism* (Westport, Conn.: Praeger, 2003).
Pendergast, Mark. *Victims of Memory* (Hinesburg, Vt.: Upper Access, 1995).
Pérez, Joseph. *The Spanish Inquisition* (New Haven, Conn.: Yale University Press, 2005).
Piekalkiewicz, Jaroslaw, and Alfred W. Penn. *Politics of Ideocracy* (Albany: SUNY Press, 1995).
Pospielovsky, Dmitry. *Soviet Antireligious Campaigns and Persecutions* (London: Macmillan, 1988).
Quigley, Carroll. *The Anglo-American Establishment* (New York: Books in Focus, 1981).
---. *Tragedy and Hope: A History of the World in Our Time* (New York: Macmillan, 1966).

Raschke, Carl. *The Bursting of New Wineskins: Reflections on Religion and Culture at the End of Affluence* (Pittsburgh: Pickwick, 1978).
———. *The Interruption of Eternity: Modern Gnosticism and the Origins of the New Religious Consciousness* (Chicago: Nelson, 1980).
———. *Painted Black: From Drug Killings to Heavy Metal—The Alarming True Story of How Satanism Is Terrorizing Our Communities* (New York: Harper, 1990).
Reshetar, John. *A Concise History of the Communist Party of the Soviet Union* (New York: Praeger, 1965).
Richardson, James T., Joel Best, and David G. Bromley. *The Satanism Scare* (New York: Aldine de Gruyter, 1991).
Robertson, Alexander, and J. Donaldson, eds. *Ante-Nicene Fathers* (Edinburgh: T & T Clark, 1989).
Robertson, Pat. *The End of the Age* (Dallas: Word, 1995).
———. *The New World Order* (Dallas: Word, 1991).
Rockwell, Llewellyn. "The Reality of Red-State Fascism," on *LewRockwell.com* (31 December 2004). Available at http://www.lewrockwell.com/rockwell/red-state-fascism.html.
Rossbach, Stefan. *Gnostic Wars: The Cold War in the Contest of a History of Western Spirituality* (Edinburgh: Edinburgh University Press, 1999).
Roth, Jack. *The Cult of Violence* (Berkeley: University of California Press, 1980).
Rousso, Henry, ed. *Stalinism and Nazism* (Lincoln: University of Nebraska Press, 2004).
Rubenstein, Joshua, and Vladimir Naumov, eds. *Stalin's Secret Pogrom: The Postwar Inquisition of the Jewish Anti-Fascist Committee* (New Haven, Conn.: Yale University Press, 2001).
Rüthers, Bernd. *Carl Schmitt im Dritten Reich*, 2nd ed. (Munich: Beck, 1990).
Schmitt, Carl. *Der Begriff des Politischen* (München: Duncker & Humblot, 1932).
———. *Brief 1930–1993* (mit Ernst Jünger) (Stuttgart: Klett-cotta, 1999).
———. *The Concept of the Political*, G. Schwab, trans. (New Brunswick, N.J.: Rutgers, 1976).
———. *Die Diktatur* (München: Duncker & Humblot, 1928).
———. *Donoso Cortés in gesamteuropäischer Interpretation* (Köln: Greven, 1950).
———. *Ex captivitate salus: Erfahrungen der Zeit 1945/47* (Köln: Greven Verlag, 1950).
———. *Four Articles: 1931–1938*, Simona Draghici, trans. (Washington, D.C.: Plutarch, 1999).
———. *Die geistesgeschichtliche Lage des heutigen Parlamentarismus* (München: Duncker & Humblot, 1923).
———. *The Idea of Representation*, E. Codd, trans. (Washington, D.C.: Plutarch, 1988).
———. "Das Judentum in der deutschen Rechtswissenschaft," in "Die deutsche Rechtswissenschaft im Kampf gegen den jüdischen Geist," in *Deutsche Juristen-Zeitung*, 41 (15 October 1936)20:1193–1199.
———. *Land and Sea*, Simona Draghici, trans. (Corvallis, Ore.: Plutarch, 1997).
———. *The Leviathan in the State Theory of Thomas Hobbes*, G. Schwab, trans. (Westport, Conn.: Greenwood, 1996).

———. *The Nomos of the Earth in the International Law of the* Jus Publicum Europaeum, G. L. Ulmen, trans. (New York: Telos, 2003).
———. *Political Theology: Four Chapters on the Concept of Sovereignty*, G. Schwab, trans. (Cambridge, Mass.: MIT Press, 1985).
———. *Politische Theologie II* (Berlin: Duncker und Humblot, 1970).
———. *Politische Romantik* (München: Duncker und Humblot, 1925).
———. *Römischer Katholizismus und politische Form* (München: Theatiner-Verlag, 1925).
———. *State, Movement, People, and The Question of Legality*, Simona Draghici, trans. (Corvallis, Ore.: Plutarch, 2001).
Service, Robert. *A History of Twentieth-century Russia* (London: Penguin, 1997).
Siegelbaum, Lewis. *Soviet State and Society Between Revolutions, 1918–1929* (New York: Cambridge University Press, 1992).
———. *Stalinism as a Way of Life* (New York: Yale University Press, 2000).
Silverblatt, Irene. *Modern Inquisitions: Peru and the Colonial Origins of the Civilized World* (Durham, N.C.: Duke University Press, 2004).
Smith, Michelle, and Lawrence Pazder. *Michelle Remembers* (New York: Congdon & Lattes, 1980).
Solzhenitsyn, Aleksandr. *The Gulag Archipelago 1918–1956* (New York, 1974).
Sorel, Georges. "Le caractère religieux du socialisme," published in *Mouvement socialiste* (November 1906), and republished in *Matériaux d'une théorie du prolétariat* (Paris: Riviére, 1919, 1923), translated version in *Hermeneutics and the Sciences: From Georges Sorel, Vol. 2*, John Stanley, ed. (New Brunswick, N.J.: Transaction, 1989), pp. 67–98.
———. *From Georges Sorel: Essays in Socialism and Philosophy*, John and Charlotte Stanley, eds. (New York: Oxford University Press, 1976).
———. *La décomposition du marxisme* (Paris: M. Rivière, 1910).
———. *Les illusions du progress* (Paris: M. Rivière, 1947).
———. *Reflections on Violence*, T. E. Hulme, trans. (Glencoe, Ill.: Free Press, 1950).
———. *La ruine du monde antique : conception matérialiste de l'histoire* (Paris: Rivière, 1933).
———. *Saggi di critica del Marxismo* (Milano-Palermo: Sandron, 1903).
Spencer, Judith. *Suffer the Child* (New York: Simon & Schuster, 1989).
Stratford, Lauren. *Satan's Underground* (Eugene, Ore.: Harvest House, 1988; Gretna, La.: Pelican, 1991).
Strauss, Leo. *Persecution and the Art of Writing* (Chicago: University of Chicago Press, 1952).
Sutton, Michael. *Nationalism, Positivism, and Catholicism: The Politics of Charles Maurras and French Catholics* (Cambridge: Cambridge University Press, 1982).
Taubes, Jacob. *Gnosis und Politik* (München: W. Fink, 1984).
Tedeschi, John. *The Prosecution of Heresy* (Binghamton, N.Y.: Medieval and Renaissance Texts & Studies, 1991).
Treitel, Corinna. *A Science for the Soul: Occultism and the Genesis of the German Modern* (Baltimore: Johns Hopkins University Press, 2004).

Triomphe, Robert. *Joseph de Maistre: Etude sur la vie et sur la doctrine d'un materialiste mystique* (Geneva, 1968).

Trotsky, Lev D. *The Young Lenin* (Devon: Newton Abbas, 1972).

Trott, Jon, and Mike Hertenstein. "Selling Satan: The Tragic History of Mike Warnke," *Cornerstone Magazine* 21 (1992):98, available from http://www.cornerstonemag.com/features/iss098/sellingsatan.htm.

Tucker, Robert C. *Stalin in Power: The Revolution From Above 1928–1941* (New York: Norton, 1990).

Tumber, Catherine. *American Feminism and the Birth of New Age Spirituality: Searching for the Higher Self, 1875–1915* (Lanham, Md.: Rowman & Littlefield, 2002).

Urban, Hugh. "Religion and Secrecy in the Bush Administration: The Gentleman, the Prince, and the Simulacrum," *Esoterica* VII (2005):1–38.

Vacandard, Elphege. *The Inquisition: A Critical and Historical Study of the Coercive Power of the Church*, B. Conway, trans. (London: Longman, 1915).

Vernon, Richard. *Commitment and Change: Georges Sorel and the Idea of Revolution* (Toronto: University of Toronto Press, 1978).

Versluis, Arthur. *Awakening the Contemplative Spirit* (St. Paul, Minn.: New Grail, 2004).

———. *The Esoteric Origins of the American Renaissance* (New York: Oxford University Press, 2001).

———. *Restoring Paradise: Western Esotericism, Literature, Art, and Consciousness* (Albany: SUNY Press, 2004).

———. *Theosophia: Hidden Dimensions of Christianity* (Hudson, N.Y.: Lindisfarne, 1994).

———. *Wisdom's Book: The Sophia Anthology* (St. Paul, Minn.: Paragon House, 2000).

———. *Wisdom's Children: A Christian Esoteric Tradition* (Albany: SUNY Press, 1999).

Victor, Jeffrey. *Satanic Panic: The Creation of a Contemporary Legend* (LaSalle, Ill.: Open Court, 1993).

Voegelin, Eric. *Autobiographical Reflections* (Baton Rouge: Louisiana State University Press, 1989).

———. *The Collected Works of Eric Voegelin*, Paul Caringella et al., eds. (Baton Rouge: Louisiana State University Press, 1989–).

———. *Die politischen Religionen* (Wien: Bermann-Fischer Verlag, 1938).

———. *The New Science of Politics* (Chicago: University of Chicago Press, 1952).

———. *Order and History* (Baton Rouge: Louisiana State University Press, 1956–1987).

———. *Science, Politics, and Gnosticism* (Chicago: Regnery, 1968).

———. *Wissenschaft, Politik und Gnosis* (München: Kösel, 1959).

Warnke, Mike. *The Satan Seller* (Plainfield, N.J.: Logos, 1972).

Weber, Eugen. *Action Française: Royalism and Reaction in Twentieth-Century France* (Stanford: Stanford University Press, 1962).

Wesson, Robert. *Lenin's Legacy: The Story of the CPSU* (Stanford: Hoover, 1978).

Winock, Michel. *Nationalism, Anti-Semitism, and Fascism in France* (Stanford: Stanford University Press, 1998).

Wolin, Richard. *The Seduction of Unreason: The Intellectual Romance with Fascism* (Princeton, N.J.: Princeton University Press).

Index

Abu Ghraib 129
Action Française 41, 44–45
Adams, John 132
Adorno, Theodor viii, 91, 95–104, 151
Agamben, Giorgio 127–128
Albigensians 57
Amitabha Buddha (more or less) 120
Amway 122
Anabaptists 46, 87
anti-occultism (as phenomenon) 103–104
anti-Semitism 44–45, 50–51, 75, 98–99, 124
Arnold, Gottfried 77
Ashcroft, John 122
astrology 100–101
Augustine 31

Baader, Franz von, 20–21, 31
Bakunin, Mikhail 61
Barkun, Michael 117
Barrès, Maurice 41–42
Bartlett, Steven 153–154
Baudelaire, Charles 108
Baur, Ferdinand Christian 76
Bennassar, Bartolomé 15, 17, 21

Benoist, Alain de 75
Berdyaev, Nicholas 62, 68, 136–140
Berlin, Isaiah vii, 23–24
Blum, Leon 45
Böhme, Jacob 62, 81–82, 149–151
Bolsheviks 62–63
Brethren of the Free Spirit 85, 87–89
Bruno, Giordano 13, 106, 147
Buchanan, Patrick 175
Buddhism 3–4, 83, 150
Bulgakov, Sergei 62, 68
Burkett, Larry 121–122
Bush Jr. Administration 50, 127–133
Bush Jr., George 120, 123, 125–133
Bush Sr., George 118

Calderon, Michael 132
Calvin, John 73
Carter, Jimmy 117
Castaneda, Carlos 106
Cathars 14, 80
Catholicism, Roman 13–18, 19–47, 136–140

INDEX

Cheney, Richard 133
Chomsky, Noam 132
Churchill, Ward 132
Clement of Alexandria 4, 5, 74
Clement V 14
Clinton, Bill 124
Cohn, Norman 85–93
Cold War, 79–80, 85
Communism (Soviet) 35, 47, 61–68, 135–140
communism 11, 18, 32, 33, 140–145, 147–155
Communist Manifesto 61, 119
Contreras Jaime 16
Coors, Joseph 122
Council for National Policy 122–123
Council on Foreign Relations 118–119, 122
Crowley, Aleister 108
Culianu, Ioan 73

Dalai Lama XIV, H.H. the, 7
DeVos, Richard 122
dictatorship 28–30, 127
Donoso Cortés, Juan 25, 27–34, 38, 41, 139
Dostoevsky, Fyodor 10, 21, 131, 136–140
Dreyfus Affair 43–44
Dzerzhinsky, Felix 64

Eckhartshausen, Karl 20
Eddy, Mary Baker 106
Emerson, Ralph Waldo 106, 108
Epiphanius 4, 5, 69, 82
Evola, Julius 177
exception, state of 8, 127–133
"extraordinary rendition" 129–130
Eymerich, Nicholas 16

Faivre, Antoine 168
Farrakhan, Louis (presented as "Gnostic") 82
Falwell, Jerry 122
fascism, viii, ix, 11, 18, 24, 25, 32, 33, 132–133, 140–145, 147–155
Fascism (Italian) 35, 47

Ficino, Marsilio 78
first and second Americas 111–112
Fornari, Cardinal 33
Fourth Lateran Council 21
Frankfurt School, 95
Freemasonry 19, 42, 44–46, 50, 120, 121
French Revolution, 19–20

Garrard, Graeme 25
Garvey, Marcus (presented as "Gnostic") 82
Geneva Convention 128, 129–130
Gnosticism 4–5, 52–59, 69–84, 106–110
Gnostics 36–38, 68, 69–84, 106–110
Gonzales, Alberto 129
Goodrick-Clarke, Nicholas 103
Gospel of Philip 74, 77
Gospel of Thomas 71, 74
Graham, John 29
Grand Inquisitor 22, 33
Gregory IX 14
Guantánamo, Cuba 128, 132
Guénon, René 51

Hanussen, Erik 102
Hegel, Georg W. F. 72
heresy 3
hermetism 71
Hertenstein, Mike 112, 114, 116
Hess, Rudolf 96
Hesse, Herman 106
Himmler, Heinrich 96
Hinduism 3
Hitler, Adolf 69, 84, 90, 127, 144
Hobbes, Thomas 50–51
Hoffer, Eric 141
Hofstadter, Richard 125
Holmes, Stephen 25
Hooker, Richard 73
Hunt, Nelson Bunker 122
Hypostasis of the Archons 77

ideocracy 7, 10
ideopathology 153–156
Illuminatiphobia 112, 116–125

Innocent III 13, 21, 58
Innocent IV 14
Inquisition
  aspects of 6–7
  history of 13–18
Irenaeus 36, 46, 69

Jefferson, Thomas 111, 112
"Jeffy" 114
Jesus Christ (nonviolence and) 56–57
Joachim of Fiore 74
John XXII 14
Jonas, Hans 69, 77
Jones, Peter 124
Julian [Emperor] 125
Justinian Marina 9

Kabbalism 50, 81
Katechon 54–56
Kelley, Douglas 154
Ketman 8–9
Kim Jong Il 144
Knights Templar 92

LaHaye, Tim 116, 120–121, 124
LaRouche, Lyndon 117
Lasch, Christopher 82
Lebrun, Richard, 24–25
Lenin, Vladimir, 35, 39, 40, 62, 84, 144
Lewis, Wyndham 35
Lucius III 13
Lukacs, John vii

Mafia 36
Maistre, Joseph de viii, 11, 19–25, 31, 32, 38–39, 43, 139, 145, 147
Manson, Charles 108, 113
Mao Tse Tung 57, 90, 144
Marcion 53
Marillion 108
Marrs, Texe 122
Marx, Karl 61, 63, 84, 119
Maurras, Charles 41–47, 139
Mayer, Jane 129
McCarthy, Eugene 85, 148
McKnight, Stephen, 77–79

McMartin preschool case 108
Meese, Edwin 122
Meier, Heinrich 49, 52
Meister Eckhart, 54, 67, 74, 88, 152
Milosz, Czeslaw 8–11, 141, 145
Moonbat Central 132
Moore, Michael 132
Müller, Jan-Wenner 49
Müntzer, Thomas, 87
Mussolini, Benito 7, 35, 39, 58
mysticism 10, 156

Nag Hammadi Library 4, 37, 71, 77, 78, 83
National Socialism 52–59
New World Order 118–121
Nicholas of Cusa 74
Nietzsche, Friedrich 71–72, 106, 108
Nixon, Richard 117
Norquist, Grover 122
North, Oliver 122

O'Regan, Cyril 81–82
Origen 4
Osbourne, Ozzy 108

pathology of humanity 153–155
Pellicani, Luciano 57
Peña, Francisco, 16
Plato 50
Plato's Cave 155–156
Platonism 71
Plekhanov, Georgy 62
Pol Pot 57, 90, 143, 144, 150
Porete, Margeurite 13, 76, 89, 152
Protestantism (seen as decline) 44, 46, 51

Quigley, Carroll 119

Ranters 85
Raschke, Carl 105–110, 112
Reagan, Ronald 127
Reptilians (from fourth dimension) 124, 172–173
Robertson, Pat 116, 118–121, 122–124, 125

Robison, John 125
Rosicrucianism 50
Rossbach, Stefan 79–80
Roth, Jack 35–36
Rumsfeld, Donald 123
Russian Revolution 24

Sade, Marquis de 106
Saint-Martin, Louis-Claude de, 20–21, 106
Saint-Simonians 37
Satanic panic (American) 111–125
Satanic panic (Swedish) 173–174
Satanism or "Satanism" 107–109, 112–116
Schmitt, Carl viii, 11, 25, 32, 41, 49–59, 96, 104–105, 127–128, 131, 139, 151
Sebba, Gregor 72, 77, 79
secular millennialism 88, 155
Servetus, Michael 153
Siegelbaum, Lewis, 164
Smith, Michelle 114
Solzhenitsyn, Alexander 65
Sorel, Georges 32, 34, 35–42, 46–47, 105, 139, 147
Spengler, Oswald vii
Stalin, Josef 47, 65–67, 143
Statton, Lauren 114
Strauss, Leo 49, 50
Sufism 148

Tedeschi, John 17
Telos 96, 175
Tertullian 4–6, 31, 36, 46, 52–59, 82, 133, 151

Todd, John 117–118
totalitarianism of right and left 135–152
Traherne, Thomas 156
Treitel, Corinna 102
Trotsky, Leon 39, 63, 65
Trott, Jon 112, 114, 116
Tumber, Catherine 82

Urban, Hugh 175

Valentinianism 81–82
Verweyen, Johannes 102
Victor, Jeffrey 115, 123–124
Voegelin, Eric viii, 69–84, 96, 101–102, 104–105, 139, 151, 155
Vonnegut, Kurt 124

Wahhabism 148
Wall Street Journal 132
Warnke, Mike 112–115, 116–117, 120
Washington, George 132
Watts, Alan 106
Weimar Republic 135, 144
Weishaupt, Adam 119, 121
Werth, Nicholas 66
Whitman, Walt 106
Winfrey, Oprah
    presented as "Gnostic" 82
    television show 113
Winock, Michael 46–47

Yoo, John 129–130

Zinn, Howard 132

Printed and bound by CPI Group (UK) Ltd, Croydon, CR0 4YY